Personal Narrative

Crafting Powerful Life Stories

Lucy Calkins, Stacey Fell, and Alexandra Marron

Photography by Peter Cunningham

HEINEMANN ◆ PORTSMOUTH, NH

This unit within the narrative writing progression

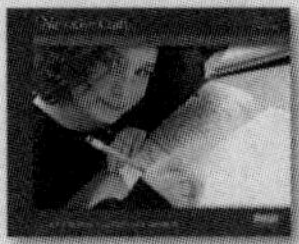

GRADE 5

In ***Narrative Craft***, students write personal narratives, making purposeful choices about the techniques, structures, and language they use to convey their meaning.

In ***Shaping Texts***, students write memoirs that combine essay and narrative structures to convey significant insights and personal themes.

THIS UNIT

GRADE 6

In ***Personal Narrative***, students write true stories, learning strategies to generate meaningful story ideas, manage pace, elaborate on important scenes, and deepen insights.

GRADE 7

In ***Writing Realistic Fiction***, students write engaging short fiction by creating action-filled plots and believable characters and by crafting nuanced, memorable scenes.

This unit within the grade 6 progression

THIS UNIT

UNIT 1

In ***Personal Narrative***, students write true stories, learning strategies to generate meaningful story ideas, manage pace, elaborate on important scenes, and deepen insights.

UNIT 2

In ***The Literary Essay***, students craft essays that make arguments about characters and themes, learning strategies essayists use to gather, analyze, and explain evidence from the text to support their claims.

UNIT 3

In ***Research-Based Information Writing***, students learn ways to research and write informational essays, books, and digital presentations or websites to teach their readers about a topic, using increasingly sophisticated ways to draw on and structure information to explain a position or make a call to action.

This book is dedicated to James Howe—thank you for being a mentor to us all.
—Lucy and Ali

This book is dedicated to Cornelia, Leopold, and Augustine, who taught me to rise early and to write fast and furiously.
—Stacey

Heinemann
361 Hanover Street
Portsmouth, NH 03801–3912
www.heinemann.com

Offices and agents throughout the world

The authors and publisher wish to thank those who have generously given permission to reprint borrowed material:

Excerpt from "Everything Will Be Okay" from *When I Was Your Age* by James Howe. Reprinted by permission of Writers House LLC, acting as agent for the author.

Cataloging-in-Publication data is on file with the Library of Congress.

ISBN-13: 978-0-325-05943-3

Production: Elizabeth Valway, David Stirling, and Abigail Heim
Cover and interior designs: Jenny Jensen Greenleaf
Series photographs by Peter Cunningham and Nadine Baldasare
Composition: Publishers' Design and Production Services, Inc.
Manufacturing: Steve Bernier

Printed in the United States of America on acid-free paper

18 17 16 15 VP 2 3 4 5

Acknowledgments

THIS BOOK STANDS ON the shoulders of the Teachers College Reading and Writing Project's decades of work developing methods of teaching narrative writing. More specifically, this book extends the trajectory of work that was set by the co-authors of the K–5 narrative *Units of Study in Opinion, Information, and Narrative Writing*, and we are grateful to Natalie Louis, Rachel Rothman, Abby Smith, Amanda Hartman, Julia Moony, Marjorie Martinelli, Maggie Roberts, Shana Frazin, and Colleen Cruz. Two of us—Ali Marron and, of course, Lucy herself—were very much a part of that series of work and were co-authors of the book that immediately precedes and sets the stage for this unit: *Personal Narrative: Crafting Powerful Life Stories*.

We're grateful to the long list of heroes in the field of writing that have informed the Project's work over all these years: to the late Pulitzer Prize–winning writer Donald Murray, who opened this field to us; and to the late Donald Graves, who helped the world understand the power of teaching children writing. Thanks too to the earliest staff members of the TCRWP who have gone on to become nationally known, including Randy and Katherine Bomer, Georgia Heard, Katie Ray, Ralph Fletcher, and Nick Flynn. Thanks to writers such as Katherine Paterson, Patti MacLachlan, Jim Howe, Eloise Greenfield, Naomi Shihab Nye, Kate DiCamillo, and so many others who have helped us and our students learn to write narratives well. We're thankful especially to the Project's middle school staff, who helped teachers pilot this narrative unit in writing workshops in thousands of middle school classrooms. Special thanks to Audra Robb, who helped orchestrate all the million of parts that make this book possible.

The entire K–8 *Units of Study for Opinion/Argument, Information, and Narrative Writing* exists today only because Kate Montgomery agreed to join in the effort. Kate has co-led all the *Units of Study in Opinion/Argument, Information, and Narrative Writing* since their inception, including the development, tweaking, and refinement of the structure, voice, mission, and coherence of the entire system. There are not words enough to thank Kate for her leadership.

We're very grateful to the entire team at Heinemann. Special thanks goes to Abby Heim, program manager, who constructs and oversees and enables the work plan for turning these words from Google Docs into books. Abby can only do this work because she has a team of people who care as much as the rest of us do. Thanks especially to Tracy Wells for her attention to detail and for her way with words, and to Elizabeth Valway, Shannon Thorner, and David Stirling for their care in every detail of production; as well as Jenny Jensen Greenleaf for design, Peter Cunningham and Nadine Baldasare for photography, and Charles McQuillen and Buzz Rhodes for marketing and sales expertise.

We're also grateful to the middle school writers at Tompkins Square Middle School who allowed us to learn from their insights, ideas, stories, and talent. These young writers and their teachers provide the specific context in which this particular unit emerged, and we are grateful to this vibrant community of highly committed teachers and of hard working students.

As in all the units in this series, the class described in this unit is a composite class, with students gleaned from classrooms in very different contexts, then put together here. We wrote the units this way to bring you both a wide array of wonderful, quirky, and unique writers, and also to illustrate for you the predictable (and unpredictable) situations and responses this unit has created in classrooms across the nation and world.

—Lucy, Stacey, and Ali

Contents

Welcome to the Unit

IN THIS FIRST UNIT OF STUDY, your students will grow dramatically as *writers*, not only as authors of personal narrative. You'll strive toward organizing a writing workshop that encourages independence and dramatic growth—a writing workshop that places high priority on setting and working toward clear goals. With this solid foundation in place, you and your students will leave this personal narrative unit expecting that their writing will continue to improve with each new unit, and that clear structures exist to support that work.

From the very start of the unit, it will be important to show students what they are trying to achieve in their personal narrative writing. When writers have strong examples and mentor texts, they can begin to crystallize their understanding of the elements of powerful narrative writing. When those same writers also have the opportunity to self-assess and set goals, they will work with great investment and will accelerate their achievement.

This unit provides you with an opportunity to teach students the work called for in the Common Core State Standards for Narrative Writing. The skills required for narrative writing align with the skills required for opinion and informational writing. Certainly the strategies differ from one type of writing to the next. Narrative writers, for example, rely on techniques such as dialogue, inner thinking, precise actions, and setting details to develop the important parts of a story, while informational writers rely on relevant facts, concrete details, definitions, and quotations to develop key parts of an article or nonfiction book. But the qualities of good writing remain the same from one writing type or genre to the next. Regardless of the terrain, to write well, one must know how to write with focus and detail, how to craft leads and conclusions, and how to use transitions and precise language effectively.

So while the focus of this unit is to teach your students how to compose powerful narratives, the impact is much more far-reaching. Ultimately, this unit will help your sixth-graders develop the skills they need to write well across all genres.

Before you embark on this unit, it will be especially important for you to be mindful of the overarching ways the CCSS raise the ante for sixth-graders. By sixth grade, writers are expected to use a variety of narrative techniques to develop their stories and, more specifically, their characters. Sixth-graders must learn to manage not only the story (conveying experiences and events precisely and vividly), but also the pacing of events. The Common Core expects that sixth-graders come to writing workshop with years' worth of strategies, allowing these young people to draw on those strategies with increasing independence and facility. To make choices, sixth-graders need to bring their interpretation skills to bear on their own emerging drafts. Just as they read fiction and nonfiction texts, thinking about the shared ideas that are forwarded in those texts and thinking also about the ways authorial decisions have been inspired by the author's intended messages, so too, sixth-graders now need to reread their own emerging drafts, making sure that they highlight the central ideas that they want readers to draw from their texts. This means it is especially important for your students to be clear about why they are telling a story so they make craft decisions with purposes in mind. The experience of angling their own stories to highlight themes will help students as they work to read interpretively, not only thinking about the central meanings in a text but also noticing how two authors may address the same theme differently.

The expectations embedded in the Common Core State Standards are especially high for narrative writing. Look at the narratives that are included at the end of this book for grade 6, and it will be clear to you that before all your students can meet these ambitious levels, they'll need to invest a lot of time and energy developing their skills. You'll want to communicate to students that it is not practice alone that leads to perfection. For students' skill levels to increase dramatically, they must learn how to practice effectively—how to practice in a way that will bring them closer to their goals. Research is clear that when students are engaged in a cycle of goal-setting, strategic work, self-assessment, and feedback, they make significant progress.

OVERVIEW OF THE UNIT

When you launch the unit, your most important job is to get all of your students inspired, feeling that their lives are worth writing about, that they can learn to write with honesty and precision, and that they are part of a community of writers who will hold them up throughout that process. As you tap into your students' motivations to put the true stories of their lives onto the page, you'll conduct an inquiry with your students, studying a few pieces of personal narrative writing that other middle-schoolers wrote. Your hope is that this inquiry will remind students of all they learned about narrative writing in prior grades so they tap all that knowledge—and then display it to you—as they write. The important message that you'll convey is that writers carry with them and draw from a repertoire of strategies.

One of the reasons that it is so important to teach for transfer, helping writers to draw on all they have already learned about good writing, is that this allows writers to be decision makers. During each day's writing workshop, writers need to assess their work, review their options, and make their own decisions about the work that needs to be done. As they do this, they draw on their complete repertoire of tools and strategies, as well as on that day's minilesson. But your emphasis on writing instruction cumulating is a way to also emphasize that the work that writers do each day is certainly not determined merely by that day's minilesson.

You will want to approach the unit anticipating that, in all ways, you'll be traveling familiar ground in hopes of raising the level of student work. You can raise the level of work by emphasizing what it means to do any strategy really well and by emphasizing that writers must make decisions based on their plans for a piece of writing, their assessment of the draft, and their full knowledge. But you will also raise the quality of writing by emphasizing the importance of meaning, of significance.

As sixth-graders enter middle school and adolescence, they especially want to do work that feels important. You can capitalize on this need and raise the level of the entire unit if you can rally students to choose story ideas that are compelling and significant to them. James Merrill said, "The stories you write first are anybody's stories. You have to make them your own." Early in the unit, you will find yourself saying something like this to your children: "Your 'I made a soccer goal' story could be anyone's story. What is your story of this soccer game? What was going on for *you* that wasn't going on for anybody else? Where's the real story here?" In an effort to help students write stories that carry significance and that are shaped like true stories, not like chronicles, you'll teach some new strategies for generating personal narrative writing as well as reminding students of strategies they already know. For example, you may teach your students that published writers sometimes think of a place that matters to them and sketch a quick map of that place, jotting all the powerful Small Moment story ideas that come from that place. Or you might teach your writers that it can help to think about a moment when you learned something important about yourself and other people.

Once the unit is well underway, and you've emphasized that writers draw on all they know as they begin a new cycle of writing work, it will be important to find ways to immediately lift the quality of students' work. Pulitzer Prize–winning writer Donald Murray, credited as the father of the writing process, has often said that the single most important quality of all narrative writing is "show, don't tell." In effective narrative writing, the entire story is shown—it is dramatized instead of summarized. As Mark Twain said, "Don't say the old lady screamed. Bring her on and let her scream." With this in mind, you'll want to remind students that to write effective narratives, they must reimagine the episode before writing it, putting it on paper as they do, so that readers will be able to experience it, too. Then, you will also teach sixth-graders that writers are especially careful about telling the details of the story *exactly* the way the narrator perceived them at the moment.

Throughout this unit, you'll also be supporting new levels of productivity, as is fitting for students who are entering middle school. The first bend of this unit is also the start of the school year, and you'll want to go to some lengths to convey your high expectations for productivity. In this bend, you'll expect students to write at least one long (two-page) flash-draft personal narrative each day, and more for homework. Your goal will be that day by day, the quality of the flash-draft narratives they produce will improve, so that when students select one of these stories to be the start to a major publication, they will have a great foundation to build upon. To raise the quality of students' writing, you'll encourage them to learn from close reading of a mentor text, "Everything Will Be Okay" by James Howe. You will teach that writers read other authors' texts not only to experience the characters' story, but also to admire, study, and emulate the quality of the writing.

In Bend II, the second part of the unit, students will choose a seed idea to take through the writing process. You'll help students to draw on all the narrative crafting techniques they have ever learned and to continue asking, "What did Howe do to write his story that I, too, could try?" Your emphasis will be on teaching students that craft and revision are always driven by an effort to communicate meaning. For example, when students rehearse for writing by generating multiple leads, they can think, "What is my story really about, and how can I begin to hint at that from the very beginning of my story?" As part of this, you will help students learn that the same story can be told differently, depending on the theme the writer wants to bring out. For example, a story about tripping and falling in a busy school hallway could be angled to show how terrifying and humiliating middle school can be; or it could be angled to show the benefits of a sense of humor and not taking oneself too seriously!

You'll remind students that it usually helps to flash-draft an entire personal narrative in one sitting, using the momentum to create cohesion and to bring voice to the piece. In this bend, as students work toward substantial revisions, you can teach them to use their writer's notebooks as a place to deliberately practice the techniques and skills they want to see in their writing. For example, using various narratives across their notebooks, they might practice elaborating or incorporating meaningful flashbacks. By the end of Bend II, students will have revised their flash-draft extensively, and in doing so, they will have gained the sense of self-efficacy that comes with making repeated and deliberate efforts to try out strategies and work toward clear goals.

Bend III emphasizes increased initiative and independence as sixth-graders begin a new personal narrative. You'll rally students to take charge of their writing process and their plan as they embark on a new cycle of writing. As students progress through the writing process, with more independence, you'll need to remind them to draw on everything they know how to do, keep an eye on their goals, and make use of their many writing tools. You'll continue to support students as they develop their skills at analyzing and annotating mentor texts and emulating the craft moves of a published author. You might draw more attention to the ways that writers slow down the problem in their story and build tension or the ways that writers create resolutions that connect to the big meaning of their story.

ASSESSMENT

Before you start this unit, we recommend that you take just a bit of time to establish a baseline understanding of your students' skills as narrative writers. This assessment is crucial. We'll provide you with instruments—learning progressions, rubrics, checklists, and a set of exemplar texts written by students—that will help you to see where in the trajectory of writing development each of your students lies. The assessment system will help you and your students see next steps. Then, too, this initial assessment is necessary for you to track each individual's progress—and to help your students see themselves improving. The improvement will be palpable. At your first parent-teacher conferences, you'll be able to say, "This is what your child's writing was like at the very start of the year. And look, *this* is what she can do now!"

For this initial assessment to provide accurate baseline data on your writers' narrative skills, be careful not to scaffold your students' work during the assessment. You'll want to simply remind students of the basic qualities you'd expect in a piece of narrative writing, then step back and leave them to their own devices. We recommend that you give students this prompt to start them off (you can find this prompt and more explanation about our assessment system in the book *Writing Pathways: Performance Assessments and Learning Progressions, Grades 6–8*, that comes with this series):

> "I'm really eager to understand what you can do as writers of narratives, of stories, so today will you please write the best personal narrative, the best true story, that you can write? Make this be the story of one time in your life. You might focus on just a scene or two. You'll have only forty-five minutes to write this true story, so you'll need to plan, draft, revise, and edit in one sitting. Write in a way that allows you to show off all you know about narrative writing. In your writing, make sure you:
>
> - Write a beginning for your story
> - Use transition words to tell what happened in order
> - Elaborate to help readers picture your story
> - Show what your story is really about
> - Write an ending for your story."

If you worry that saying, "Welcome to a new year. I want to begin by evaluating you," might seem harsh, you might soften this by saying that you can't wait until the end of September before having some of your students' writing to display on bulletin boards. Or perhaps you can make this on-demand writing feel celebratory by saying that you realized from things they've said that many of them are entering your classroom already knowing a lot about writing, and you want to give them all a chance to show off. Just be careful that you don't find yourself being so chatty about this whole endeavor that you end up teaching them a quick course on narrative writing prior to the assessment, unless your whole school has agreed to do that. You will want the various classrooms in a grade to do this on-demand assessment in ways that are consistent across the classrooms.

We encourage you to duplicate your students' on-demand narratives and to give one copy to each student, asking each writer to tape his on-demand writing into the first page of his writer's notebook, where it can serve as a reminder to the writer and to you that this is the level of work that the writer was able to do at the very start of the year. By keeping the on-demand writing close at hand, you can help writers hold themselves to the job of making sure all their subsequent writing is progressively better. As students collect narrative entries in the days ahead, ask them to look back frequently at their on-demand piece, making sure that they are getting palpably stronger in comparison.

You will also need to assess where each writer falls in the Learning Progression for Narrative Writing and to note where the bulk of your class falls, letting that information inform your teaching in the upcoming unit of study. To do this, we suggest you read each student's writing, comparing it to the exemplar texts provided at each grade level, and then read the descriptors to hone in on the specific ways that a student can improve. No text will match a grade level in its entirety, so don't be knocked off-kilter if a piece of writing seems to be generally one level, but there a few criteria it does not meet. The descriptors of the criteria will be particularly useful as you help writers know concrete steps they can take to make their writing better. That is, if a writer's narrative writing is grade 6, you and that writer can look at the descriptors of, say, character development for grade 6 and note whether the writing adheres to those. If so, tell that child—or your whole class, if this is broadly applicable—"You used to develop the people in your stories by . . . ," and read the descriptors from the prior grade level, "but now you are . . . ," and read the grade 6 descriptor. "Can I give you a pointer about a way to make your writing even better? Try . . . ," and read from the grade 7 descriptor. You can even say, "Let me show you an example," and to do so, you can cite a section of the grade 7 benchmark text.

One final word: the baseline assessment is not assessing you. It is assessing the background your students have when they enter your classroom. But when this unit ends, you'll repeat this assessment exactly, and when you collect the student writing and look between the first on-demand and the second, the progress that you see will allow for an assessment not only of your students but also of your teaching and of this curriculum, too. We have found that when you teach, knowing that assessment will be based upon what writers do without any input from you (or us) in an on-demand situation, this serves as a reminder to you. It reminds you that the goal of any writing instruction is not to produce strong writing. It is to produce strong writers. Our goal is to teach in ways that not only lift the level of today's piece of writing, but that also leave writers able to do better work another day, on another piece. When you look back on the baseline data you collect at the start of this unit and at the work students eventually produce, you'll be able to say, "Look at this progress!"

GETTING READY

Because in this unit students will be using a writer's notebook, you will want to create a certain fanfare around this professional writing tool. You will also want to make sure you have your own writer's notebook (or one borrowed from a colleague or downloaded from a famous writer on the Internet) filled with various personal narratives that have been sparked by thinking about memorable moments with special people or events that happened in special places. If you plan to have your students decorate their notebooks with photos and pictures that might spark stories, then you should decorate yours also in a similar way. If you want your students to carry their notebooks with them always, then you should also, sharing stories of how you were able to jot down events right after they happened or how disappointed you were when there was a time you didn't have your notebook with you. You may be the first living, breathing author they know firsthand, so everything you do as a writer will inspire them to do the same.

You will also want to gather examples of sixth-grade writing so your students have a vision of the kind of writing they will be doing. You can find some examples on the CD-ROM, but the best are examples that come from your own students or the students of colleagues because that way you know the inside story behind the stories, which students always find intriguing. In addition, throughout the sessions, we suggest returning to the same author, Jim Howe, and the same text, "Everything Will Be Okay," so that students can become used to reading closely like a writer. Of course, you can choose any author and book you love that has the qualities of good writing you hope to teach, but in either case, the important thing is to have an author who becomes like your coteacher in the room, sitting on your shoulder, whispering writing advice into your ear and eventually into your students' ears.

Launching Independent Writing Lives and Generating Personal Narratives

BEND I

Session 1

Setting Up to Write

IN THIS SESSION, you'll teach students that writers can study finished work, imagining the strategies that other writers probably used, and then try these strategies with their own work.

GETTING READY

- ✔ Each student will need his or her own writer's notebook and a writing tool.
- ✔ A personal narrative from Ai's notebook to be projected (or enlarged on chart paper) (see Teaching)
- ✔ Chart entitled "How to Write Powerful Personal Narratives" (see Teaching)
- ✔ Sample of Ai's writing, with copies for each student (see Active Engagement)
- ✔ Excerpt of Ai's personal narrative (see Link)
- ✔ Several writer's notebooks from former sixth-graders (see Link and Conferring and Small-Group Work)
- ✔ Chart paper for tables (see Link and Mid-Workshop Teaching)
- ✔ Chart titled "My Writing Goals" (see Share)
- ✔ We recommend that you create some kind of meeting area. Usually it's a combination of kids on the floor and kids in chairs, and in some cases kids literally just move their chairs a little bit so they're facing the right way.

COMMON CORE STATE STANDARDS: W.6.3, W.6.4, W.6.5, W.6.10, RL.6.2, RL.6.3, RL.6.5, RL.6.6, SL.6.1, L.6.1, L.6.2, L.6.3, L.6.4.a

AS YOUR SIXTH-GRADERS ENTER YOUR CLASSROOM, they also enter adolescence and, in many cases, middle school. They come with questions: "What will school be like, now that we're sixth-graders? What will writing be like?" The unspoken question is, "What will I be like?" In many ways, life is like a drama; each person plays a role in that drama, and the roles people play shape the ensuing actions and interactions. In these early days of sixth grade and of your writing workshop, your students are stepping into roles within the new context of middle school and, more specifically, of your classroom. It will be important for you to do everything possible to make it acceptable—even inviting—for students to identify themselves as people who like to write.

Let's face it. Luring teenagers to enjoy writing personal narratives will take some finesse. This will be the case if your students have grown up within writing workshops, with personal narrative writing as a staple of their language arts work, because the prospect of writing yet more personal narratives in sixth grade could feel lackluster. And luring students to enjoy writing personal narratives will take even more finesse if your sixth-graders have *not* grown up in writing workshops, because they'll be apt to think, "Nothing interesting happens in my life" and to resist turning around on their own tracks to make something of their experiences. Of course, chances are that some of your students will come to you familiar with writing workshop, while others will be uncertain about what it means to write a personal narrative or to work independently across a publishing cycle. All of this is par for the course for the sixth-grade writing teacher.

Going forward, your job is to get all of your students inspired, feeling that their lives are worth writing about, that they can learn to write with honesty and precision, and that they are part of a community of writers who will hold them up throughout that process. Because the most important work for today will be that of tapping into your students' motivations to put the true stories of their lives onto the page, it will be crucial that you enter this session clear in your own mind why the work of this unit is grand, challenging, significant work. We've talked about this in the introduction to this book; for now, we'll say only that Donald Murray—the Pulitzer Prize–winning writer who is credited as the father of the writing process and who coached journalists at both the *Boston Globe* and the Poynter Institute—always began his writing courses for college students and adults in just the way that you will be beginning your yearlong course of study.

Frankly, the very reason why adolescents will resist personal narrative writing is the reason this work matters for them. Your students are entering an epoch that will be marked by new self-consciousness, a new interest in self-definition, a new effort to distance themselves from parents to answer that age old question, "Who am I?" They will not want to discuss this—heavens no—but the work of thinking, "What is my life story?" "How does this moment fit into the whole of my life?" "What role do I play in those interactions?" "What are the central tensions in my life and how do I deal with them?"—this is significant work indeed.

"Right from the get-go, you'll want to induct students into the rituals and routines and expectations of your classroom."

For today, however, your only job is to start the work of luring your students to want to write. Your job is to help them construct identities for themselves that embrace writing. As you do this, you'll also be working to create that all-important learning culture in your classroom—what educator and scholar Charlotte Danielson refers to as Domain 2. Right from the get-go, you'll want to induct students into the rituals and routines and expectations of your classroom.

We've designed this session as an inquiry. You'll say to your students, "Let's study together to learn the sort of work that middle school writers do when writing personal narratives," and then you'll channel students to examine a few pieces of writing that have been written by other middle-schoolers. Your hope is that this inquiry will remind students of all they learned in prior grades about narrative writing, so they tap all that knowledge (and display it to you) as they write, and that the inquiry will also fill them with respect for the work they are undertaking. The texts they'll study are effective ones—quirky, adolescent, well written.

The saying "A picture is worth a thousand words" could be expanded to "An example is worth a thousand words." Hopefully by studying these texts, students will learn far more than you could impart in a launching lecture. Hopefully students will see that the exemplar texts are a far cry from being chronicles of "The day my team won the championship" or "The day I moved." That is, writers could absolutely write about a winning game or moving from one home to another, but the texts you give students to study will be true stories in which the main character (the writer) has motivations, runs into challenges, and finds ways to overcome these challenges. The texts will advance ideas—interpretations—of experience. Today, then, as you launch your sixth-grade writing workshop, you'll ask your students to study student-written personal narratives so that they are more apt to select story ideas that are compelling and significant to them.

Of course, a writing workshop needs to include time for writing. Although part of today will be reserved for reading and talking about writing, you'll use the mid-workshop teaching as a time to say, "Now it's your turn." Your students presumably will only write about half of a narrative today, finishing the story for homework so that they come to school tomorrow ready to write yet another personal narrative entry. Although you won't tell students this today, your goal will be that day by day, the quality of the flash-draft narratives they produce will improve, so that a week from now, when students select one of these entries—one of these stories—to be the start to a major publication, they will have a great foundation to build upon.

MINILESSON

Setting Up to Write

CONNECTION

Create a drumroll for the writing workshop by emphasizing that the work of writing compelling true stories will require students to help each other and to draw on all they already know.

I gestured to one table of students, asking them to come quickly and directly to the meeting area and to sit on the carpet, benches, and desks close to me. Then I convened the other tables of writers. Waiting for students' attention, I began. "Writers, a couple of months ago I got the list of your names, and since then, I've been researching each of you, trying to piece together some clues about the sort of person you are so that I could plan our year together. What I've learned is that *some* of you—but not all—have *already* learned that professional writers know how to take small moments of their lives and write these not just as," and I shifted my voice to exaggerate total boredom, "'The Day I Won the Game' stories but instead," now my voice shifted to show what a wonderful option this was, "writing about the small moments in ways that make those true stories really important. Will you give me a thumbs up if you've had a teacher, sometimes in elementary school, who tried to teach you about crafting powerful true stories from the small moments of your life?"

A portion of the class signaled that yes, they'd had a teacher who taught the craft of effective narrative writing. Nodding, I continued. "Let me tell you something. This is going to be a big year for you. Becoming a full-fledged middle school author is serious business. But you know what? I'm not worried about you. And do you know why? Because we have expertise in this room—we have people with experience writing the small moments of their lives, and I can already sense that you will be game for helping others in this room who haven't yet tried this kind of writing."

"Am I right that you all are willing to help each other produce powerful true stories? The important thing for you to know is that in sixth grade, expectations skyrocket. I'm going to expect that each of you, as a writer, can fill a page and a half or so of your notebook every day with a compelling true story. That's ambitious, and you're going to need help, so it is great that some of you have experience at this and can help others."

◆ COACHING

Today's session launches the yearlong writing workshop, and therefore it will be especially important for you to take the time to induct writers into the routines that will allow today's workshop—including transitions to and from the meeting area—to be efficient. Keep in mind that a minilesson not only requires that you use methods of teaching—your students also need to use methods of learning. Today you'll not only teach writing; you'll also teach students about the roles they play, the methods they use to learn during a minilesson.

It may seem surprising that in a minilesson that aims to tap students' energy for writing, you emphasize the challenges that lie ahead and the need for students to help each other meet those challenges. This is deliberate. Any entering class of students wants to feel that the work has become more significant, more challenging—and of course the prospect of giving and receiving help among peers is a welcome one for sixth-graders, who are hoping to establish a place for themselves in the social fabric of this classroom.

Name the teaching point.

"Today I want to teach you—to remind you, really—that as a writer, you can get help not only from each other and from me, but also from texts others have written. To learn from finished texts, you need to study them, imagining the strategies the writer probably used so you can then try those same strategies on your own writing."

TEACHING

Illustrate the concept of looking at finished work and imagining the strategies a writer probably used by telling about how you admired a fancy cake, speculating on the recipe.

"Have you ever seen those really amazing wedding cakes that have *tons* of layers? I saw one this summer, and found myself thinking, 'Whoa, how did the pastry chef keep those layers from tipping or from sliding?' It'd be really crazy if, right in the middle of the wedding reception, the cake started leaning over farther and farther until it collapsed all over the floor!

"I'm telling you this because writers study other people's finished writing in just the same way that I studied that towering wedding cake. Writers think, 'Whoa. How did somebody make this?'"

Recruit writers to join you in studying a narrative entry, highlighting the way you first read for content, then pause to name what the writer did well, then speculate on what the writer did to achieve the effect.

"Let's start our year by studying a personal narrative that another middle school writer has made—and see if we can try to figure out the recipe for this piece of writing, the steps that the writer seems to have taken, so we can make writing that is equally powerful. When I'm trying to learn from a piece of finished writing, *first* I just read the writing like it's a book in the library, enjoying it. *Then* I think, 'What did this writer do that worked?' And I look more closely at the piece to try to figure this out. So let's first just read the start of Ai's piece—and then we'll pause and think, 'What works in this writing?' 'How did she pull that off?'"

I read the first portion of an entry from Ai's notebook, which I'd enlarged onto chart paper (see Figure 1–1).

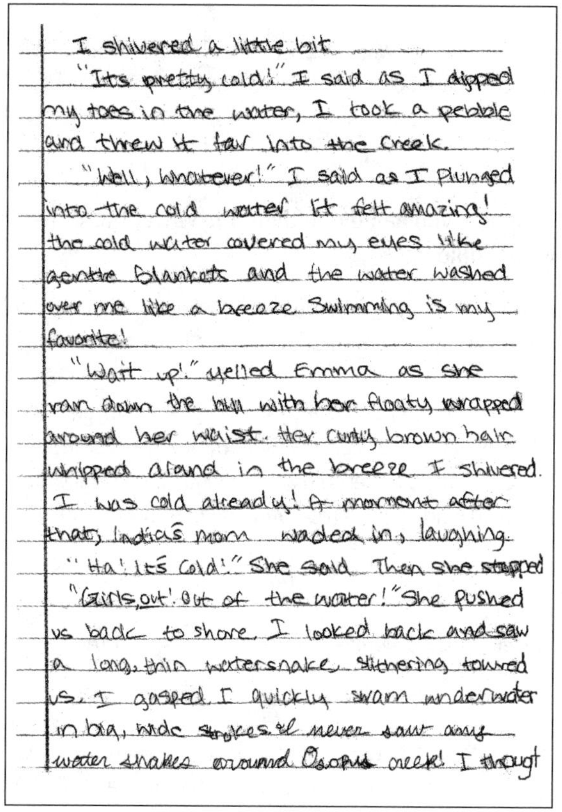
I shivered a little bit
"Its pretty cold!" I said as I dipped my toes in the water, I took a pebble and threw it far into the creek.
"Well, whatever!" I said as I plunged into the cold water it felt amazing! the cold water covered my eyes like gentle blankets and the water washed over me like a breeze. Swimming is my favorite!
"Wait up!" yelled Emma as she ran down the hill with her floaty wrapped around her waist. Her curly brown hair whipped around in the breeze. I shivered. I was cold already! A moment after that, India's mom waded in, laughing.
"Ha! It's cold!" She said. Then she stopped
"Girls, out! Out of the water!" She pushed us back to shore. I looked back and saw a long, thin watersnake slithering towred us. I gasped. I quickly swam underwater in big, wide strokes. I never saw any water snakes around Osopus creek! I thougt

FIG. 1–1 An excerpt of a personal narrative from Ai's notebook, enlarged on chart paper

Notice that I do not phrase the teaching point this way: "Today I want you to read and think about some finished manuscripts." That wording would have simply given an assignment to students, and that is not the goal here. A minilesson is not intended to tell students what you want them to do in the upcoming workshop. Rather, the goal of a minilesson is to explicitly teach students the skills and strategies of good writing—tools that students can draw on often, whenever they write.

Sometimes you will step away from writing to bring home a point about writing. When you do this, try to be quick about it. You don't want your minilesson to detour for too long into grand and glorious accounts of amazing wedding cakes! Make your comparison and then flip back to writing right away. The line, "I'm telling you this because writers . . ." will be one you use often when you want to flip from a real-life comparison back to writing.

You can use one of several methods during the teaching section of a minilesson. Here you use the most common method—demonstration. First, you ask students to join you in doing something—even though, in truth, you are going to pull ahead of them, showing them how a pro works. Students will watch and learn from you more intently if they are engaged in the same work that you are demonstrating, which is why you start off the demonstration as if this will be shared work.

I shivered a little bit.

"It's pretty cold!" I said as I dipped my toes in the water. I took a pebble and threw it far into the creek.

"Well, whatever!" I said as I plunged into the cold water. It felt amazing! The cold water covered my eyes like gentle blankets and the water washed over me like a breeze. Swimming is my favorite!

"Wait up!" yelled Emma as she ran down the hill with her floaty wrapped around her waist. Her curly brown hair whipped around in the breeze. I shivered, I was cold already! A moment after that, India's mom waded in, laughing.

"Ha! It's cold!" she said. Then she stopped. "Girls, out! Out of the water!" she pushed us back to shore. I looked back and saw a long, thin water snake, slithering towards us. I gasped. I quickly swam underwater in big, wide strokes.

"Writers, remember that to learn from finished writing, you first just read it, which we've done. Then you think, 'What part worked for me in the piece?' After that, we can think, 'How did she do that?'

"Hmm . . . What did get to me in the piece?"

Once students are engaged, demonstrate by showing them how you name one thing the writer has done. To highlight what you notice, juxtapose it with what the writer could have done.

"I like how she took this one time in the summer, and wrote a *whole story* about what probably lasted only twenty minutes. This isn't one of those 'My Whole Summer' stories. It is focused, and that makes it better, more detailed.

"Let me reread and see if I can find specific evidence of what I mean when I say that by focusing, she was able to be more detailed," I said, and this time as I reread, I annotated the text, adding a marginal note beside the first few sentences saying, "I can picture this exactly." Then I muttered, as if to myself, "I better think about what she actually did to make it so I can picture this section. What's the recipe for this sort of writing?" I reread and added to my annotation:

I shivered a little bit.

"It's pretty cold!" I said as I dipped my toes in the water. I took a pebble and threw it far into the creek.

"I can picture this exactly. She started with a tiny action and with the exact words she said. She showed the place." Then, turning to a second piece of chart paper, I said, "Writers, remember, I am studying Ai's writing to learn what we can do to make powerful personal narratives—starting today. So let's list what we're learning":

You will notice that I haven't pulled off miracles. Instead, I've named what works in the piece of writing in ways that probably match the thinking that kids were doing (if they have grown up in writing workshops). When demonstrating, think about the piano teacher—she doesn't sit beside a novice pianist and say, 'Watch me' and then proceed to play a complex sonata with great flourish while the kid sits there, dumbfounded. The piano teacher plays just a notch above the student, showing him something he can do with a bit of effort. Although my observation is fairly obvious, it is also foundational, and I want to be sure all sixth-graders know this matters.

How to Write Powerful Personal Narratives

- Focus on one episode, write with detail (don't summarize a stretch of time).
- Help readers picture the episode—a small action and exact dialogue.

Debrief to accentuate the replicable work you've done. Remind your students to use these strategies whenever they are studying narratives to write their own.

"Writers, did you see that I read the text, then paused to think, 'What works that this writer has done?' Then, after I got some start of an answer in my mind, I reread the text, looking for more evidence and more specifics. I annotated the text with the things I noticed and began collecting a list of steps writers can all take to write similarly powerful stories.

"Are you ready to continue reading like a writer, this time on your own?"

ACTIVE ENGAGEMENT

Read the next section of the exemplar student piece, asking students to annotate what works.

Distributing copies of Ai's writing, I said, "Let's read on. Remember, let's first just read like this is a great library book, taking in what she said. Then we can pause to think, 'What got to me in this piece? What works for me?'" I reread the first portion, and then read on:

> I shivered a little bit.
>
> "It's pretty cold!" I said as I dipped my toes in the water. I took a pebble and threw it far into the creek.
>
> "Well, whatever!" I said as I plunged into the cold water. It felt amazing! The cold water covered my eyes like gentle blankets and the water washed over me like a breeze. Swimming is my favorite!
>
> "Wait up!" yelled Emma as she ran down the hill with her floaty wrapped around her waist. Her curly brown hair whipped around in the breeze. I shivered, I was cold already!

I left some silence, then said, "Are you thinking, 'What got through for me?' Try to put into words what, exactly, Ai has done that you think works." I again left a pool of silence, then prompted. "If you find yourself coming up with a quick and easy label for what she has done, push yourself to be more specific. What exactly did she do to pull this off? Be specific enough that you come up with a recipe that you can follow that will work equally well for you." Again I left some silence, knowing that the students were rereading.

"I'm glad to see so many of you underlining and annotating, marking up specific things in the text. Let's reread this one more time, and as you listen, think about all the strategies that teachers in prior years taught you. Maybe Ai has used some of those in ways that really work."

LINK

Channel students to disperse to their writing places, only this time instead of writing, to spend time continuing to read, annotate, and learn from what other writers have done.

"So, writers, today you start your first sixth-grade writing time. In a few minutes, you'll have a chance to start your own writing, but first, take some time to continue reading, annotating, and learning from Ai's draft. When I send you off to your writing places, bring your copy of Ai's writing with you. You can tape it right into page 1 of your new writer's notebook if you want, or tape it onto a blank sheet of paper. In any case, take some time to continue reading, noticing what works, thinking, 'How did she do that?' and rereading to study her craft. You'll learn more from this work if you do it with another person—someone sitting near to you—but you can work alone if your prefer. The important thing is to read Ai's writing in a way that gets you ready to do your own, equally powerful piece of writing.

"But here's one more thing you'll have a chance to do. I'm going to give each table a writer's notebook that a sixth-grader (from last year) filled with the kind of writing you'll soon do. Just as you'll study Ai's draft, you'll also look across the pages of these notebooks to think, 'How are writer's notebooks organized? What seem to be the rules for writer's notebooks? What kinds of ideas for writing am I having now?' You'll have large pieces of poster paper to make charts, listing all the smart things you're noticing about the work these writers have already done that you'll strive to do. When we study the work of other writers this way, it can give us tons of ideas for how we'll do this kind of work, too."

Notice that I am deliberately not reading the good part, when the snake slides into view, when tension picks up, when the characters encounter trouble. Because the plan is for students to continue reading analytically after the minilesson, doing that work with more independence, we're leaving the best part of the text—and the easiest parts—for them to encounter later, when they do not have the support of a read-aloud or of working with each other.

For now, simply pair up students who are sitting near each other in the meeting area. You'll formalize partnerships in the next session.

CONFERRING AND SMALL-GROUP WORK

Helping Writers Build a Vision

FOR THE FIRST PORTION OF TODAY'S WORKSHOP, your sixth-graders will work in pairs, mostly, to continue investigating Ai's personal narrative draft and sample writer's notebooks from previous sixth-graders. You'll want to coach your students to bring a variety of lenses to this work. To do this, move from one table group to the next. At one table, you can channel your sixth-graders to ask, "What seem to be the 'rules' for keeping a writer's notebook?" Of course, you'll also steer them to notice a few things that merit attention. For example, you may find yourself saying, "I'm so glad you noticed that none of the notebooks have pages ripped out of them. You are right, too, that students used legible handwriting, but that it also looks like they were writing quickly. That's a tough combination!"

It's likely that your students will list the topics they see addressed. You'll want to channel them to go from simply noting that the writer writes about this or that topic—say, "best friends"—to helping them see that the writer has zoomed in on particular small moments spent with that person. "You are right that although that friendship spanned years, this writer has focused on a specific memory of one terrible fight with his best friend. It sounds like this whole story of the fight, from where he started telling it until where he ended it, was probably only a half hour or so of time."

As students notice what the writer has done, help them to imagine how they will do similar work. "Are you getting ideas for small moments you might write about? Will you start like this writer seemed to have done by thinking about a best friend or some other person and then coming up with moments spent with that person?"

As you move from table to table, strive to let each student know the ways you already anticipate their contributions. Warmth and words of welcome do matter. "You look like you're really deep into that personal narrative—you must be appreciating all of the details! Make sure to notice how your writer elaborates by moving between characters' actions, their dialogue, and what they are thinking. It's never just one kind of detail, right?" Or "I just noticed that you flipped back to an earlier entry—I love the

(*continues*)

MID-WORKSHOP TEACHING **Making Charts that Our Community of Writers Can Use Independently**

As soon as students at most of the tables had jotted some observations on their charts—and before the students' interest in studying the texts waned—I convened their attention. "Writers, may I please have your eyes? I'm impressed by your respect for these sixth-graders' writing. You came up with some thoughtful observations—but here's the thing. I'm the only one who got to roam around admiring your work. I shouldn't be the only one who gets to learn from the observations you've made. So take three more minutes to finish jotting your thoughts and observations, and then we're going to turn this classroom into a museum and let you study what others have done."

After a few minutes, I asked writers to leave their work on display and to roam around the room, noticing what others had done. And if seeing other people's comments about Ai's narrative draft and the notebooks gave them ideas, I encouraged them to "grab" them, as if pulling those ideas right off the chart and putting them in their pockets for a story they'd soon write.

The students didn't come close to finishing this before I said to them, "You have twelve minutes exactly until writing time is over today. Use that time to get started right now, writing your own first personal narrative, your own true story. Write this in the next page of your writer's notebook. Go!"

way you seem to be trying to figure out this writer's process! And, I overheard you reading aloud that bit of dialogue from the narrative—you really put a ton of feeling into it!"

As you talk with writers, acknowledge the writing experience they bring with them, and try to convey your confidence in them as writers. "That was really sharp to add the generating strategy that your mentor writer is using to your chart—I'm sure you have a few of your own favorite strategies that you go to when you're collecting story ideas!"

If one of your goals is to establish that first highly welcoming contact, another goal is probably to convey your absolute respect for this exemplar writer's practice and commitment to the writer's notebook. This is a time for a bit of drama—open your eyes wide, nod your head in amazement, cluck over the filled pages of the notebook—do all you can to show your students that writer's notebooks are incredible tools, that the writing never ceases to move us, that we learn so much from other writers' story ideas and writing moves. Hopefully, your students will notice more specific "rules" or guidelines for keeping a writer's notebook and add those to their group's chart. They will probably notice the format of the notebook, how the writer dates each entry and leaves the back of pages blank. They might then analyze the ways the writer comes back to those blank pages to jot notes or do some revision work. Most likely, they will discuss the length of entries, noticing that some entries are as much as three or four pages. They may also notice the way the writer uses quick lists throughout the notebook or the way the writer may draw a simple line within an entry to begin storytelling a new story idea.

SHARE

Taking Stock, Clarifying Goals, Creating Authentic Writing Tasks

Convene the writers in the meeting area, and ask them to take stock of where they are as writers right now and where they feel inspired to go.

"Writers, what is one thing you can imagine working even harder at? I've put two of my goals up here, they are both things that I'm already doing well, but I want to turn my strength into a *superpower*." I gestured to the chart:

My Writing Goals

- *Use details that totally transport my readers into my story so they feel like they have traveled back in time to the neighborhood where I grew up.*
- *Write stronger and longer entries–two and a half or three pages in a sitting–not pausing to adjust every sentence.*

"Can you take a minute to begin your own list of the ways you can imagine working hard? I know you won't finish, but you'll have a good start for your homework. Remember to start with something that you feel strong in, and then picture yourself learning from one of the writers you admired today. What is one thing you could learn to do even better?"

SESSION 1 HOMEWORK

DECLARING YOUR WRITING GOALS

"Sixth-graders, for homework tonight, you'll need to finish declaring your own writing goals. Continue to study Ai's personal narrative and notice the writing moves that inspire you and make you want to work hard, as a writer, this year. Finally, using all you know and all you have just learned about generating personal narrative drafts, continue the draft that you began in class in your notebook tonight. I expect you will write about a page and a half, in total. And you'll have another chance to share in the next class."

Session 2

Calling On All Strategies to Write Up a Storm

IN THIS SESSION, you'll teach students that writers call on a toolkit of strategies for finding ideas for their stories and that they can use those ideas to launch into fast and furious writing. You'll also teach students that narrative writers sometimes generate story ideas by thinking of places and the meaningful episodes that occurred in them.

GETTING READY

- ✔ Each student will need his or her own writer's notebook and a writing tool.
- ✔ Chart titled "How to Write Powerful Personal Narratives" from Session 1 (see Connection)
- ✔ Chart titled "Strategies for Generating Personal Narrative Topics (see Connection and Teaching)

Common Core State Standards: W.6.3, W.6.4, W.6.5, W.6.10, RL.6.2, RL.6.3, SL.6.1, SL.6.5, SL.6.6, L.6.1, L.6.2, L.6.3

TODAY YOU WILL TEACH STUDENTS to map places that matter to them as a strategy for finding ideas for personal narratives, and you will teach this as just one of many strategies a writer could draw upon, emphasizing that published writers call on a whole toolkit of generating strategies for help getting themselves started. Your sixth-graders are settling into their identities as adolescents and mature writers, and trust me, it matters to them that these are not just "kid" strategies for generating personal narratives. These are strategies that also work for Newbery Award–winning authors!

As part of establishing their burgeoning identities as writers, you'll want to take a minute to acknowledge the work students did for homework. Writers write, after all, and you'll want to make sure that each and every student understands that homework is not something separate from the workshop but is an integral part of becoming stronger, more prolific writers.

After giving students a moment to share last night's work, you'll begin the new work of the day. To begin the session, you will discuss celebrated author Jack Gantos's map of the neighborhood where he grew up in Florida, the same map that served as his jumping-off point for writing *Heads or Tails: Stories from the Sixth Grade*. Jack speaks often to groups of middle school students and teachers, inspiring the readers who love his books to write their own stories and sharing tips for capturing compelling story ideas and crafting them into powerful personal narratives. When presenting, Jack regularly shares the maps that figure prominently in his own writer's notebooks, acknowledging how much he values this generating strategy. He explains this on his website, with an example of a neighborhood map: http://www.jackgantos.com.vhost.zerolag.com/wp-content/uploads/2011/06/The-Next-Level-Booklinks-article.pdf.

After discussing Jack's neighborhood map together and seeing how the act of remembering one moment often brings to mind another and another, your writers will be eager to get started on their own maps of places that really matter to them. This particular strategy is always a big hit with sixth-graders, many of whom already attack the white space in their notebooks with personally significant doodling. The other appeal of this strategy is the forum it offers sixth-grade writers to document the quirky and humorous details of their lives, the ones that they remember with such clarity and are eager to share within their new writing community.

"Take care to ramp up the level of students' independent work now, setting high expectations early on."

Take care to ramp up the level of students' independent work now, setting high expectations early on. It will be of the utmost importance to emphasize that sketching and labeling a map is just another way to *quickly* list personal narrative story ideas. Nudge your students to be like Jack Gantos and move quickly from the topics they generate when sketching to the beginning of a story. For this reason, you'll use today's mid-workshop teaching point to push your students' volume, to teach them ways they can write more and write faster in one sitting.

In your small-group conferences, when you pull kids together to share their own observations and learning, you'll use the time to point out that sophisticated writers have criteria for weighing story ideas. For example, for all the stories that Jack did jot on his map, there must be many more that he deemed not worth adding. You can teach your writers to assess story ideas by asking themselves if these are truly moments of strong emotion.

This is an important journey for the sixth-grade writer. Some students will think they can only write about the time they broke an arm roller-blading or rolled down the school stairs on the way to the gym. In middle school, you are trying to move them toward moments that are psychologically intense, not merely action-driven. Otherwise, students risk thinking they don't have anything worthwhile to write about if they haven't experienced a dramatic incident or accident. You do not want your students to miss the opportunity to use writing to figure out how they feel *and what they have come to understand* about the more typical, daily moments of their lives—the friend who didn't sit with him at lunch, the team he didn't make, the family interaction that still confuses him.

For more concrete examples of choosing psychologically intense moments over physically daunting ones, you may find it helpful to take another look at sixth-grade student writing samples in *Writing Pathways*. As you reread the stories, notice how each story owes its meaning and tension and brings the reader into the rather ordinary emotional drama of day-to-day life.

MINILESSON

Calling On All Strategies to Write Up a Storm

CONNECTION

Compliment students on their productivity yesterday, referencing the year's new chart.

"Sixth-graders, I have to confess that our very first writing workshop was pretty thrilling for me. I know the pressure is on, that you are feeling the high expectations. Well, yesterday, I saw you step up in a big way. As I watched you annotate Ai's story with your observations and your ideas about what it took for her to arrive at that finished text, I thought to myself, 'Holy moly. These kids already know how to learn from each other.' Normally I'd spend today teaching you the most crucial things about personal narrative writing—but you guys learned those things, on your own, from Ai and the other sixth-grade writers you studied yesterday." I pointed to yesterday's anchor chart.

How to Write Powerful Personal Narratives

- Focus on one episode, write with detail (don't summarize a stretch of time).
- Help readers picture the episode–a small action and exact dialogue.

"Right now, in a flash second, will you show the person beside you the notebook work you've done so far? You might start by sharing the goal you set for yourself at the end of yesterday's workshop and the writing work you did last night to achieve it."

Acknowledge that students already know strategies for generating narrative writing. Channel them to add more strategies to their repertoire by studying another author—this time a published one.

"As you moved from studying Ai's narrative to writing your own, it was clear to me that many of you already know strategies for coming up with true stories—ones that are worth writing. That is, you know the work writers do *before* they get down to the business of writing strong narratives." I gestured to the anchor chart. "You know how to come up with personal narrative *topics*. Yesterday, some of you, like Ai, thought of a person who matters to you, listed small-moment

◆ COACHING

Time is of the essence in the fast-paced world of middle school. Because of this, you will want to keep your lessons short and focused, giving students as much time as possible to write independently. I urge you, however, to take a few seconds several times a week to bring homework into the world of the classroom. It is all too easy for students to see homework as a time-filler (or time-waster). By acknowledging it in the lesson, you help your sixth-graders see that homework is a relevant and important extension of the work they do each day as writers.

stories connected to that person, then wrote one of those as a whole long story." I gestured to a new chart on generating personal narrative topics (to be used for just a couple of days) and pointed to that strategy, listed as the first bullet. "So you now have two charts to consult as you work, one for coming up with ideas and one for writing powerfully."

Strategies for Generating Personal Narrative Topics

- Think of a person who matters to you, list Small Moment stories, choose one, and write the whole story.

"Some of you turned to other strategies to get yourselves started, and once you start sharing those with each other so they become shared strategies, we can put them onto this chart as well. The great thing, though, is that you grabbed a strategy and used it to get yourself writing fast and furious. How many of you—between yesterday and last night—have filled a page and a half or so of your notebook with your own compelling true story?" I demonstrated a discreet thumbs up to clue them as to the signal I wanted.

Some writers signaled they'd done this—fewer than I wished—but I carried on.

"Today I thought you might want to learn from another writer—this time, Newbery Award–winning author Jack Gantos." I held up a couple of books from Jack's popular Joey Pigza series.

Name the teaching point.

"Today I want to teach you that published writers sometimes think of a *place* that matters to them and make a quick sketch—a map, actually—of that place, jotting all the powerful Small Moment story ideas that come from that place."

TEACHING

Project the image of a neighborhood map, and model studying one author's process.

"Writers, yesterday you learned that to learn from someone else's writing, you first just read it, then you think, 'What did that writer do to pull that off? What's the recipe for this kind of writing?' So let's follow that same plan to learn from Jack Gantos's map."

I added, "Let's just read this map, just enjoying it. Remember as you do, though, that we'll pause soon to think, 'What has Gantos done that we could try?'" I displayed his map, and immediately the room buzzed as students talked about parts of it.

Typically you will create and use one or two anchor *charts in our units of study—charts you and your students will build on over the course of the unit. In addition, you will sometimes create more temporary charts—charts that you will use for just a day or two to jot ideas in the moment that don't necessarily help anchor the overall unit. Note that today's chart is a little different. While it functions as a temporary chart as you and your students gather strategies for generating topics, you will soon (in Session 4) synthesize the ideas you gather on this chart to a single bullet and transfer that to your anchor chart.*

After a moment, I asked for the students' attention. "I can tell you are as taken by this as I am. But remember that as writers yourselves, you need to read the work that others have done in a special way. You ask, 'How has he pulled this off? What did he do that I could try as well?'"

Then I said, "So let's look back at this again, and this time, let's notice things Gantos did that any one of us could try. Hmm . . ." I looked at the map. Around the room, hands shot up. I quelled the students' urge to blurt out whatever they were noticing, saying "You'll get a chance soon."

Then, shifting my eyes to the projected image of Jack's map, I said, "So let's figure out what Jack did that you could do as well. Hmm . . . I'm thinking about those boxes right in the middle of the map, aren't you? I think those are the rooms in the house in which he grew up, and this is the canal that ran behind his backyard. So even though there are lots of pictures and captions packed into this drawing, the map is still of one very specific place: the house and yard where he grew up.

"That means that first, this writer had to choose just one place to map, a place where he spent a good amount of time, one that held lots of stories. And, holy cow, there are a lot of stories here! I guess it is true that people have a million stories about the place where they grew up."

Nodding my head as though I was really starting to figure something out, I continued, "There's something else about his map that really stands out to me. It shows a drawing of Jack's dog, BoBo, with a sad, unhappy face. I think that actually this drawing is here as a placeholder for this awful story Jack once told some teachers about a time when one of the mean alligators in the canal actually ate BoBo! Can you imagine that Small Moment story?" Then I said, "So Jack puts little drawings onto the map that each stand for a whole story of 'one time . . .'"

Debrief, reiterating how mapping can be a powerful generating strategy for writing stories.

I exhaled a big breath to show that I was pulling myself out of Jack's story world, and then I said, "Writers, remember, I am studying Jack's map to learn how writers use this generating strategy to make powerful personal narrative writing. It looks like once Jack had a really important place in mind, he remembered Small Moment stories that occurred there and drew quick little pictures representing the stories he could write. Every picture on his map is actually a personal narrative, just waiting to be powerfully written. I wonder if he looks at his map and hears them shouting, 'Pick me! Tell me! Hey Jack, over here—write me next! Writers, let's add Jack's strategy for generating powerful personal narrative topics to that chart."

I didn't tell the students this, but the picture of the drooly dog in the corner stands for another story Jack told a group of teachers. He explained that there were many mean dogs in his neighborhood, and one time, this particular dog bit him and he was terrified. He was convinced the dog gave him rabies!

Strategies for Generating Personal Narrative Topics

- Think of a person who matters to you, list Small Moment stories, choose one, and write the whole story.
- Think about a place that matters, use pictures and quick notes to jot about the small moments that occurred there, choose one, and write the whole story.

"Are you ready to try generating another personal narrative by thinking of a place that matters to you?"

ACTIVE ENGAGEMENT

Set students up to give this strategy a try, scaffolding them through just the first steps.

"Let's try it. Right now, think of a place that matters, a place where you have lived a lot of your life." I stopped talking to give the students a chance to think.

"Okay, writers, you have two minutes to tell the person beside you what place you're choosing and what some of the things will be that you sketch onto your map. Go!"

Remind writers to move quickly from generating topics to writing stories.

"Writers, you'll have time today to write. Some of you will not make a map at all—you already have an idea, just from the map you imagined making. Some of you will reuse yesterday's strategy of thinking of a person who matters to you and writing Small Moment stories connected to that person. All of these strategies are what Jack Gantos calls 'jumping-off points for writing.'"

LINK

Send students off to quickly sketch their maps, generate ideas, and write.

"So remember, when writers are stuck and need ideas about what to write about, one thing they can do is to look at other writing to see what another author may have done. And they can always think of a place and the meaningful

Notice how, over the course of a unit and even a week, I vary the method of practice during the active engagement. Whereas yesterday I set students up to work independently while I guided them through quiet thinking, today I ask them to turn and talk with a partner. On other days, I will ask students to practice my teaching point in writing.

You will notice that I rarely make the work of the minilesson a directive. Rarely is it "I jump," then "You jump." Rather, I typically direct students to add whatever I've taught to their repertoire of strategies and encourage them to make their own, thoughtful decisions about what strategies they will use. In today's case, what matters to me is that everyone comes up with topics and writes stories, not that everyone creates a map of a place. The latter is merely a strategy for moving toward the end goal, and not everyone need draw upon the same strategy.

events that happened there. So go ahead and sketch, label, or write. Put your pen to the paper—go!" Again, for a few moments, I kept my eyes on my own notebook, concentrating on my writing, while most of the students began writing.

I motioned to writers who were writing up a storm to move back to their tables.

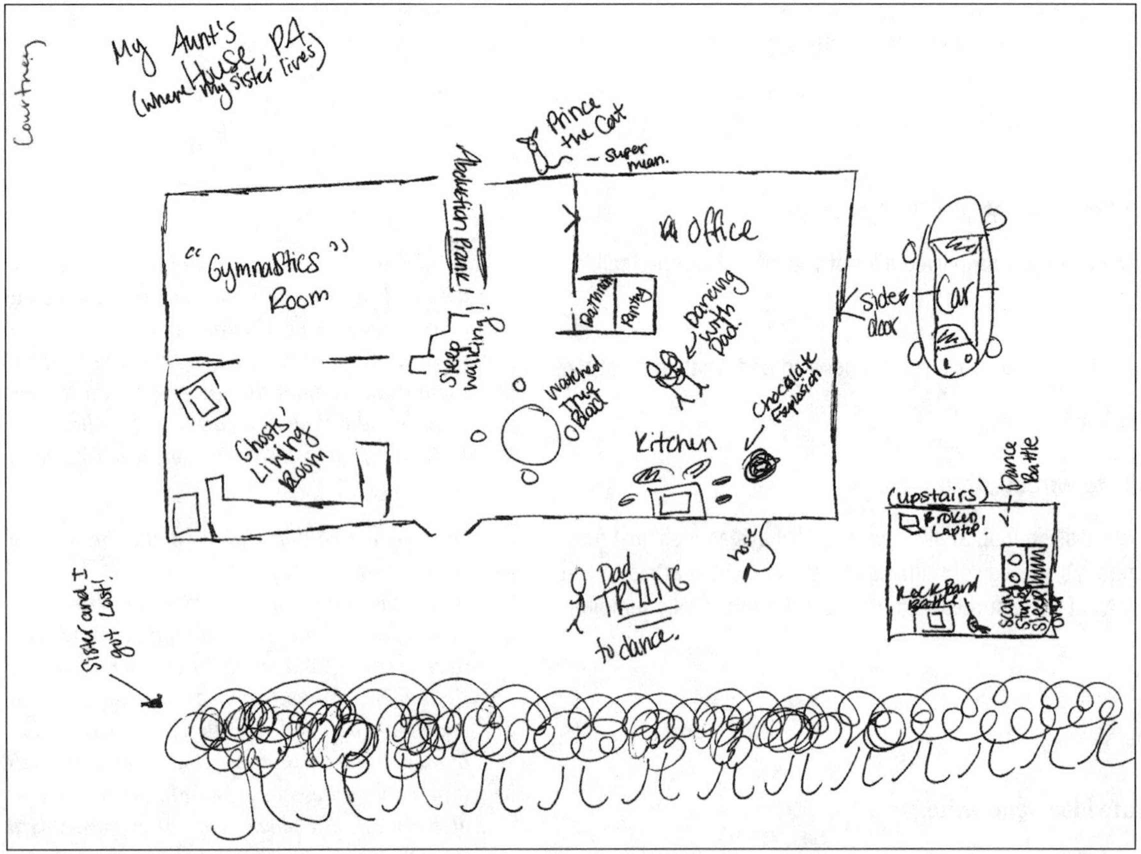

FIG. 2–1 Courtney makes a quick sketch of her aunt's home and jots some of the Small Moment story ideas that come from that place.

CONFERRING AND SMALL-GROUP WORK

Finding Ideas Worth Writing About

WE HAVE TALKED ABOUT THE IMPORTANCE of fostering a safe and supportive writing community and emphasized that this kind of community is a prerequisite for the kind of risk taking and honesty that writing requires. As you look over your writers' shoulders, you'll likely find yourself asking questions like "Is wiping out on his bike last summer *really, truly* what occupies Tim's mind space? Is this the memory that speaks volumes about him and his life?" The answer is most likely a resounding "no," but risk taking takes time, reassurance, and some strategies for writing with depth.

In fact, as you circulate around the room today, you are apt to see many students thinking hard about which moments to include on their maps (or lists or webs). What you may not see yet is much discrimination between ideas. Students may not yet realize that for all the stories that Jack Gantos did jot on his map, there must have been many more that he deemed not worth adding. In tomorrow's session, you'll emphasize an important message about the collecting process: collecting ideas for personal narrative is *not* about thinking up any old topic. Instead, it is about generating ideas that say something about ourselves and our lives. This means that we are apt to disregard some memories and choose others. It may be that you decide to teach that concept to certain students today, ahead of time, to give them more time to work with this important concept.

If you decide to do this, your conferring may go something like the following conference.

I pulled up next to Jelena, who was diligently sketching moments onto a map of her home. "This is where my little brother threw up on the wall," she told me, laughing. "And here's where my mom burned her hand cooking. That was an awful mess." I glanced over Jelena's map, worried that she was playing it a bit safe—grabbing at the first memories that popped into her head. I wondered whether these moments would bring out anything profound about her or yield powerful stories. After complimenting Jelena on her diligence as a writer, I set to work trying to help her develop a more potent topic.

"Jelena," I said, "you know how the books we read usually have a mix of intense feelings? Characters want things. They struggle. They try and try again. Sometimes they fail, but usually in the end they learn some sort of lesson." Jelena nodded and I

(*continues*)

MID-WORKSHOP TEACHING **Building Volume**

"Writers, I'm sure you remember that I said I would expect each of you to fill a page and a half or so of your notebook every day with a compelling true story." When students began to nod, I continued, "Well, that's not entirely true. I actually expect that you'll soon be filling closer to two pages of your notebook every day!

"I think that most of you are getting awfully close to that goal. But I have a practical tip for many of you. I noticed that even when you're writing fast and furiously, getting a stretch of sentences down, you tend to take a break after that stretch. And that break isn't doing you any favors! Today can be the day you get rid of that habit.

"So now, everybody get ready! First, eye the place in your notebook that is a full two pages from where you'll start and mark it with a Post-it®. Now, get there by writing, writing, writing. Resist the urge to stop for a break. Use your strong writing muscles, and forge ahead two pages."

continued on. "Our lives aren't much different. The best stories are those that involve some sort of want, a struggle, or times when we've learned something important. While the moments you've sketched are fun, I worry that they aren't the memories that are most meaningful to you."

I coached Jelena as she went back to her map, reconsidering memories from her home. This time, we focused on times when she wanted something, times when she struggled, or times when she learned a lesson. Before long, Jelena had uncovered a couple of potential seed ideas: the time she pretended to not see her best friend at the bus stop and the time she cut her own hair the night before school pictures. "Jelena, what you've just done is intense work. Personal narrative writers make choices about the moments they'll share from their life, and they know that the most intense moments are those that yield the most powerful stories. It means putting yourself on the line, taking a risk and writing about something that is a bit more personal, but the payoff is huge. I hope that you continue to take risks as a writer and to show others in our class how writing and bravery go hand in hand. And remember, when you're stuck for a potent topic, you can always think back to times when you've wanted something, times when you've struggled, or times when you've learned a lesson."

SHARE

Celebrating, Sharing, and Keeping Ideas Flowing

Celebrate the fact that students are beginning to take risks and write about powerful moments from their lives.

"Your goal this week is to dig into your own and each other's expertise and to produce powerful personal narratives *every day*. It's only our second day of writing workshop, but you've already written drafts that reveal so much about you and your lives—writing that clearly deserves to be shared.

"Some people call this a 'popcorn share' because when you heat up a pan of popcorn, the kernels begin to pop, one right after the other. And that's what you'll be doing: sharing one right after the other. To get ready, you'll need to choose a short excerpt from your notebook to read aloud. Practice reading the words in your head to show their meaning, just the way I read aloud to you from Ai's narrative yesterday." I looked down at my notebook for a minute, to choose and silently rehearse my tiny excerpt of writing, gesturing for them to do the same.

"I think we're ready! I'll point at each of you to share, and remember, it's a *popcorn* share, so it's going to move quickly." I gestured at Ruby, and she read this excerpt from her writing:

> "Well, let's get on with swimming . . ." I nervously said, voice hoarse. I'm not good with waves. <u>Especially</u>, huge waves. The waves slammed the ground so hard it made a huge BOOM-CRASH! The waves were like huge tongues rolling in, out, in, out.

Then I nodded at Garrett and he read a bit from his writing.

> When I got downstairs I felt a cold January breeze. I ran to the black Honda right through the snow. I climbed into the car and closed the door. "Dad, I think we're going to win." This is basically my motto, something I say before every game. My dad laughed. Then he stepped on the gas pedal and started to ride through the January ice and snow.

After a few minutes, I stopped gesturing at students and placed my hands in my lap. "Wow. Can you feel the power of your words? Amazing!"

KEEP THE IDEAS FLOWING AND KEEP WRITING

"I bet this is getting you energized to write more. So that's your job tonight, to keep going. You are the boss of your writing life, and it seems to me like you have a few choices here—go on with one of the personal narratives you started or start a new one. Right now, make a quick plan, and tell your partner what you're going to do tonight. Be ambitious and see if you can set a goal that will push you even further as a writer. Could you aim to write about two pages?" I looked around the room. "I'm thinking most of you could." I gave students a minute to set goals and jot them at the top of their notebooks.

Session 3

Writing from Moments that Really Matter

LEARNING NEW STRATEGIES for generating story ideas is essential for any writer. Jack Gantos turned to the strategy of sketching his neighborhood because it allowed him to overcome the terrifying blank page. In other words, mapping allowed Jack *to get started*. As Jack explains on his author website, "When you look at a blank piece of paper on your desk, or open a diary and see a blank spread, it's really hard to get started. All that perfect white space is intimidating. It's begging you to improve upon it. And it's hard, because every time you put that pencil down on the page, you sort of mess it up." Strategies are the entry points that make it okay for writers to mess up the page and get the memories and words flowing onto the page. The work of the last two sessions has been to push your writers to learn from the writers around them, especially by imagining the strategies those writers used, and to nudge them toward trying those same strategies in their own writing.

In today's session, you will teach students that when writers ponder and jot moments that have really mattered in their lives, they often turn to moments when they realized or learned something significant. In keeping with the goal of moving your students toward small moments that are emotionally intense, not only action-driven, you will teach them to consider the times when they have felt especially strong emotions and may have learned life lessons as a result. By teaching this additional strategy for generating ideas, you are continuing to equip students with that all-important repertoire for facing down the blank page and getting started. However, the most important work of today's session is not the particular strategy but the idea that writers select compelling story ideas that hold the promise of a larger meaning and conflict, elements of most really good stories.

When you teach this, or any, new strategy for generating writing, continue to remind writers that you do not expect they will *all* draw upon it during the day's writing workshop. Keep praising your sixth-grade writers for turning to all of the strategies they have learned in previous years and are now learning from their peers and published writers. Plus, expect that some students have internalized generating strategies and can move right into a flash-draft narrative without visibly generating.

IN THIS SESSION, you'll teach students that to come up with ideas for personal narratives, it can help to think of small moments that matter deeply. Writers often do this by turning to moments when they realized or learned something significant.

GETTING READY

- ✔ Each student will need his or her own writer's notebook and a writing tool.
- ✔ The "Strategies for Generating Personal Narrative Topics" chart from Session 2 (see Connection)
- ✔ Prepare your own example of a time when you realized something important (see Teaching).
- ✔ Begin some notes titled "Moments I Realized Something" (see Teaching).

Common Core State Standards: W.6.3, W.6.4, W.6.5, W.6.10, RL.6.3, RL.6.6, SL.6.1, SL.6.6, L.6.1, L.6.2, L.6.3, L.6.6

MINILESSON

Writing from Moments that Really Matter

CONNECTION

Support students' identities as writers by telling them that you've already begun to notice their individual processes

"All morning, I've been thinking about how most of you, like Jack Gantos, thought of a place that really matters to you and then sketched a quick map, jotting down all the powerful Small Moment stories that took place there. I'm a teacher, so of course I am excited when I see you making use of something I have just taught!

"But I am also excited to see that some of you studied and admired Jack's strategy but then made different choices about how to proceed with your own personal narratives. Some of you returned to the strategy of thinking of a person who matters to you and listing Small Moment stories connected to that person," I said, as I gestured to our chart, "Strategies for Generating Personal Narrative Topics."

"Some of you turned to other strategies you've learned over the years. And some of you moved to your seat, with your story idea already in hand, and just began to write, write, write. You already had your Small Moment story idea and were ready to go. Because you are in sixth grade now, I'm especially pleased to see that you are keeping in mind the real goal—to write compelling stories, to write a lot, to make each day's story better than the day before's—and you are realizing that you can and must make some decisions about how to meet that goal.

"Let's take a minute to share with your partner how you continued to make those important decisions for last night's homework. Open up your notebook to the fast and furious writing you did at home yesterday. Remind your partner of the goal you set for yourself, at the end of yesterday's workshop, and then share how you went about generating your personal narrative topic." The meeting area filled with the hum of students showing off their work to each other.

Teach and recruit students to join you in trying another strategy for generating narrative writing.

"You each may want to make your own personal 'Strategies for Generating Personal Narrative Topics' chart in your notebook. Some of you have ideas that aren't even on the class chart!

"Listening over your shoulders, I heard some of you sharing the strategy of generating quick lists of the first and last times you did something. I went ahead and added that strategy to our class chart. But you also reminded me that *some*

◆ COACHING

Notice that, as I launch today's session, I quickly list out some of the strategies that students used to arrive at their story ideas. From the get-go, I want to remind students that they must take charge of their own writing process.

first and last times are especially powerful because they are moments when you realized something important. That strategy of remembering when you have realized things is worth tucking into your toolkit of strategies."

Strategies for Generating Personal Narrative Topics

- Think of a person who matters to you, list Small Moment stories, choose one, and write the whole story.
- Think about a place that matters, use pictures and quick notes to jot about the small moments that occurred there, choose one, and write the whole story.
- Think of first times or last times you did something, list Small Moment stories you could tell about each, choose one, and write the whole story.
- Think of moments that really mattered because you realized or learned something, list those moments, choose one, and write the whole story.

Name the teaching point.

"Today I want to teach you another strategy that helps people write powerful true stories: jotting moments that have really mattered. Although they *could* be first or last times, what really works is to think about moments when you learned something important about yourself and other people and life. Then write the whole story, fast and furious."

As students develop facility with these strategies, the strategies will become internalized to the point that ideas for writing will blossom even outside of the writing classroom. Your students will start noticing and remembering those important moments that they might want to write about later. If they have their notebooks or digital devices with them, they could jot down a few notes to save for later. This is what real writers do—they are constantly observing, noticing, learning, being surprised, realizing, jotting ideas, recording bits of conversation. Before long, your students will enter your classroom with exciting writing ideas ready to go.

TEACHING

Demonstrate the step-by-step sequence of using this strategy: generate ideas for personal narratives by remembering and listing times when you realized something important.

"Let me show you how I use this strategy—thinking of times when I realized something important—because this can be a way for me to uncover the Small Moment stories from my life that really matter. Pay close attention to my steps, because you'll be trying this work in just a minute.

"To start, I can ask myself, 'What are the moments I can recall when I realized something important?' Hmm . . . that's not so easy, I really need to think. Often, the moments when you come to understand something are pretty emotional ones, so it can help to think about when you have felt strong, strong emotions and learned a lesson as a result.

"There is one time I am remembering. I was absolutely frantic, just completely overwhelmed, and I was racing around trying to fix a terrible mistake I had made after ignoring my dad. When my dad arrived and saw the situation, he didn't get angry, like I expected. Instead, he took a long look at me and said in this really calm, soothing voice, 'It's okay, honey. We can fix this. I'll help you.' I can still remember how tightly he hugged me as he said that. In that moment, I realized something enormous, something that I have always carried with me. I realized that even when I don't listen to my dad and make bad choices, even when I really mess up, my father will help me sort it out." I jotted quickly in my notebook, which I projected for the class.

Moments I Realized Something

The time I was frantic, after destroying the garden, and my dad stayed calm and reassuring. I realized he would always help me, even though I didn't always listen to him.

Debrief, focusing on the steps you took to use this strategy and how it can lead to ideas for writing a powerful personal narrative.

"When I want to choose a powerful topic for a personal narrative, I sometimes brainstorm times when I came to an important realization. Then, I do a quick assessment, looking for the one small moment from the list that feels the most compelling to write out long, in detail.

"I have to tell you that I often return to this strategy because I have discovered that the stories I write about times when I've had really strong feelings followed by an important realization tend to make good personal narratives! Just as importantly, they are the stories that are about more than just the action that is happening—they hold a deeper meaning, one that I can try to bring out as I'm writing."

As students go further into writing personal narratives, they'll realize that the act of writing about a significant realization can often lead them to a richer, more nuanced understanding of what happened and what they learned. Writing can help deepen the thinking process, uncovering new thoughts or feelings about an experience as words and ideas flow on the page.

ACTIVE ENGAGEMENT

Set students up to try the strategy.

"So now I want you to try it. On the next page in your notebook, make a quick list of the times when you realized something important. Remember, to recall those times, it helped me to remember moments when I felt really strong emotions and learned a lesson."

Channel students to do the work alone, voicing over to coach into their work.

"Writers, try to focus in on the moment when you were feeling those emotions most intensely, the moment when your realization was most acute. If you look over your list, and it looks like you are planning to tell a whole, very long story, use the margins of your list to jot the thing you really understood in that moment.

"Do some more jotting quietly for now, and then you can talk with each other."

LINK

Send students off to write their next personal narrative drafts in their notebooks, reminding them to continue to draw from their whole repertoire of strategies to get themselves writing.

"Writers, I know it's hard to tear yourself away from talking about your small moments, but you'll want to save some of that energy for the fast and furious writing you are about to do. I can see that this strategy of thinking of moments that have mattered to you in life is really working for you right now. That's great to remember, because that strategy is there for you to use for the rest of your life!

"Once you are set and ready to write, head back to your seats and carry on. For today you can look over the list you just brainstormed and write one of those stories, or you might go back to another strategy or story idea you've been meaning to put on paper."

It's worth reminding your students that they each carry a repertoire of strategies—the ones they learned today or very recently and the ones they learned in the past. Each day's learning is cumulative. Students are in charge of their own work and should be able to evaluate their personal collection of strategies and apply the ones that fit the work at hand.

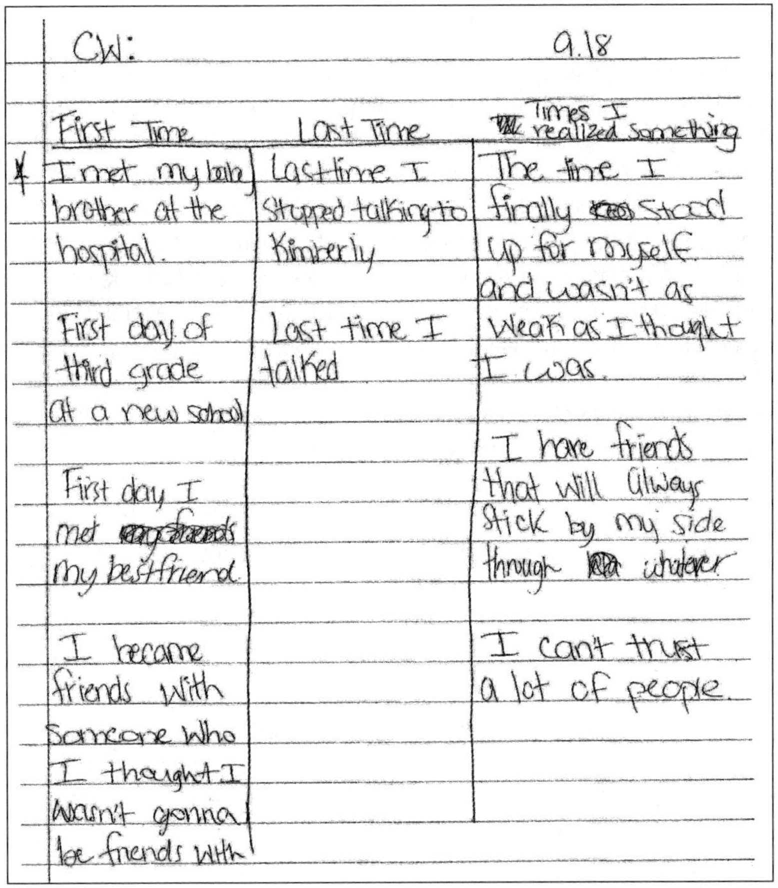

CW: 9.18

First Time	Last Time	Times I realized something
I met my baby brother at the hospital.	Last time I stopped talking to Kimberly	The time I finally stood up for myself and wasn't as weak as I thought I was.
First day of third grade at a new school	Last time I talked	I have friends that will always stick by my side through whatever
First day I met my best friend		I can't trust a lot of people.
I became friends with someone who I thought I wasn't gonna be friends with		

FIG. 3–1 Fionna quickly generates ideas for personal narratives.

CONFERRING AND SMALL-GROUP WORK

Anticipating and Addressing Predictable Problems as Students Draft

As you confer with students today, your hope will be that they, like you, will have found a moment that rises to the surface of their memory banks because it got through to them in a big way—because it left them with an indelible understanding or feeling. Your hope will be that they take that moment and turn it into a narrative that flows easily and quickly onto the page.

The reality, of course, is that not all kids will have this experience. Even though they've been writing for a few days now, as they try on new strategies meant to deepen their writing, some students' writing may in fact veer in the other direction. Some may think too literally about today's teaching, recalling times they learned something concrete, like a new karate move or a knitting stitch, rather than gained an insight into themselves or others. Be careful not to dismiss these kids' ideas. Something meaningful may lurk beneath the memory they select. Instead, nudge them to say more. "You've learned to do a lot of things by now, right? From tying your shoes, when you were maybe four, to braiding your hair, to making a goal, doing math, writing an essay . . . So what is it about learning ___ that's stuck with you all these years?" And "What else came out of that moment that really stuck with you?" If the student is hard-pressed to answer, help her understand what it was about the tight hug your father gave you and the words he spoke in that one moment that stood out from all other hugs and words. Then encourage the student to sift once more through her memories for such a moment. You may need to share more examples of moments that illuminate truths, foster beliefs, evoke emotions. Once these students are on the right track, get them going writing quickly down the page. Sometimes it just takes a little elaboration to turn a bare-bones story into one that has depth. Just as in the previous session, you pointed out that for every story idea an author chooses to develop, there are many he discards, you could encourage students to draw out any details that feel especially significant—ones that highlight why the moment mattered so much.

Meanwhile, you'll have in your room students who easily recall moments that mattered enormously to them—ones in which they discovered how much a parent valued them

MID-WORKSHOP TEACHING **Writing to Bring Out a Feeling**

"Writers, eyes up here for a minute. Max just asked me an important question. He said, 'I know what I felt in that moment, but how do I get the people reading it to feel the same way?' This is one of those age-old questions writers ask themselves. Here's what I know for sure: if you don't feel it, your reader won't either. So put yourself back into that moment. Remember what it felt like to be that earlier version of yourself—whether this means yourself at five or yourself last week. Were you nervous? Sad? On top of the world? Get that feeling into your whole body. It needs to be there for you to bring it out. You won't necessarily write, 'I felt overjoyed' about meeting a baby sibling. But you need to *feel* overjoyed, as you're writing, just as you did when you first laid eyes on his outstretched hand.

"Here's another tip: the bigger the feeling, the smaller you write. The most powerful writing isn't loaded with endless fancy descriptions and clichés; it's full of tiny, precise details. When in doubt, replay the scene in your mind. What did you see? Did the fingers on the baby's outstretched hand curl around your thumb? Did you feel the velvety soft skin, smell the new baby smell? Hear its heartbeat? How did you react? What did you feel? Give us the tiniest details of the moment—the ones that made a lasting mark on you, ones that made it worth sharing."

as the oldest kid of five or what it means to have a friend who's like a brother. These students may write with real zest today. They'll write as you've asked them to, fast and furiously. You'll want to let them go to it, understanding that what they produce will be a first draft, not a polished one. You may find, in peering over their shoulders, that the moment they told you about with such emotion loses its power on the page. Don't despair. You'll have plenty of opportunities to help these kids hone their writing as they try out different strategies for tapping into voice and craft. For now, it's enough that they have found a moment that feels deeply personal to them. Remember, if it doesn't matter to them, it won't matter to the reader. Of course, it's never too early to give tips on strong narrative writing, so don't hold back from reminding kids of the power of "show, not tell" or of including lots of specific details or mixing in dialogue with actions.

Chances are, you'll have students who are ready to write a newly selected memory that's come easily to mind, who nonetheless struggle to get words onto the page. They may need simple reassurance that this draft need not be perfect—in fact, it would be a miracle if it were! Tell them that some writers generate fifty drafts of a single story before it is published. Some students may be hesitant to put into writing something that is so personal. Remind them that all writers take risks when they write. Stories that reveal something deeply personal are often the best kind, and this year, the whole class of writers will take this risk together. Encourage these kids to trust their guts and to write with abandon.

SHARE

Thinking "Who Am I as a Writer?" to Bring Out Meaning

Admire students' collective work and individual writing styles.

"Writers, as I've been peering over your shoulders, it's been easy to admire your writing. You're drawing not only from your memories, but also from your understanding of how powerful stories go—and it shows. What I've noticed is that even though we now have a shared sense, as a class, of some things that make a story strong, each one of you is bringing your own particular understanding of this to your work. I can see that Xander prefers crisp short sentences. His style reminds me of Hemingway's. Hemingway is a famous twentieth-century American writer, known for his tight prose. What strikes me is that Xander's way of writing reflects so much who he is, not only as a writer, but as a person. I see his fingerprint in his work, and I see Xander. And so it's easy to put myself into his narrative and to get a sense of why that moment mattered so much.

"Jasmine, meanwhile, clearly favors long, descriptive writing. Reading her narrative, I can see exactly where she was, and I can feel how life-changing this moment was for her. There's such a sense of mood here. I can tell that the physical place she was in played an important role in her memory."

Ask students to reflect on their writing styles and intentions and then to turn and talk to a partner about their insights.

"Rather than sharing bits of your writing, as you did yesterday, I thought you might take a minute to think about your particular style of writing—and how it reflects who you are, what you learned in that moment, what you're hoping to make your reader feel. Take just a little bit of time to reflect."

After a pool of silence, I said, "Now turn and talk to your partner about what you noticed. Maybe it's your writing style or the particular strategies you seem to use again and again to make your writing powerful. Maybe it's that you push yourself to hone in on the tiniest of details, the ones that pull readers right into the moment."

BRINGING OUT YOUR STORIES' MEANING

I reconvened the class. "I'm glad I asked you to do this. I can tell it's got you thinking. Part of learning how to write well is knowing who you are as a writer—what your voice is, the kinds of things you tend to want to write about, your style of writing. Tonight, I want you to take this exercise a step further. I want you to think not only, 'Who am I as a writer?' but 'How can I use this understanding to dig even deeper into the story I'm telling? How can I use this understanding to bring out my meaning?' Then use that knowledge either to develop one of the personal narratives you've written so far or to begin a new one. Remember, your goal is to write *at least* two pages in a sitting, as much as you can."

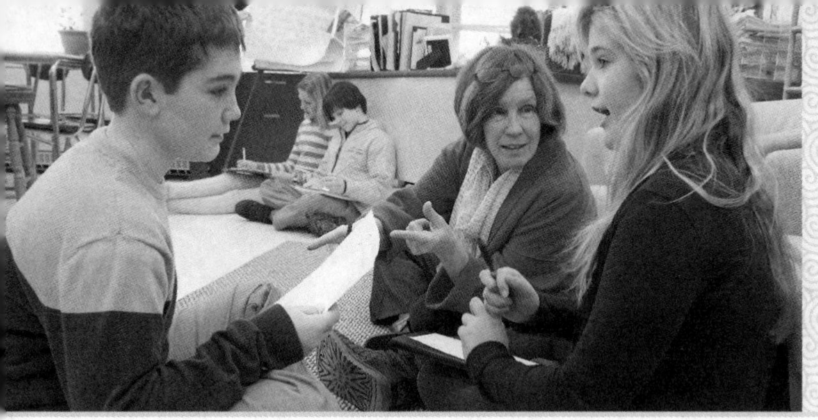

Session 4

Telling the Story from the Narrator's Point of View

IN THIS SESSION, you'll teach students that to write effective narratives, writers reimagine the episode as they put it on paper, so that readers will be able to experience it, too.

GETTING READY

- Each student will need his or her own writer's notebook and a writing tool.
- A story "before" and "after" revision, one in which you first slip out of the narrator's point of view and then fix the problem (see Teaching)
- An oral story on which students can practice imagining the episode before rewriting it (see Active Engagement)
- A revised version of the anchor chart "How to Write Powerful Personal Narrative," with the ideas from the temporary chart "Strategies for Generating Personal Narrative Topics" synthesized into a single bullet and added to the top of the anchor chart. Also add to the bottom of the chart the strategies taught in today's lesson (see Link).
- Two excerpts of a student's personal narrative, before and after revising, to project for the class or copied onto chart paper (see Share)
- "Questions to Ask Yourself as You Edit" checklist (see Homework)

COMMON CORE STATE STANDARDS: W.6.3.a,b,c,d,e; W.6.4, W.6.5, W.6.10, RL.6.2, RL.6.3, RL.6.6, RL.7.6, SL.6.1, SL.6.4, SL.6.6, L.6.1, L.6.2, L.6.3

IT IS ONE THING to *hear* that the writer should tell a story in ways that help the reader experience it, adding words and details to replay the story bit by bit, but it is an entirely different challenge to write from inside the story and actually do this well. You'll find, therefore, that although other teachers in previous years taught your students to story-tell, you'll end up teaching this again, and then again. After all, with repetition and practice comes deeper and deeper understanding.

Earlier, you urged students to search deep down for moments that really matter, writing in ways that show heart. In this session, you'll build on that intention, teaching students to search once more, this time reimagining that story, reliving that moment, reexperiencing those feelings and retelling it from the inside. You'll be teaching students to maintain a point of view as they write and to be able to reread their rough draft entries and notice times when the point of view doesn't ring true, moving to sweeping summaries rather than in-the-moment accounts, or unrelated descriptions that distract the reader. I recall one such writer who, in midst of telling a story about meeting her newborn baby sister for the first time, interrupted with a description of the cold, rainy weather outside. When I reached for the words to capture why this passage didn't work, I realized that the details reflected the fact that she found it difficult to maintain a point of view, to truly tell the story as if she had experienced it once again. I suspected she had included these details about the weather perhaps because she had learned the strategy of adding sensory details, not yet fully grasping how to harness this technique to drive the heart of the story, and instead plugged in details where there was space.

In today's session, you will teach students that telling a story through a narrator's eyes means keeping a consistent point of view throughout the piece. Over the past few days you've been encouraging students to write with their full attention on the heart of their story, writing about moments that truly matter. This session focuses on point of view and extends the larger message.

MINILESSON

Telling the Story from the Narrator's Point of View

CONNECTION

Celebrate the way students have learned to search for moments that yield deep and meaningful personal narratives.

"I want to celebrate something before we begin today's lesson. I'm so proud of the ways you're growing so quickly as writers. You may not realize it, but you've already come to understand something critical in the life of a writer. Do you know what that is?" I paused for a moment to build a bit of suspense. "Writers are incredibly brave people—they take risks each time they put their pen to paper and tell a story.

"I think you are coming to realize, as you make decisions about which small moments to choose as topics for your personal narratives, that there is tremendous payoff in those moments of strong emotion and struggle and profound realization. It isn't always easy to revisit those kinds of tense life moments, but you are figuring out that it is worth it. In my eyes and the eyes of your writing community, that makes you brave, too.

"This makes me think it's time to ratchet up the level of that work even further so that the drafts you write get better and better, each day."

Name the teaching point.

"As writers of true stories, you already know how important it is to write from inside the story moment, telling the story as it unfolds, but today I want to teach you that writers are especially careful about telling the details of the story *exactly* the way the narrator perceived them at the moment."

TEACHING

Tell a story that demonstrates the moves you had to make, as a writer, to stay inside your narrator's point of view.

"When people talk about *point of view*, they are talking about the way the narrator tells the story through his or her eyes and other senses. The details in the scene need to be the ones that the narrator can take notice of—otherwise, they don't belong there.

◆ COACHING

Notice that even with our compliments we are teaching students how to become powerful writers, not only how to produce one given powerful piece of writing.

Note that the term point of view *is not used here in the sense of first- or third-person storytelling. Instead, it is meant more literally, seeing through the eyes of the character and considering what the narrator saw, heard, and felt in the actual moment, as well as what details the narrator did* not *notice, so as not to include them in the writing.*

"When I think about writing inside a point of view, I always think back to when I was writing about changing my squirmy baby sister's diaper. At that moment, our father walked through the door with a large box. I wanted to run over to help open the box, but of course I couldn't leave my sister half-diapered on the changing table.

"At first, I wrote the story like this," I said, and began reading my story aloud.

> I was still at the changing table, my sister squirming beneath me, when my dad put the box on the kitchen table and then, peeling off a long strip of tape and pulling back one of the flaps, looked in on a jumble of family photos, with little photo albums scattered throughout. The photos showed me and my sister when we were little—they were the ones he'd lost.

As I talk, I hold my arms out, acting out how physically tethered I am to the baby in this moment. I want students to grasp that while I am busy with my sister at the changing table, my dad is opening the box. I am hoping that as they watch me acting out my part of the scene and hear my intonation, it will become obvious why I could not have known, in that moment, what was inside the box.

"But wait, this couldn't have been possible! I was at the changing table, right in the middle of a serious diapering operation. I couldn't move an inch. My dad and the box were across the room. How would I know what he was seeing inside the box? It helps my readers if I tell the story exactly the same way I experienced it. Let me think about this again. I'm standing at the changing table, trying to get my squirmy sister's diaper fastened, barely able to glance at my dad as he opened the box. So the story, as I (the main character and narrator) experienced it, goes more like this":

> I was at the changing table, my sister squirming beneath me, when my Dad came into the kitchen and dropped a heavy carton on the kitchen table. I heard him rustling about, and then I heard him mutter, "Unbelievable, just unbelievable." He looked up from across the room and called, "Remember all those lost photos from our farm? They're all here!"

Debrief, reiterating the moves you made to clarify and strengthen your story's point of view.

"Writers, do you see the major adjustment I made in the second version? Only my father could reveal the contents of the box! When writing, I have to step back in time and write from my point of view at that time. I can only capture what I saw, heard, or felt from my particular perspective."

If some students struggle to grasp how to write from within the narrator's point of view, suggest that they act out being the narrator as you just modeled. They could move, observe, listen, talk, feel, and think as the narrator would in a situation. Some students need to make this kind of concrete, physical connection—into their very bones—to truly understand how to write personal narrative.

ACTIVE ENGAGEMENT

Set students up to practice telling a small moment through the main character's eyes, exactly the way he experienced it. To start, ask them to listen to a draft where the point of view is not consistent, pointing out where revision is needed.

"Once you get used to the concept of stepping back in time and writing only from one perspective, it's easier to spot moments when you fall out of perspective. Let's practice noticing when a writer slips out of his or her perspective by mistake. As you listen to my draft, decide, 'Is the point of view consistent?' in which case, give me a thumbs up, or 'Did the narrator just fall out of one point of view?' In that case, give me a thumbs down." I read aloud from my notebook:

I made my way slowly toward the front of the line, as one by one, kids in soggy bathing suits sat at the edge of the water slide before disappearing suddenly down the chute. I was next in line and the thumping in my heart was almost audible. "I can do this," I thought to myself. I took one step forward . . .

I looked up at the students. "Am I still inside the story or have I fallen out? Thumbs up or thumbs down so far?" They all put their thumbs up, signaling my point of view was accurate. I continued to read:

Soon I was at the edge of the slide. I leaned forward just enough to peer down below at the small, blue rectangle of a pool dotted with the heads of swimmers below. I shut my eyes quickly, dizzied from the height.

Again, I paused, and the students were quick to give me their thumbs up.

I carefully sat down, feeling the cold rush of water beneath me. My hands gripped the edges of the slide. "Ready?" the attendant asked. "I think so," I replied, still unsure. [Thumbs up.] My cousin waited at the bottom wondering what was taking me so long.

I read the last line with a little more emphasis and then paused, looking meaningfully at the students to see if they had realized that I had just lost my perspective as the narrator. A few students glanced around and then gave a thumbs down. Soon, the other joined in. "That's right, this last part does not work, because I couldn't have possibly known what my cousin was thinking at that moment."

In my story, I intentionally use words that make it clear when I'm writing from within my point of view and when I step outside of it. Intonation helps me emphasize this as well. There are only a few minutes for students to practice the concept I've just taught, so I strive to set them up for as much success as possible.

LINK

Remind students of the importance of maintaining their narrator point of view as you send them off to write.

"Writers, take just thirty seconds to decide on the powerful Small Moment story you'll begin drafting in today's workshop. If you need help getting a topic, I synthesized our ideas from our temporary chart, 'Strategies for Generating Personal Narrative Topics,' and added them to the top of our anchor chart, 'How to Write Powerful Personal Narratives.' I also added the new technique I just taught you," I said, pointing to each item on our chart.

How to Write Powerful Personal Narratives

- **Think of a person, place, or moment in your life (maybe a first or last time, or a time when you realized something) that matters, and write a story about it.**
- Focus on one episode, write with detail (don't summarize a stretch of time).
- Help readers picture the episode–a small action and exact dialogue.
- **Climb inside the moment and write within the narrator's point of view.**

"So right now, think of a topic, and think about how you will begin your story." I looked down at my own notebook while they reflected. "Now that you have your story, travel back in time, back into your point of view, at that time.

"Right now, as you move back to your desk, use this strategy—this strategy you can use from now on in your writing life: hold tight to that picture you have in your mind. Zoom into the tiny details of the place—the ones you can see from exactly where you are in the story. What are you saying? What are you doing?"

As students moved from the meeting area to their desks, I waited. Once many had settled, I said, "If you've made it to your seat, then your notebook is open and your pen is flying. Get started on your next personal narrative!"

CONFERRING AND SMALL-GROUP WORK

Using Details that Convey the Meaning We Intend

As you move among your students, reading over their shoulders, you will probably see that many of them are making an effort to write detailed narratives. That will please you. But it is also likely that often their details will feel off to you, leaving you unsettled. Did your teaching help? It will be important for you to remember that when your students work to do some new things as writers, they will be novices at those things. You still want to support their attempt to outgrow themselves. You also want to give added feedback. The minilesson is not your only forum for instruction, and once writers are attempting some work, they are especially ready to extend their skills.

If the details that some students insert into their narratives do not ring true, chances are good that the student has yet to really learn what you were trying to teach in this minilesson. As Gabe rang the doorbell at his friend's house, did he *really* take notes of the fact that the door was wooden and brown? As Sarah scanned the cafeteria for an available seat, did she really notice one red metal chair? Didn't she instead see an empty chair, only to notice it was next to some seventh-graders?

The details that work in a narrative are those that the writer actually saw and thought about and noticed when experiencing that event. You can encourage writers to self-assess, asking questions such as "Is this something I really would have noticed?" and "Does this detail serve a purpose—does it help my reader to feel or imagine something that is important to my story?"

You will also want to help writers get started on a pathway that produces details that ring true. The best way to do this is to ask that writer to retell the memory, starting with the beginning, telling it with specifics. "Where were you, exactly? What did you notice, sitting there? What did you do next? Exactly how did you do that?"

You might also share an excerpt from a text so that students can study effective detail. Even a short excerpt will work. At the Teachers College Reading and Writing Project, one of our favorite excerpts comes from Jean Fritz's memoir, *Homesick* (1982). In this passage, Jean is describing her entrance into her home, describing the hallways in a

(*continues*)

MID-WORKSHOP TEACHING **Writers Choose What They Will and Will Not Include**

"Writers, let me stop you for a moment. I see many of you are writing from inside your stories, reliving the experience and writing to capture the events, feelings, and details on the page. As you do this, I want to remind you that writers are a picky bunch. Writers don't just slap any ol' details or any ol' dialogue onto a page. Instead, writers make calculated decisions about the details to include.

"Let's take my diapering story. There were a million things I could have included. I could have told my reader that my sister's tummy felt warm or that I heard her cooing as she wiggled or that my dad was wearing jeans or that the box he carried was brown. All of this would be true, but it wouldn't help my reader understand the meaning behind the moment—that I wanted to be done with diaper duty to be part of what my dad was doing. So instead, I chose to include details about holding my sister in place as I leaned forward to see what my dad had in the box, and about my dad pulling back the long strip of tape. I wanted to show that I was dying to see what was in the box. Do you see how I made choices and how those choices were driven by what I most wanted my reader to know and understand?

"As you continue writing, ask yourself what you most want to show your reader. Then, be picky about the details you include, adding only those that help your reader to experience what your story is really about."

way that reveals not only the hallway, but also what she wants her readers to understand about her as a person.

> *I flung open the iron gate and threw myself through the front door.*
>
> *"I'm home!" I yelled.*
>
> *Then I remembered that it was Tuesday, the day my mother taught an English class at the Y.M.C.A. where my father was the director.*
>
> *I stood in the hall, trying to catch my breath, and as always I began to feel small. It was a huge hall with ceilings so high it was as if they would have nothing to do with people. Certainly not with a mere child, not with me—the only child in the house. Once I asked my best friend, Andrea, if the hall made her feel little too. She said no. She was going to be a dancer and she loved space. She did a high kick to show how grand it was to have room.*

Notice that the details in this passage are not details about the setting, but about the writer's actions. These are details that ring true. Those of us reading them are brought back to that moment, and to the feeling the author had at that moment.

SHARE

Living Inside the Details of the Moment

Share an example of a student's personal narrative and how he reworked the sensory details to make them the ones the character would have truly noticed in that moment.

"Writers, I want to show you how last year, one of my students, a boy named Kei, spotted some details in his personal narrative that just didn't ring true." I projected an excerpt from Kei's unedited personal narrative for the class, then continued. "He was rereading the narrative he wrote about when his dog, Jamp, swallowed a sewing needle. He wasn't just rereading—he was self-assessing, asking himself, 'Are these all details I really would have noticed right then, in the moment?' Read along with me and see if the details make sense."

> We ate lunch and just sat down watching the T.V. as a family. We usually just leave Jamp wandering in the house so he has freedom.
>
> My great-grandmother likes to sew and do many cool things with fabric. She's been doing it all her life. While we were watching T.V., Jamp went to my great-grandmother's small shelf that had all the things that she used for sewing.
>
> Then Jamp came running out of the room to us. "Ahhh!" I screamed as I saw Jamp cough up some blood on the floor. He had swallowed a needle and was running around the room screeching in pain. My mom picked him up and took him to the vet quickly.

"Turn and talk, what do you think?" The room filled with the students' animated talk, as they quickly realized that Kei could not have known, at that point in his story, that Jamp had rummaged around his great-grandmother's sewing shelf or that he had swallowed a needle!

I spoke above the students to pull them back together. "Just like Kei, we are all noticing that his storytelling just doesn't make sense here—it's out of order and confusing, so it pulls you, the reader, out of the moment. So Kei went back in his mind to that memory and tried to tell it more specifically. He tried to remember where he was and where Jamp was and what happened step by step. Then, he wrote that scene again. Take a look." I projected an excerpt from Kei's revised personal narrative for students to read along.

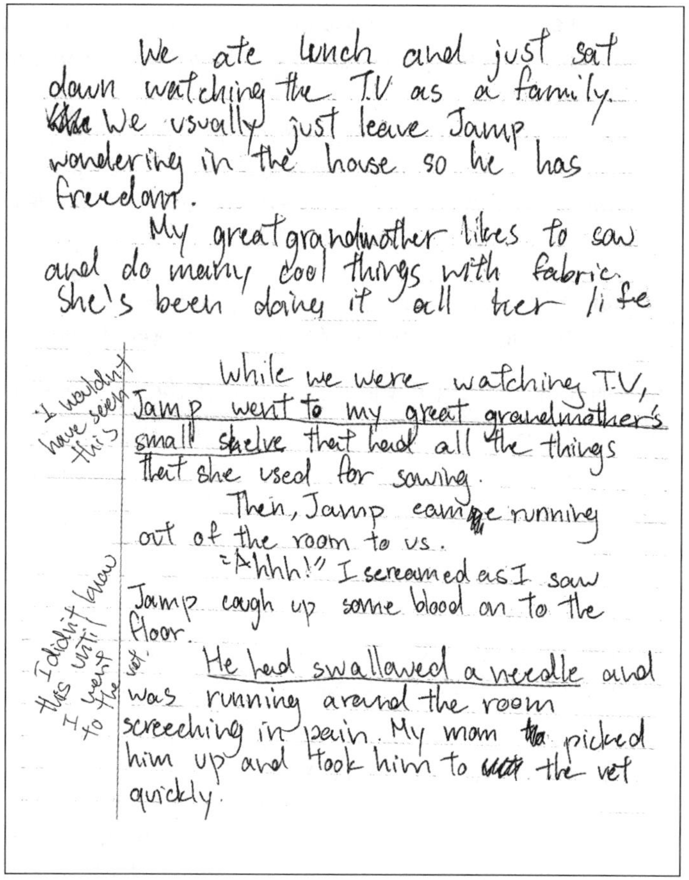

We ate lunch and just sat down watching the T.V as a family. We usually just leave Jamp wondering in the house so he has freedom.

My great grandmother likes to sow and do many cool things with fabric. She's been doing it all her life

I wouldn't have seen this

While we were watching T.V, Jamp went to my great grandmother's small shelve that had all the things that she used for sowing.

Then, Jamp came running out of the room to us.

"Ahhh!" I screamed as I saw Jamp cough up some blood on to the floor.

I didn't know this until I went to the vet.

He had swallowed a needle and was running around the room screeching in pain. My mom picked him up and took him to the vet quickly.

FIG. 4–1 An excerpt from Kei's writer's notebook, before revision

I was sitting on the left side of the couch with my mom sitting next to me on the right. My great-grandma and grandma were sitting on the cushioned seats across from us. Jamp was between my mom and me, snuggled between the cushions. My grandma smiled toward us and said, "Let Jamp get off the couch." I knew Jamp wanted to wander around the house.

I pet him and he jumped off the couch. As I turned to watch the television, I heard Jamp's footsteps go into my great grandmother's room.

Just a few minutes later, Jamp came running out of the room. His choking cough grabbed my attention. I looked over and saw him coughing blood. "Ahhhh!!!" I screamed. I quickly stood up on the couch. I was too shocked to care about my grandma's rules.

"Do you see how, this time around, Kei manages to keep his story on track? His details put you right into his world, and they work well because they sound like the true details that he would have noticed in that moment."

Ask students to share their own writing and to talk about where the sensory details do and don't ring true, as well as the ones the character would actually notice.

"Will you read a portion of writing to each other, choosing a part where you've included sensory detail, and will you and your partner think about which of your details do work, and which don't yet work?"

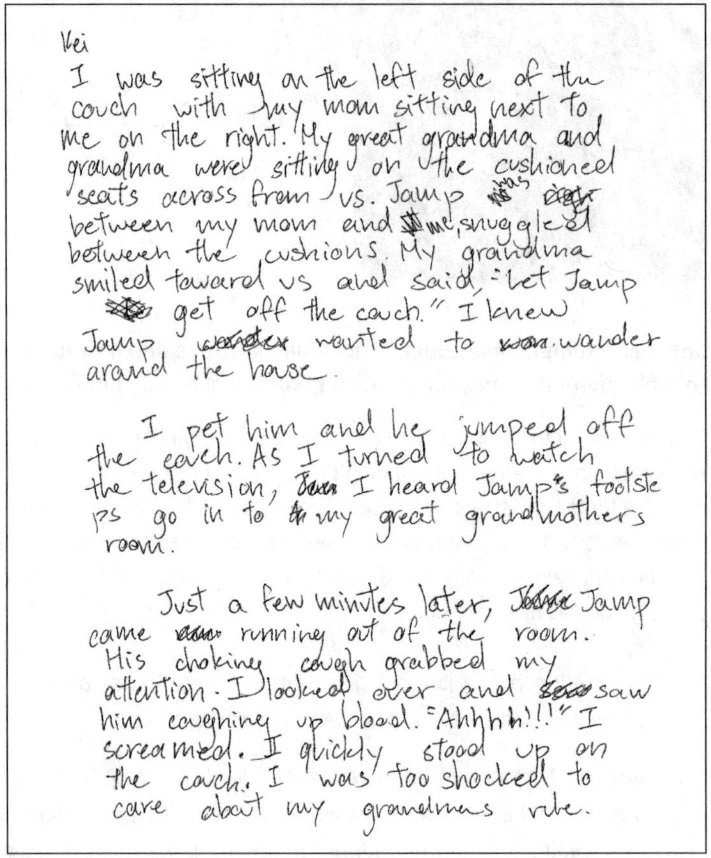

Kei
I was sitting on the left side of the couch with my mom sitting next to me on the right. My great grandma and grandma were sitting on the cushioned seats across from us. Jamp was between my mom and me, snuggled between the cushions. My grandma smiled toward us and said, "Let Jamp get off the couch." I knew Jamp wanted to wander around the house.

I pet him and he jumped off the couch. As I turned to watch the television, I heard Jamp's footsteps go in to my great grandmothers room.

Just a few minutes later, Jamp came running out of the room. His choking cough grabbed my attention. I looked over and saw him coughing up blood. "Ahhhh!!!" I screamed. I quickly stood up on the couch. I was too shocked to care about my grandmas rule.

FIG. 4–2 An excerpt from Kei's writer's notebook, showing his effort at revising to make his details ring true.

SESSION 4 HOMEWORK

EDITING AS YOU WRITE

"Sixth-graders, as you know, strong writers are in the habit of editing *as they write*. That means that even as you draft in your notebook, you are always looking back over your writing and asking, 'Am I using my best spelling, punctuation, and grammar to make my writing as readable as possible?'

"Tonight you'll move forward with your personal narrative, or begin a new personal narrative, but you'll also make time to look over your prior drafts and do some editing. Here is a checklist to help you."

Questions to Ask Yourself as You Edit

1. Does this make sense? Are any words or parts missing?
2. Are all my sentences complete? Have I checked for run-ons and fragments?
3. Have I used correct capitalization (for names and the beginning of sentences)?
4. Have I used commas and quotation marks for dialogue?
5. Have I checked to see that all my verbs and subjects agree? Are my verbs in the right tense (past, present, future)?
6. Do the words all seem to be spelled right? Do they look right? Have I checked any I'm uncertain of?
7. Have I checked for frequently confused words (to, too, two; there, their)?
8. Have I paragraphed and indented?

1. Does this make sense? Are any words or parts missing?
2. Are all my sentences complete? Have I checked for run-ons and fragments?
3. Have I used correct capitalization (for names and the beginning of sentences)?
4. Have I used commas and quotation marks for dialogue?
5. Have I checked to see that all my verbs and subjects agree? Are my verbs in the right tense (past, present, future)?
6. Do the words all seem to be spelled right? Do they look right? Have I checked any I'm uncertain of?
7. Have I checked for frequently confused words (*to, too, two; there, their*)?
8. Have I paragraphed and indented?

Session 5

Reading Closely to Learn from Other Authors

IN THIS SESSION, you'll teach students that one way writers raise the level of their own writing is by imitating the personal narrative writing that inspires and moves them.

GETTING READY

- ✔ On an earlier day, students need to have listened to you reading aloud "Everything Will Be Okay" by James Howe. Today you need a marked-up text of "Everything Will Be Okay" with the powerful parts of the story circled in red (see Teaching).
- ✔ Chart paper to create the chart "Lessons from Mentor Narratives" (see Teaching)
- ✔ Excerpt from "Everything Will Be Okay" to project or copied onto chart paper (see Active Engagement)
- ✔ A copy of "Everything Will Be Okay" for each student to bring to the meeting area and annotate during the workshop (see Active Engagement)

COMMON CORE STATE STANDARDS: W.6.3.a,b,c,d,e; W.6.5, W.6.9.a, W.6.10, RL.6.1, RL.6.2, RL.6.4, RL.6.5, RL.6.10, SL.6.1, SL.6.6, L.6.1, L.6.2, L.6.3, L.6.6

AS A YOUNG CHILD with plenty of older siblings and cousins, I spent a lot of time studying the big kids. I imitated the way one older sister blew her bangs out of her eyes with a sharp exhale, I turned the pages of books at the exact same pace as my older brother, and I spent too many hours striving to crack my gum like my teenage cousin. I was often ribbed for being a "copycat," but I wasn't simply copying, I was gathering images and ideas of what it meant to be a big kid, and I was trying bits and pieces on to see how they fit.

I eventually shed my childhood identity as the family copycat, but I continued to value how much someone can learn through careful observation and emulation. This was most obvious to me when I was a student teacher and spent many hours studying the craft and personas of master teachers. As eager as I was to write my own lessons and begin teaching the class, I understood that there was so much to learn from watching experienced and highly skilled teachers in action. Learning through close observation is the heart of any apprenticeship program, and history has proved that it is a highly effective system for training novices and setting them on the road to becoming masters. Your sixth-grade writers will benefit tremendously from learning to apprentice themselves to all the written words and works of other authors who have come before them.

To launch this bend, you taught students that they can learn from former sixth-graders' manuscripts by studying that finished work and imagining the strategies the writer probably used. Your hope was to remind students of all they learned in prior grades about personal narrative writing and to nudge them toward selecting story ideas that are compelling and significant to them. In today's session, you will again teach students to study a mentor text—this time, "Everything Will Be Okay" by Jim Howe—but the new work will center especially on using a study of mentor texts to lift the level of student narrative writing.

MINILESSON

Reading Closely to Learn from Other Authors

CONNECTION

Use a metaphor to illustrate that apprentices are always trying to imagine the process behind the finished product.

"Sixth-graders, if you have ever seen my daily lunch spread, you may have figured out that I am a serious 'foodie.' For me, food is more like a hobby than just a basic need.

"So when I eat at a restaurant, I am in research mode! The thought bubble above my head sounds something like this: 'Hmm . . . That's an interesting presentation for the salad. It looks like the vegetables have been shaved with some kind micro-peeler to create these translucent ribbon shapes. And would you look at this sprinkle of purple and red carrots? The colors contrast so nicely with the greens in the salad. I am going to remember this technique.' I won't simply copy the dishes I admire. Instead, I will bring some of the chef's methods into my own cooking and let that chef influence the taste and sight of my dishes.

"I'm telling you this because writers study other authors' published writing in the same way that I study professional chefs' dishes—to learn new tricks of the trade."

Name the teaching point.

"Today I want to teach you that writers read other authors' texts not only to experience the characters' story, but also to admire, study, and emulate the quality of the writing."

TEACHING

Demonstrate that when they want to make writing especially powerful, they can begin by finding a mentor text and asking, "What has this writer done to affect me so profoundly that I can try it in my own writing?"

"Yesterday, when I read Jim Howe's 'Everything Will Be Okay' aloud to you, everybody in this room was deeply moved by the narrator's story. But it was more than just the compelling topic he chose—it was also his incredible craft as a

◆ COACHING

You'll need enough copies of "Everything Will Be Okay" for each student in the class to have a personal copy to study and annotate. To save time, I put the copies on the students' desks before they arrived at class and asked them to bring their copies, along with their writer's notebooks, to the meeting area.

You can personalize this metaphor by thinking of your own experiences as an apprentice who imagines the steps leading to a completed product or an achievement. Studying a painting to see how the artist applied her brushstrokes. Stopping in a garden to see how a gardener grafted a plant. Closely observing how a champion tennis player anticipates and reacts to her opponent's shots. Listening to the riff of a jazz saxophonist and then trying to replicate his cool sounds when you practice your own music.

writer. Whenever a story takes your breath away, that is your cue to pause and to study what the writer did that was so powerful. It helps to ask, 'What makes this writing so powerful and amazing right here? How did the author make this?' The goal is to bring all that you learn from your mentor text into your own writing."

I showed the students my marked-up copy of "Everything Will Be Okay." "As you can see, every time I reread 'Everything Will Be Okay,' I notice parts that are especially powerful to read. I keep track of the parts that I notice by circling them.

"It is like Howe is one of my writing teachers. He expects me to study parts of his story that I admire and ask, 'What is he doing as a writer that I can try?' Let me show you what I mean—here is one part that I circled":

> *"Come on," Paul says in his take-charge voice, "get that box now. Bring it on in here."*
>
> *He flicks on the light in the waiting room. "You're coming in back with me," he commands. "I'll need your help."*
>
> *"What are you going to do?" I ask. I am holding the box tight against my chest. I feel Smoky moving around inside.*
>
> *"What do you think?" he says. "You heard your mother. That kitten is sick, bad sick."*

"Straight off, I notice that passage affects me as a reader—when I read it, I really dislike Paul and I really feel compassion for Jim. Now that I notice I am affected, I ask, 'How did he do that?' I'd ask that question if this part made me laugh, if it made me furious. Either way, my point is to study the craftsmanship that allowed the text to get through to me.

"So, how did he do that? Hmm . . ." Then I said, "I'm noticing there is dialogue, and I know it is supposed to sound realistic, and when the narrator and Paul talk, it does sound true, but it's more than that. I think what I notice is that *the way* Howe makes Paul talk makes me sense that Paul is condescending and insensitive—maybe even cruel. I think Howe wrote this dialogue in a way that shows Paul's feelings. Let me reread a bit of Paul's talk to you."

As I read Paul's talk, I made my voice impatient and bossy:

> *"Come on, get that box now. Bring it in here."*

Then, I made my voice slightly more exasperated:

> *"What do you think? You heard your mother."*

"Yes, I think that's it! The way Paul is speaking to his brother—his tone—is coming through in the dialogue, and it's giving me all sorts of ideas about the kind of brother Paul seems to be. Are you also feeling that from his tone, his way of talking?"

To help convey the author's craft here, use your acting skills and read aloud the lines with appropriate dramatic flair. When you're reading aloud Paul's lines, visualize someone you know who's bossy and condescending, and make sure your body language and voice express bossy, take charge, condescending.

Name what the author has done and highlight that the same craft move is transferable to other texts.

"So it looks like Howe really thinks about the kind of person the character is, and then based on what he wants to reveal about the character, he makes the character talk in a particular way. Just think how it would change your impression of Paul if, instead, he said to his brother, 'I know this is hard—really hard—for you, Jim. But sometimes, when an animal is too sick to get better, the kindest thing we can do is put an end to its suffering. There's no rush. Take a minute to think about this.' Do you see how when I imagine Paul saying *those* lines, my whole tone shifts to a more caring and gentle voice and Paul emerges as a different kind of brother altogether?"

Name what you have learned in ways that are transferable to other drafts, other days.

"As writers, you might try Howe's technique. You can make your characters talk in the tones that let their personalities come through and that hint at the bigger meaning of the moment." I wrote out the first bullet on the class chart:

The focus of this session refers to reading standards RL.6.4 and RL.6.5, which ask for readers to notice the impact of word and craft choices on meaning and tone.

Lessons from Mentor Narratives

- When characters talk, writers make them say the words and use the tone that shows their personalities and hints at the bigger meaning of the moment.

ACTIVE ENGAGEMENT

Ask students to continue their study of the mentor text, noticing precisely what the author has done that they can try, as writers.

Projecting an excerpt for the class and gesturing for students to pull out their copies of it I said, "Let's study more of 'Everything Will Be Okay.' I'm going to continue reading from where Paul says, 'You heard your mother. That kitten is sick, bad sick.' Try to listen like a reader and a writer, meaning that you should let this part of the story affect you, but then you should follow up by asking, 'How can I do that in my writing?' Jot anything you notice onto your copy." I read aloud:

> *"She's your mother, too."*
>
> *"Well, she happens to be right," Paul tells me. "With an animal that far gone, you don't have a choice. It's got to be put to sleep."*
>
> *I think the tears I jam back into my body are going to kill me. I think if I don't let them out they will kill me. But I won't let them out. I won't let Paul see.*
>
> *"You do have a choice" is all I say. I hug the box for dear life and move to the door. Paul moves faster.*
>
> *"Come on now," he says, gently taking hold of my arm, "be a man."*
>
> *"I'm not a man," I tell him. "I don't want to be."*
>
> *"You've got to do what's right. That kitten is half dead as it is."*

"Then it's half alive, too."

He shakes his head. "You always have to one-up me, don't you?" he says.

I don't know what he means, but I do know that no matter what I say he is going to do what he wants to do.

A few minutes later, we are in the back room. The box is empty. Smoky is inside a big old pretzel can with the hose attached, clawing at the can's sides as my brother pumps in the gas. He is telling me it is good for me to watch this, it will toughen me up, help me be more of a man. Then he starts to lecture me about different methods of putting animals out of their misery, but all I can hear is the scratching. And then the silence.

"On your own, study this part closely to figure out what the author has done that you could try in your writing." The room was quiet as the students worked on their personal copies of the text.

Facilitate a quick share of the students' findings, and add their observations to the class chart.

I gave the students enough time to jot down a few observations and then told them to share with their partners. As the partners talked, I listened for observations they might share with the whole class.

A minute later, when I asked Jesse to repeat what he had shared with his partner, he said, "He explains why the narrator keeps his tears jammed inside when he says, 'I think if I don't let them out they will kill me. But I won't let them out. I won't let Paul see.' You can tell he feels a lot of pressure to be tough in front of his brother."

Jesse made a sharp observation about the effectiveness of the way Jim Howe narrates his character's thoughts and feelings, but it is important that students see these techniques as transferable qualities. I pressed him to rephrase his finding.

"So what exactly did the author do that you can try in your writing?" I asked. I touched the class chart to prompt him to begin with, "Writers . . ." Jesse nodded and tried to clarify: "Writers try to explain why characters do whatever they do."

Ai added, "And he puts in those really little details—like Smoky clawing at the inside of the can—that really gets to you and makes you know exactly how he's feeling." Other students nodded in solidarity.

Lessons from Mentor Narratives

- When characters talk, writers make them say the words and use the tone that shows their personalities and hints at the bigger meaning of the moment.
- Writers explain why the characters act the way they do.
- Writers zoom in on the small but powerful details that really capture big moments and feelings.

LINK

Reiterate the teaching point and send students off to study mentor texts.

"Sixth-graders, we learned today that when writers read the work of other authors, they first read to experience the story. They then reread the text, asking themselves, 'What did this author do that I could try in my writing?' Writers are always trying to figure out ways they can add to and improve their own repertoire of strategies and techniques. I'm realizing that everything we're learning by studying our mentor is a technique for writing powerful personal narratives, so tonight, I'll transfer our thinking from today's chart to our anchor chart, 'How to Write Powerful Personal Narratives.'

"When you go off today, you'll want to read over 'Everything Will Be Okay' again. Try to find new lessons that you can take away from Howe's writing and that you could imagine adding to our chart and then trying in your own writing. List everything you find in your notebook. In a bit, I'll stop you to remind you to switch back to being personal narrative writers. I can't wait to see how you'll use some of the new techniques you've learned from studying a mentor text."

CONFERRING AND SMALL-GROUP WORK

Helping Students Discover New Lessons from Mentor Texts

TODAY, AS YOU CIRCULATE, support your students' efforts at a close and analytical reading of "Everything Will Be Okay." Expect a good deal of tentativeness when you ask a student to point out the section of text he is admiring. If you agree wholeheartedly with the student's choice, you'll encourage the student to continue learning from whatever he has noticed (and actually, any portion of the text is worth studying). Say something like, "Wow, you are right about that being a powerful part."

You might add, "Let me read it aloud for us, so we can really feel how it affects us." When you read that section aloud, resist analyzing the writing techniques, and just focus on reading the passage incredibly well to convey its meaning. This will help students realize how the passage is getting through to them and help them understand the importance of rereading deeply as a first step to learning from other authors.

After I joined Maizy in reading aloud a section, I first modeled how readers name the effect the passage created. I tried to speak as directly and honestly as possible, saying, "I can feel this part right in my gut. When he says, 'I won't go with him. I don't want him teaching me anything anymore,' it's just so final and harsh—like a door closing." Maizy nodded, and I waited, confident that she would add what she was thinking if I gave her the time and space. When Maizy began to share, I nodded and encouraged her to say more by responding, "I definitely know what you mean. And what else?" Once I was confident that Maizy was immersed in that section of the mentor text, I then nudged her toward unpacking and naming the writing techniques that she might also try in her personal narrative.

MID-WORKSHOP TEACHING **Make Time for Writers to Write**

"Writers, you will not have finished annotating 'Everything Will Be Okay,' but you need time to write your next personal narrative. In just another couple of days, you'll choose one of your stories to shape into a publishable piece of writing, so it is important you keep generating these entries.

"As you move forward today, keep 'Everything Will Be Okay' and the lessons you learned from Jim Howe near to you. Try some of his techniques. Remember, you want your writing to affect your readers just as Howe's story affects you. You want to raise the hairs on the back of your readers' necks, you want to take away your readers' breath.

"So draw on strategies for generating ideas," I gestured to the chart, "and get started writing your next personal narrative."

SHARE

Setting Your Own Assignments

Remind students to keep writing at home.

"Writers, most of you are running out of time during your independent writing. Your stamina for writing longer and longer drafts in one sitting is growing, and our writing workshop time passes so quickly that I have to interrupt your writing at the end of class. I am sorry!

"But, the good news is that you have time tonight to pick your pen back up and continue writing your personal narrative. Is that what you'll do for tonight's homework? Or will you start a new personal narrative? Right now, think about what you are going to do tonight and jot that assignment at the top of your page."

Then I called for their attention again and said, "Now turn and tell your partner what you'll work on for homework tonight and why that feels like the right assignment for your goals as a writer."

> "Come on, we're gonna be late!" my mom shouted as she tried to get us out of the apartment. I groaned and made my way out the door. It's Saturday, and I have to go to school! I bet everyone else is still sleeping.
>
> I was starting Chinese school and I had to start at the lowest level since I barely knew how to read and write. I was probably the oldest there. I was 10 years old and going to first grade Chinese school! I could imagine me walking into a room filled with kids half the size of me, and I would be so out of place.

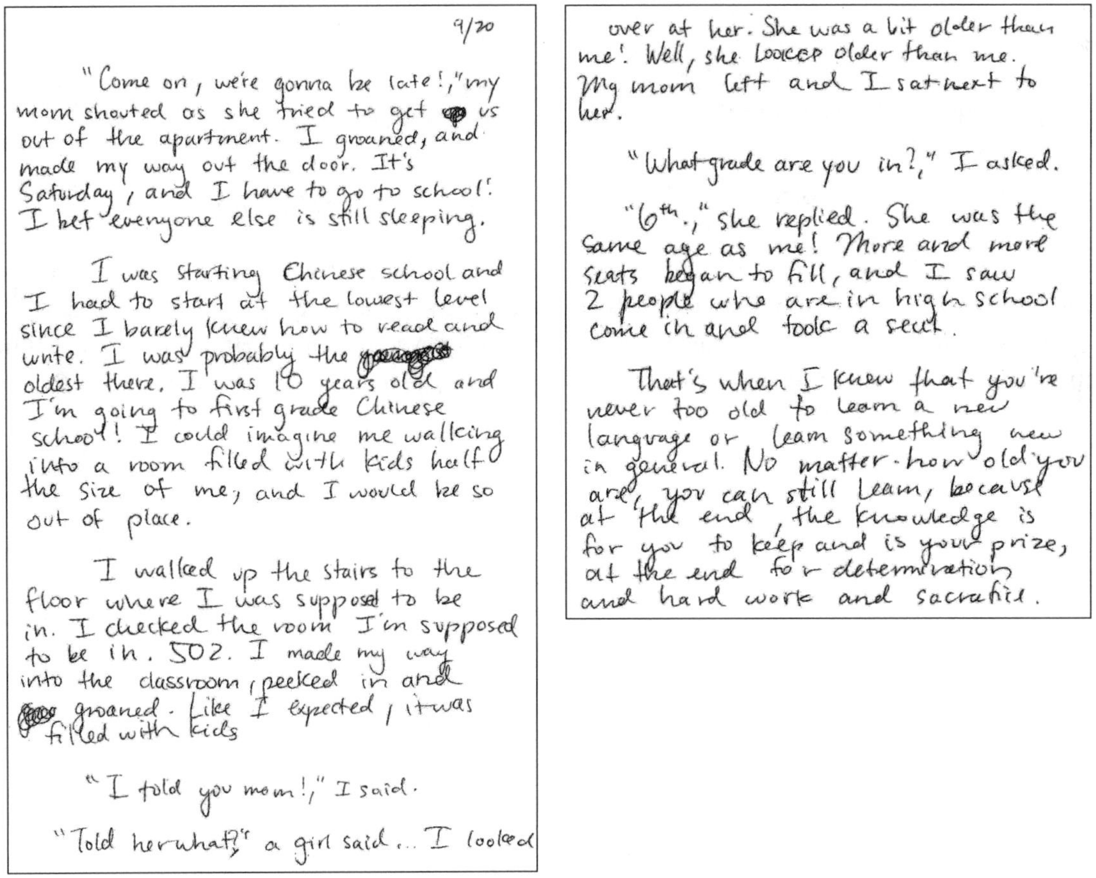

9/20

"Come on, we're gonna be late!," my mom shouted as she tried to get us out of the apartment. I groaned, and made my way out the door. It's Saturday, and I have to go to school! I bet everyone else is still sleeping.

I was starting Chinese school and I had to start at the lowest level since I barely knew how to read and write. I was probably the oldest there. I was 10 years old and I'm going to first grade Chinese school! I could imagine me walking into a room filled with kids half the size of me, and I would be so out of place.

I walked up the stairs to the floor where I was supposed to be in. I checked the room I'm supposed to be in. 502. I made my way into the classroom, peeked in and groaned. Like I expected, it was filled with kids

"I told you mom!," I said.

"Told her what?" a girl said... I looked over at her. She was a bit older than me. Well, she looked older than me. My mom left and I sat next to her.

"What grade are you in?," I asked.

"6th.," she replied. She was the same age as me! More and more seats began to fill, and I saw 2 people who are in high school come in and took a seat.

That's when I knew that you're never too old to learn a new language or learn something new in general. No matter how old you are, you can still learn, because at the end, the knowledge is for you to keep and is your prize, at the end for determination and hard work and sacrafice.

FIG. 5–1 Fionna writes, inspired by "Everything Will Be Okay."

I walked up the stairs to the floor where I was supposed to be. I checked the room: 502. I made my way into the classroom, peeked in and groaned. Like I expected, it was filled with kids.

"I told you, Mom!" I said.

"Told her what?" a girl said. I looked over at her. She was a bit older than me! Well, she looked older than me. My mom left and I sat next to her.

"What grade are you in?" I asked.

"6th," she replied. She was the same age as me! More and more seats began to fill, and I saw two people who were in high school come in and take a seat.

That's when I knew that you're never too old to learn a new language or learn something new in general. No matter how old you are, you can still learn, because at the end, the knowledge is for you to keep and is your prize at the end, for determination and hard work and sacrifice.

SESSION 5 HOMEWORK

SETTING A PURPOSEFUL AND CLEAR WRITING TASK

"While you are assigning yourself a homework task, jot some margin notes to remind yourself to write a full two pages. Or maybe you want to jot a note about trying a particular technique you just learned from your mentor text. Or maybe you need to remind yourself to look over your draft and do some editing." I motioned for the students to make those margin notes and gave them a minute to work.

Session 6

Taking Stock

Pausing to Assess and Set Goals

FROM THE START OF THE SCHOOL YEAR, you have been teaching your students the strategies they need to become more skilled narrative writers. You have created the supportive space and structures that allow your students to practice the work of the minilessons with regular feedback and coaching. With each day of writing workshop, you hope their focused practice will accelerate their growth and achievement.

Hopefulness matters, but it won't be enough. It is important for you to clarify for students what they are trying to accomplish in their writing. They may tell you they are trying to write "really great personal narratives," but can they tell you what makes a personal narrative "really great"? As a step toward developing a cohesive response to that challenging question, your students need more opportunities to study examples of what they are working toward.

"It is important for you to clarify for students what they are trying to accomplish in their writing."

In this session, you will build on the work you have done since the very first session when you shared an exemplar student-written personal narrative and asked students to set their own goals for themselves as sixth-grade writers. Today you will continue to help your students solidify their concept of what makes for an effective and powerful personal narrative, to self-assess, and to set accessible goals.

You can help your students see that when they pause to self-assess, look back on the progress they have made, and make decisions about what to work on next, they are taking charge of their learning and achievement. They should feel empowered by their important role in the process.

IN THIS SESSION, you'll teach students that writers sometimes pause to consider their progress, using a checklist to assess their own growth and set new goals.

GETTING READY

- ✔ Each student should bring his or her notebook and a writing tool, as well as perhaps the initial on-demand writing, to the meeting area for the minilesson.
- ✔ A copy of the Narrative Writing Checklists, Grade 5 and 6, placed on each student's desk (see Link) and a version for class display with only a few categories unveiled (see Teaching)
- ✔ A copy of "Look Up and Watch the Show" for each student and a copy to project for the class (see Teaching)
- ✔ "How to Write Powerful Personal Narratives" chart with the work from yesterday's session on mentor texts added to the chart (see Link)

COMMON CORE STATE STANDARDS: W.6.3, W.6.5, W.6.10, RI.6.1, RL.6.2, SL.6.1, SL.6.4, L.6.1, L.6.2, L.6.3

MINILESSON

Taking Stock

Pausing to Assess and Set Goals

CONNECTION

Explain to your sixth-graders that in today's minilesson, they will be assessing themselves as writers and setting goals.

"Writers, you know that our most important goal this year is to become better writers. All you need to do is flip back to your first personal narrative and then look at your most recent one, and most of you can quickly see that your hard work is paying off." Unable to resist, the sixth-graders began to do just that, and I gave them a moment to recognize their accomplishments.

"Getting better at writing might *feel* mysterious and magical, but I want you to know that there is a tried-and-true method to make sure you improve. It's the same trick that works for all the athletes and artists we admire in the world. The trick is to set super ambitious goals for yourselves and then work like crazy to reach those goals. By deciding on specific ways that you can improve your craft, concentrating on those goals, and then working toward them, you can get better at anything.

"You've already shown me that you aren't afraid of hard work. Each day, you come into our writing workshop and you fearlessly take on another blank page, writing powerful stories fast and furiously. It's time for me to share some new tools with you, ones that will help you continue to improve the quality and power of your writing."

Name the teaching point.

"Today I want to teach you how helpful it is to pause at times and to reflect on the progress you've made as writers. You can use a checklist to guide you as you look back at your writing and ask, 'In what ways am I getting better?' and 'What is the next thing I can work on improving?'"

◆ COACHING

We've all heard the old adage, "practice makes perfect." But it turns out that in life, practicing the same thing over and over again may not necessarily lead to perfection or even growth. The cardiac surgeon who has been performing heart surgery for twenty years may not be more proficient than the rookie surgeon who has been doing this work for five years. The reason for this is that many people reach a certain level of proficiency and then hit a plateau. To continue growing and improving, people must be deliberate about their learning. They must set concrete goals and work toward them, self-assess their work against established benchmarks, and receive specific feedback. This session encapsulates that idea.

TEACHING

Introduce students to the Narrative Writing Checklist, a tool that will help them measure their progress.

"Writers, over the past few days, some of you have brought your writing to me and asked, 'How am I doing? Is this good for sixth-grade writing?' I think it's wonderful that you are asking these questions, but I want to give you the tools that will help you answer those questions yourself. There are two tools, in particular, that I know you will find useful: one is an example of a really strong sixth-grader's personal narrative to help you see what you should be aiming for, and the other is a checklist to help you measure your own writing progress.

"I actually have two checklists here, grade 5 and grade 6, because the checklist shows what a writer should be able to do at the *end* of each grade. Your writing is already more powerful than when you entered our classroom, so I think many of you are quite ready to reach toward the expectations for the end of sixth grade—and some of you will soon exceed those sixth-grade goals and work toward seventh-grade goals as you write!

By studying and analyzing exemplar writing, students can develop a vision for good writing. The checklist provides them with the tools to evaluate writing: the words to name what they see and the language to express what they are working toward. You'll need to make a choice about whether to give the students grades 5, 6, and/or 7 checklists based on what you have noticed so far about their writing and what you'll need to teach.

Narrative Writing Checklist (continued)

	Grade 5	NOT YET	STARTING TO	YES!	Grade 6	NOT YET	STARTING TO	YES!
	Development				**Development**			
Elaboration	I developed characters, setting, and plot throughout the story, especially the heart of the story. To do this, I used a blend of description, action, dialogue, and thinking.	☐	☐	☐	I developed realistic characters, and developed the details, action, dialogue, and internal thinking that contribute to the deeper meaning of the story.	☐	☐	☐
Craft	I showed *why* characters did what they did by including their thinking and their responses to what happened.	☐	☐	☐	I developed some relationship between characters to show *why* they act and speak as they do. I told the internal, as well as the external story.	☐	☐	☐
	I slowed down the heart of the story. I made less important parts shorter and less detailed and blended storytelling and summary as needed.	☐	☐	☐	I wove together precise descriptions, figurative language, and some symbolism to help readers picture the setting and actions, and to bring forth meaning.	☐	☐	☐
	I included precise details and used figurative language so that readers could picture the setting, characters, and events. I used some objects or actions as symbols to bring forth meaning.	☐	☐	☐	I used language that fit my story's meaning and context (for example, different characters use different kinds of language).	☐	☐	☐
	I varied my sentences to create the pace and tone of my narrative.	☐	☐	☐				
	Conventions				**Conventions**			
Spelling	I used what I know about word families and spelling rules to help me spell and edit.	☐	☐	☐	I used resources to be sure the words in my writing are spelled correctly.	☐	☐	☐
	I used the word wall and dictionaries when needed.	☐	☐	☐				

"Writers, I know you are eager to use the checklists to measure one of your own personal narratives, but first, let's look at a personal narrative another sixth-grade student has written, 'Look Up and Watch the Show.'" I projected this for the class. "You should know that many teachers worked together to decide that 'Look Up and Watch the Show' is a very good example of what most sixth-graders should be able to write as an on-demand, by the end of sixth grade. Of course, I know that you'll study 'Look Up and Watch the Show' and think to yourself that you are working really hard right now, *at the beginning* of sixth grade to write this powerfully.

In the near future, students will assess their work against the complete narrative checklist. But for now, you are asking them to pay attention to just two important categories. This allows students to take in the checklist in more accessible, bite-sized chunks. Also, this is the focus of students' most recent work, and by promoting these parts of the checklist, you can guide them to work toward goals within these categories. If you see things on the checklist that you have not yet taught, don't worry. Because these are end-of-sixth-grade standards, that is just as it should be. Be assured that throughout the unit you will touch on everything addressed in the checklist.

"For today we'll look at just two categories on the checklist: elaboration and craft." I projected those two categories from the grades 5 and 6 checklists. "And I think you'll recognize some of the qualities that you have been really focusing on bringing into your personal narratives. Take a moment to read these points under elaboration and craft, and then turn to your partner. What do you notice?"

Demonstrate how to use the checklist to thoughtfully assess a benchmark personal narrative for sixth grade.

After giving the students a minute to read and discuss the excerpt from the checklist, I gave them their own copies of "Look Up and Watch the Show" and explained, "Now I am going to read this strong sixth-grade personal narrative aloud, and I want you to really listen for examples of the checklist points that you just discussed with your partner. When you hear the writer doing those things on the checklist, go ahead and mark it on your copy of the story."

Look Up and Watch the Show

I walked up the stairs of the subway. We were almost there! I had been waiting to see this for my whole life!

Five years before this I had been asking,

"Mom, can I go to the fireworks?"

My mom always replied, "No honey, maybe next year."

"Dad, can I go to the fireworks, all my friends have."

"You are too young and it is too late." This went on for the next five years.

Finally I asked and they said, "YES." I jumped up and down and kissed and hugged them eight times. They said I was now old enough. I couldn't wait to tell my friends.

And here we are an hour early, staring eagerly at the star lit sky. I looked at the barges straight ahead of me. They were ready to fire! I imagined streams of color floating out of them in every direction. Like ten hoses with ten different colors of water.

For the next hour I asked my parents at least 100 times, "When is it starting?" My parents were giving me dirty looks. They were annoyed, but I really couldn't help myself.

Then BOOM crackle, crackle, BOOM, red, orange, yellow, green, blue, purple, and white, all seemed to be falling on me screaming, "Hi nice to meet you." They were saying to most of the other people, "I remember you from last year."

I glanced straight ahead of me and bats were flying away from all the commotion, and noise. It was eerie and exciting.

Amazing shapes, colors, and noises were bursting out of the four barges. Large booms from previous fireworks echoed from one building to another behind us.

Now the time I had been waiting for, to see the grand finale. Smiley faces and 100's of shooting stars shot high in the sky with large booms. Everyone was oohing and aahing. But I knew I oohed and aahed the loudest. I was sure I was more excited than anyone else.

It was now over. Silence rang in my ears and a heavy smoke lingered in the sky. The smoke carried away with it all my dreams of this, because now I had seen and I experienced my first ever, up close showing of the fireworks.

I hope my old dreams of seeing the fireworks for the first time is carried over to someone. And just like me they can have this great first time experience and tell their friends all about it.

Now I have done it. I can tell myself I will never forget the first time I ever saw the fireworks. Now I understand what people mean when they say how magical the fireworks are.

"So, let's see how the writer of 'Look Up and Watch the Show' is doing, according to those points on the checklist." I read the first few paragraphs of the narrative aloud and then paused to consult the checklist. I tapped one portion of the checklist, and then, nodding, I tapped the parts of "Look Up and Watch the Show" that corresponded to those points. "I can definitely see how she tells the story bit by bit through thoughts, action, and dialogue. And the flashback at the beginning hints at what this story is really about." As I spoke, I quickly underlined those parts and annotated my observations in the margins. Then, I touched another point on the checklist and asked the students, "Now, about the characters—would you say the writer creates characters who feel realistic? Hmm . . . What do you think?"

Make sure students notice that you are not whipping through this, just going check, check, check. Demonstrate close analytical reading, and show that you hold yourself accountable for providing evidence for each conclusion you draw. It would be just as effective to do this work with a text that is not entirely up to standards—but we wanted to introduce "Look Up and Watch the Show" to the class for other reasons. This narrative will resurface in later minilessons.

I nodded encouragingly at Beatrice, and she pointed out a couple of places where she thought the readers got to know the main character. I underlined them as she spoke and then responded, "Absolutely! I have such a strong sense that not only is she excited to finally see the fireworks, but she's also thrilled to be considered *old enough* to be part of that special group of people who go to the fireworks each year. The character's actions—her jumping up and down and hugging and kissing—plus her thinking about being old enough and wanting to tell her friends really show that the writer is about to take a big life step. Some people like to say 'coming of age' to describe that big step from being a little kid to becoming a tween, right?"

I pointed once more to the checklist. "I just want you to notice that it says, 'I developed realistic characters . . . ' with an *s*—so that's *characters*, plural. Could you please go back to the story to reread and think about that?" When the students began to look up again, I directed them to talk with their partners and then I reconvened the class. "A lot of you were saying that the writer develops both parents, as well. Her dialogue with both the mother and the father show what kind of people her parents are." I underlined the part of the text where the parents deny the narrator's repeated requests to go to the fireworks. "It looks like these are the kind of parents who have pretty firm rules for their daughter. It sounds like they don't give in easily to whining or begging." Then looking at the checklist, I said, "If I were going to score 'Look Up and Watch the Show' for these categories, I would definitely say that it does match most of the sixth-grade descriptors."

Debrief in ways that help students extract transferable lessons from what you just taught.

"You probably noticed that it didn't take me very long to figure out what this writer did and didn't do in her story. I took a quick look at the checklist to see what sixth-grade writers are aiming to do as writers, and then I checked to see how the author of 'Look Up and Watch the Show' measures up for those skills. But I didn't just say 'yes' or 'no'—I found specific places where I saw her doing that work and jotted what I saw in the margin."

ACTIVE ENGAGEMENT

Ask students to work with a partner and use the checklist to assess each other's writing.

"I want you to try this right now. First, talk with your partner about what you noticed in 'Look up and Watch the Show,' and then with your partner, reread one of your personal narratives together. Talk to each other about where you see evidence of elaboration in the draft. Push yourself to be a super supportive partner, to really help your partner notice where good work has happened in the draft. Turn and talk right now."

It's important to hold students accountable for identifying specific places where they have achieved what's described in the checklist. Encourage students to examine their work critically, identifying the good work they have done, as well as the work they still need to accomplish.

LINK

Remind students that pausing to take stock of what they have accomplished and what they need to work on is key to their growth as writers.

"Writers, I realize many of you are still assessing your writing with your partner, but I am going to stop you. As wonderful as it is to see you and your partner really helping each other, this is actually work that you need to mostly do on your own, and on a regular basis. I have already put a copy of the full Narrative Writing Checklist on your desks, so that when you go off today, you'll be able to look through your personal narrative writing and determine which skills are 'starting to' and which skills are 'not yets' for you. Once you self-assess and set some specific goals for yourself, take a quick moment to decide on today's writing plan. Will you go back to one of your personal narratives and revise it, based on the goals you set today? Will you start a new personal narrative, with your new goals fresh in your mind as you write? You decide.

"One more very important thing. Keep in mind that tomorrow you'll be choosing one personal narrative as the seed idea that you will work on for the next couple weeks. You only have today and tonight's writing time, so really use that Narrative Writing Checklist to push yourself to do your strongest writing." I added our newest strategy to the class chart—as well as the three techniques we identified yesterday when studying our mentor text.

How to Write Powerful Personal Narratives

- Think of a person, place, or moment in your life (maybe a first or last time, or a time when you realized something) that matters, and write a story about it.
- Focus on one episode, write with detail (don't summarize a stretch of time).
- Help readers picture the episode–a small action and exact dialogue.
- Climb inside the moment and write within the narrator's point of view.
- **Make characters say the words and use the tone that shows their personalities and hints at the bigger meaning of the moment.**
- **Explain why the characters act the way they do.**
- **Zoom in on the small but powerful details that really capture big moments and feelings.**
- **Use the Narrative Writing Checklist to ask, "As a writer, what are my strengths? What are my needs?" Then, plan your next steps as a writer.**

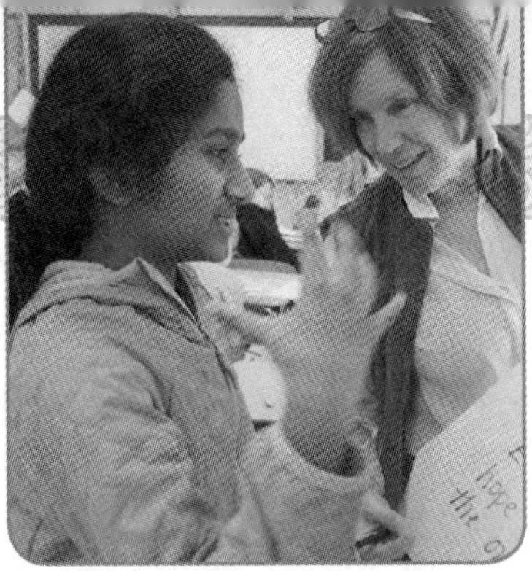

CONFERRING AND SMALL-GROUP WORK

Helping Your Writers to Set Goals

TODAY WHEN YOU ASKED WRITERS to self-assess and to set realistic goals, you taught them the importance of looking back on their writing and reflecting on their progress. Your writers are developing a sense that they are not just doing a lot of writing but are aiming to improve with every sentence, every page. Of course, setting strategic goals takes practice, and some of your students will need your guidance. In anticipation of that, you will want to have "just right" goals in mind for each student. For much of today's small-group and conferring work, you may need to direct students toward the goals that you think are especially key for their development.

To get started, look over your students' personal narratives and use the checklist to look for patterns. You might first look for skills that many students seem to need and note that these would be areas for your whole-class teaching. Then, look for smaller groups of students who could use similar support in their writing, and plan the small-group work you could do with them across the next few days. Challenge yourself to make quick assessments of your students. Instead of spending hours after school poring over notebooks, try moving from table to table while the students are writing independently. Glance over their busy shoulders, and note where they are in their

(*continues*)

MID-WORKSHOP TEACHING **Crafting Systems to Keep Track of Goals**

"Writers, let me stop you for a moment. I've met with a few of you today and asked the same old question I always do, 'What are you working on as a writer?' What was so beautiful was that so many of you were able to tell me about the specific work you're focusing on right now—like Fatima, who is working to make her story more compelling, so that her readers are perched on the edge of their seats. Not only could you name your current work, but most of you could also tell me the goals you'll tackle next.

"The thing is, most of you are keeping these to-do lists in your heads. And while that may work for today, you are apt to forget some of your goals by tomorrow and certainly by the following day. Right now, I'd like you to think about a system you can use to keep track of your goals: the ones you've accomplished, the ones you are working on right now, and the ones you've yet to tackle. Let me give you a few ideas to get you started brainstorming."

I moved to the white board and began sketching a few quick possibilities. "One way to keep track of goals is by keeping a dated list." I quickly sketched a T-chart on the board. "You put the date in the left-hand column," and I filled in that day's date as I talked, "and then your goal in the right-hand column. Once you've completed a goal, you check it off and go on to the next. If you choose to do something like this, you'll probably want to find a clean page in your notebook that will be just for goal-setting."

I saw several students begin to create a T-chart, but continued on, eager to share one more possibility. I taped a copy of the Grade 6 Narrative Checklist on the board. "Another option is to keep several copies of the Narrative Checklist in your writing folder. You'll need to develop some system for marking your goals and showing when you've succeeded in reaching them. Perhaps you'd do something like this." I thought for a moment and then circled several boxes on the checklist. "I've circled the goals I have for myself, and I can cross them off once I've worked on them." With that, I drew a few quick *X*'s over the boxes I had circled.

"Writers, the choice is yours, but I'd like each of you to develop some system for keeping track of your goals. This will ensure that the goals you set are not just for today, but for the entire unit."

development. It helps to focus on just one part of the assessment rubric at a time. For instance, you might circle the room once, looking only for students who have summarized rather than told a story, jotting their names on a list as you go. Then take a second spin around the room, this time jotting down notes on those who need work with paragraphing, then those who have an overabundance of dialogue, and so on.

One thing you are bound to notice is that students tend to set goals that feel too small, with little thought about *why* that goal is important or *how* it might be accomplished. For instance, you'll probably find several students haphazardly adding transition words into their stories without much thought given to why authors use such words. You'd be wise to seize such an opportunity to teach that when writers set goals, they name why they will work on this particular goal and then make a plan for how they will do it. In the case of transition words, you might help students get started with this work by steering them back to their mentor text. "First," you might begin, "writers find it helpful to study how other authors have used these words. To study this mentor text together, let's first highlight the transition words we find, and then we'll figure out what the transition words do, how they make the writing better."

After a brief inquiry, students might compile a quick chart about the roles transitions can play in a piece of writing. Help students to recognize that these are big, powerful words, capable of clarifying relationships, linking sections of text, creating cohesion or sequence, signaling shifts in time or setting, and even building suspense. Then, ask students to turn to their own pieces of writing and ask, "Where are some places where my story would benefit from the use of transition words?" In this way, you have set students up to do big, purposeful work.

SHARE

Clarifying Goals and Making Plans for Meeting Them

Channel students to share their self-assessments and their goals for moving forward with their drafts.

"Writers, tomorrow you will do the very important work of rereading your notebook—of rereading all of your personal narratives—and picking a seed idea to take through the writing process. As you draft and revise that one story all over again, you will need to keep the goals you just set in mind.

"Right now, take a few minutes to show your partner how you assessed your own writing today. Share your checklist and what you realized about the work you are starting to do and the work that still needs to happen. Point out your evidence for particular skills. Then, share your goals. What are you going to push yourself to work on next, and what is your plan for making that happen?"

SESSION 6 HOMEWORK

SETTING YOURSELF UP TO DO YOUR MOST POWERFUL WRITING

"Sixth-graders, for homework tonight, you'll have one last chance to write a drop-dead powerful story. Give yourself one more incredible personal narrative to choose from when I ask you commit to your seed idea—make your selection process that much more challenging.

"Take a moment to set yourself up. You might look back at our chart of generating strategies and decide how you'll get yourself started, or you might just jot down that story idea you have been meaning to get down on paper. Perhaps you want to visualize where you'll do your best writing tonight and plan to hold yourself to writing in that place tonight. What have you learned about what you need to do your most focused writing? Do you need to turn your phone over to your parents? Do you need to turn on or off the music? Do you need to write at the kitchen table? You know best, so make a quick plan and carry it through for homework."

Moving through the Writing Process and toward Our Goals

BEND II

Session 7

Rehearsing

Experimenting with Beginnings

IN THIS SESSION, you'll teach students that writers generate multiple leads as a way to rehearse a story.

GETTING READY

- ✔ Each student should bring his or her writer's notebook to the meeting area for the minilesson.
- ✔ Four cups filled with enough paper clips for students to mark the seed ideas they select to turn into a story (see Connection)
- ✔ Lead from "Everything Will Be Okay" to project or copied onto chart paper (see Teaching)
- ✔ "Techniques for Writing Memorable Leads" chart, to be created with students (see Teaching)
- ✔ "How to Write Powerful Personal Narratives" chart from Session 6 (see Mid-Workshop Teaching)

Common Core State Standards: W.6.3, W.6.5, W.6.10, RL.6.1, RL.6.5, SL.6.1, SL.6.4, L.6.1, L.6.2, L.6.3

You spent the first bend of the unit getting all the students launched as writers of personal narratives, helping them to feel that their lives are worth writing about and that they can write about compelling moments with insight and craft. In today's session, the start of the second bend in the road of this unit, students will turn from generating many personal narrative story ideas toward developing one narrative into a publishable piece of writing. This will be a noticeable shift for your students as they move from writing a new narrative each day to committing to just one story and taking that story through the whole writing process.

Today you will ask students to pick a seed idea, and then you'll teach a strategy for rehearsing for writing that students can add to their repertoire of rehearsal strategies. As with teaching strategies for generating powerful personal narratives, your hope is that this minilesson will give students yet another strategy to draw upon at this stage of their process. That is, the essential take-away is the concept that writers do, in fact, rehearse prior to writing, not the particular rehearsal strategy.

"The essential take-away is the concept that writers rehearse prior to writing."

Remember that earlier, you taught your students that writers turn to strategies for generating story ideas because it allows them to overcome the terrifying blank page. In a similar manner, today you will teach students that even once writers have a powerful story idea, it can still be difficult to know how and where to start storytelling. Writers can feel like they are facing that frightening blank page all over again, and rehearsal empowers them to take charge and figure out the best way to start to tell the story.

MINILESSON

Rehearsing

Experimenting with Beginnings

CONNECTION

Tell students that today is the start of the second bend in the unit, and preview how their writing work will change. Then, channel students to reread their notebooks and consider which personal narrative they want to develop into a publishable piece.

"Writers, you have to know that today is an exciting day! Today, instead of generating new personal narratives, you'll need to look back over your whole collection of stories and choose just one. Writers often call that a seed idea, meaning you'll nourish and grow that seed idea into a published piece of writing.

"It's a little daunting to wrap your mind around all you have written and choose just one, isn't it? This is a time when you really have to pay attention to that little voice as you reread—the one that whispers that there is just *something* about this story, that this story idea has the potential to become a really important piece of writing. Remember, that doesn't mean that the personal narrative is *already* an incredible piece of writing. It might just be an idea that you think you can develop into a powerful and meaningful story.

"I'll stop talking now, so you can reread your notebooks and start to notice which stories could function as your seed idea. Get started." As the students worked, I voiced over. "I love how thoughtful you're being, really taking the time to reread. This is what real writers do."

I gave students a few more minutes, and then I set out cups of paper clips in the four corners of the meeting area. "Writers, I'd like you each to take a paper clip and mark your seed idea."

As the students finished clipping, I gathered their attention. "Congratulations, writers, and welcome to your seed idea."

Convey that most writers don't just pick a story idea and then write the book; they get ready to write by rehearsing.

"You probably remember from years past that writers don't settle on a seed idea and then jump into writing the book or story. They warm up and take a few practice runs, just like dancers before a performance or musicians before a concert. One of the best ways to rehearse your story is to do some storytelling.

◆ COACHING

Usually, at the start of a new bend in the unit, you'll want to let students know the path of the work ahead—let them know where they are headed.

Perhaps only a few students are rereading, but when I voice over simple compliments like this, I am bringing important strategies to everyone's attention. That is just enough teaching for more students to join in and do the same.

"Partner 1, get ready to try this. You're going to *tell the story* that is your seed idea. I want to hear you using the same dramatic storytelling voice you use in the hallway, when something unbelievable has just happened to you and you bump into your best friend and tell him or her all about it. Partner 2, lean in and expect to get goose bumps!" I listened in as students told their stories, prompting, "Keep going. And then what happened?" As Jonah told Beth his story of getting caught stealing gum from the corner store, he deepened his voice to imitate the store clerk. I gave him a thumbs up and kept circulating.

"Writers, can I stop you? That was amazing—your stories really came to life just now! It seemed to me that as you told your stories, you started to figure out what you wanted to show about your characters and how you wanted to make your partner react to certain parts of the story." I paused for them to nod and then confirmed, "That is exactly why we might story-tell our story before we put it on paper."

Name the teaching point.

"Today I want to teach you that writers also rehearse for writing by trying out several different leads."

When students work on their leads early in the writing process, they can become aware of new directions their stories might take. Students are often surprised to see how starting a story in a different place can change the way the rest of the storytelling unfolds. Plus, they tend to be more open to exploring those directions if they haven't already written a whole draft.

TEACHING

Study Jim Howe's lead together and name what writers can do, at the start of their stories, to pull the reader right into the story.

"Writers, you know how much the first sentences or paragraphs of a story—what writers call the *lead*—matter. The first bit of text on a page has the big job of grabbing the reader's attention, making that reader want to put everything else aside so he can just hunker down and read, read, read.

"Authors try out different leads, looking for the one that will set them up to write a great story. Let's go back to our mentor author, Jim Howe, and see what this famous writer did at the start of 'Everything Will Be Okay' that makes his lead so powerful. Remember, whenever a story takes your breath away, that is your cue to pause and study the writer's moves. Your goal is to bring all that you can learn from your mentor text into your own personal narrative writing."

Notice that I am using this as an opportunity to reinforce my earlier teaching about how to use mentor texts effectively. In this session, I want the students to learn from Howe's lead, but my larger goal is still for them to use mentor texts independently and throughout the writing process, for all aspects of craftsmanship.

I showed the students the first page of my marked-up copy of "Everything Will Be Okay" and continued, "I definitely noticed how powerful Howe's lead is. Let's study his beginning together and ask ourselves, 'What is he doing at the start—the lead—of his story that I can try?'" I read the lead aloud:

> *The kitten is a scrawny thing with burrs and bits of wood caught in its hair, where it still has hair, and pus coming out its eyes and nose. Its big baby head looks even bigger at the end of such a stick of a body. I found it in the woods at the end of my street where I play most days with my friends. This time I was alone. Lucky for you I was, I think to the kitten. Otherwise, David or Claude might have decided you'd be good practice for their slingshots. Those two can be mean, I think to myself. I don't like playing with them really, but they live at the end of the street and sometimes you just play with the kids on your same street, even if they're mean, sometimes even to you.*

"What has Howe done that I could do?" I muttered to myself. "The first thing I'm noticing is that he is right in the moment of his story, recalling and zooming in on these tiny details that must have actually caught his attention at the time: the missing fur, the leaky eyes, the stick-skinny body. Howe must have really replayed the scene in his mind bit by bit, to remember what he saw and felt at that time, for those details to ring so true. I held up one finger, to show I'd need to keep track of more than one observation.

"And I'm also noticing that, in his lead, Howe has the narrator talking to the kitten in his mind, telling him how lucky he is and how he feels about the neighborhood kids." I nodded and held up a second finger. "This inner thinking, right at the start of the story, certainly pulls me into his world and makes me curious about him. It makes me want to keep reading! Hmm . . . but why is that? Well, I notice his inner thinking is really a kind of dialogue. He's actually talking to the kitten—just silently, in his head—but I think what's really powerful about his inner thinking at the start of the story is the way it allows him to drop some hints about what his story might really be about. When he's thinking about how David and Claude can be mean, it seems like he is showing us that this is a lonely time in his life. Aren't you getting the feeling, right from the lead, that the narrator could really use a little more love in his life—even from a scrawny, sick kitten?"

Name what the author has done to craft this lead, and highlight that the same move is transferable to the texts they are writing.

"So what I'm noticing is that leads can pull us right into the story by including very precise details from the moment. It looks like leads can also include the main character thinking in a way that touches on the heart of the story.

"As a writer, I might try Howe's technique in my own lead. I can actually highlight the importance of what is happening when my story starts by climbing inside my story and zooming in on those small but very telling details. I can also include inner thinking to begin to express the bigger meaning of the moment." I wrote out the first two bullets on the class chart:

Techniques for Writing Memorable Leads

- Writers might include the smallest details of the moment, the ones that ring true for the narrator.
- Writers might include inner thinking to hint at what the story is really about.

Debrief. Repeat how writers study what great authors do and then try to use the same moves in their own writing.

"Remember, I am rereading just the lead of 'Everything Will Be Okay' to notice what the author has done in his lead that I could try too. So I'm not going to stop here. I need to keep studying his lead and adding to what I just noticed. When I go off to rehearse a few leads for my personal narrative, I'll be able to try out what Howe is teaching me about starting stories."

ACTIVE ENGAGEMENT

Ask students to continue studying the start of the mentor text, noticing precisely what Jim Howe has done in his lead that they can also try.

"Let's study a bit more of the start of 'Everything Will Be Okay.' I'm going to continue reading, and you try to notice what else Howe does in his lead. Get ready to tell your partner, 'One thing I notice that he did that I could try is . . .'" I read aloud:

> *The kitten makes a pitiful noise.*
>
> *"Don't worry," I tell it, stroking its scabby head until the mewing is replaced by a faint purr. "Everything will be okay. I'm going to take you home, and my mom will give you a bath and some medicine."*

I stopped reading and said, "What else does Jim do in the start of his story?" As the partners talked, I listened for observations they might share with the whole class.

Facilitate a quick share of the students' findings, and add their observations to the class chart.

A moment later, I prompted Marlene to repeat what she had shared with her partner. "Well, the author has the kitten making noise, and then the character pets him. So we know what they're both doing."

Marlene's partner, Pablo, added, "He's not just petting the kitten, he's also talking to it—and this time, he's not just talking in his head. He's actually saying all of these words in quotation marks, about how his mom is going to help him."

I nodded. "Wow, I'll add all of those important points to our chart right now," and I quickly added the next bullets:

Techniques for Writing Memorable Leads

- Writers might include the smallest details of the moment, the ones that ring true for the narrator.
- Writers might include inner thinking to hint at what the story is really about.
- **Writers might include the precise actions of the characters, helping readers to see how one action leads to another.**
- **Writers might include the exact words the characters are speaking, in dialogue.**

LINK

Restate your teaching point and send students off to try a few different leads.

"Sixth-graders, keep in mind that writers are always trying to figure out ways they can add to and improve their own repertoire of moves. Look how much we learned from Jim Howe today about techniques for crafting a great lead.

"When you go off to write today, try a few different leads. If you first start with a bit of dialogue, to quickly bring your characters to life for your reader, then next you might begin with inner thinking to hint at what the story is really about, or the smallest details of the moment or precise character actions, just like Howe did."

CONFERRING AND SMALL-GROUP WORK

Crafting a Lead that Draws Readers to the Heart of the Story

As you circulate around the room today, you will find students who are successfully trying out multiple leads for their stories. You may want to pull a small group of these writers to push them to consider not only *how* to begin their stories but *where* to begin their stories. A strong lead is essential to setting up the heart of the story, but often, when writers try different starting points—not just different techniques for starting—some new insight or angle emerges.

Say to this group, "Writers, I pulled you together because I noticed you've already drafted a few different leads. While you're thinking about which lead feels right to you, I'd like to tell you about another way that professional writers rehearse their leads as they strive to tell their stories in the most compelling way possible. Writers experiment with starting their storytelling at different places within the story, to see if they end up telling the story more powerfully.

"Let me share a bit about one of my personal narratives to show you what I mean. You'll probably recognize the story from my 'Last Times' list. If I were writing the story of seeing my grandmother for the last time, I could definitely start on the edge of her bed when I was holding her hand in the last moments of her life. If I did that, I could start with the action of squeezing her hand or with the words I spoke to her or with the thoughts swirling inside my own head. But I could also start my story *several hours earlier*, when we were celebrating my grandmother's 90th birthday. In that lead, I could start with the two of us sitting side by side, laughing together as friends and family members told favorite stories about my grandmother. It's hard to believe, but just a few hours later, I was at her bedside, holding her hand as she slipped away. But you know what? I could even begin my story *the night before*, when my grandmother and I lined up all of her bottles of nail polish—the ones she kept in an old metal tin beneath her bathroom sink—and painted our nails matching colors. I would have to plan how to

MID-WORKSHOP TEACHING **Carrying Everything You've Learned into New Writing Situations**

"Writers, eyes on me, please. We've already spent a good amount of time this year studying mentor authors—both student and published—and talking about how to write powerful personal narratives.

"I know we started a new chart today on writing memorable leads, and certainly you'll want to reference that one as you work on your leads. But it's critical that you carry what you learn on one day to the next and the next—to realize that what it means to write well on one day and in one situation will help you write well in other situations, too.

"So let's all take a minute to reread our anchor chart," I said, gesturing to "How to Write Powerful Personal Narratives." "Let me quickly add our work today on leads, and then talk with your partner about a couple of things from these charts that you will hold close to you today, as you work on your leads."

move time in my story to get to that scene at her bedside, but when I got there, I would remember how, as I held her hand, I ran my fingers over her painted nails and relished the memory of us painting our nails together the night before.

"Wow. I now realize that is the story I want to write. Whenever I visited my grandmother, we pulled that metal tin from her bathroom and filed and painted our nails together and caught each other up on our lives. So now, my story is not just about her death, but also about her life—about something special we often did together. Had I not tried different *places* to start alongside different *ways* to start, I would not have found the story I really want to write about the last time I saw my grandmother."

While you will support many writers with their leads, some might be ready to dive into their drafts. You might remind them that the same strategies they used to start their stories can be used to keep their stories going. Writers begin with precise details, action, dialogue, and inner thinking because it pulls readers into the moment from the very first lines of their story, but then they continue to use these same techniques as they write from inside the story moment, telling the story as it unfolds.

How to Write Powerful Personal Narratives

- Think of a person, place, or moment in your life (maybe a first or last time, or a time when you realized something) that matters, and write a story about it.
- Focus on one episode, write with detail (don't summarize a stretch of time).
- Help readers picture the episode–a small action and exact dialogue.
- Climb inside the moment and write within the narrator's point of view.
- Make characters say the words and use the tone that shows their personalities and hints at the bigger meaning of the moment.
- Explain why the characters act the way they do.
- Zoom in on the small but powerful details that really capture big moments and feelings.
- Use the Narrative Writing Checklist to ask, "As a writer, what are my strengths? What are my needs?" Then, plan your next steps as a writer.
- **Craft a memorable lead.**

SHARE

Sharing Powerful Beginnings

Gather students back to the meeting area to share their leads and recognize how their rehearsals are helping them to develop their seed ideas.

"Sixth-graders, I want to share something Austin pointed out during his conference. He noticed how his second lead, is going to make it possible for him to tell the rest of the story really powerfully. He said, 'I liked my first lead, but it's a good thing I didn't just stop there. I made myself try something else, and it turned out that it works even better for my story.' Many of you experienced something like this today. You pushed yourself to write a first, a second, a third lead, and you were surprised to see how much starting your story in a different place can affect the quality of your storytelling.

"Will you look over your leads and make a quick decision? So far, which of your leads is setting you up best to tell the rest of your story really powerfully?"

Ask students to share one of their leads with their partner.

After giving them a moment to reflect on their leads, I said, "Partner 1, will you please use your best storytelling voice when you read your lead to your partner? And Partner 2, get ready to listen really closely and tell the writer how that lead grabs you and makes you want to hear the rest of the story." I gestured to the Techniques for Writing Memorable Leads" chart to remind the listeners to see if their writing partners were trying any of those same techniques.

"Writers, can I have your eyes, please? Some of you have written leads you feel quite proud of today. Others of you want to try starting your story another way, because none of your leads feel just right yet. That's okay, too! Published authors often draft thirty—not three—leads before they find the 'right' one."

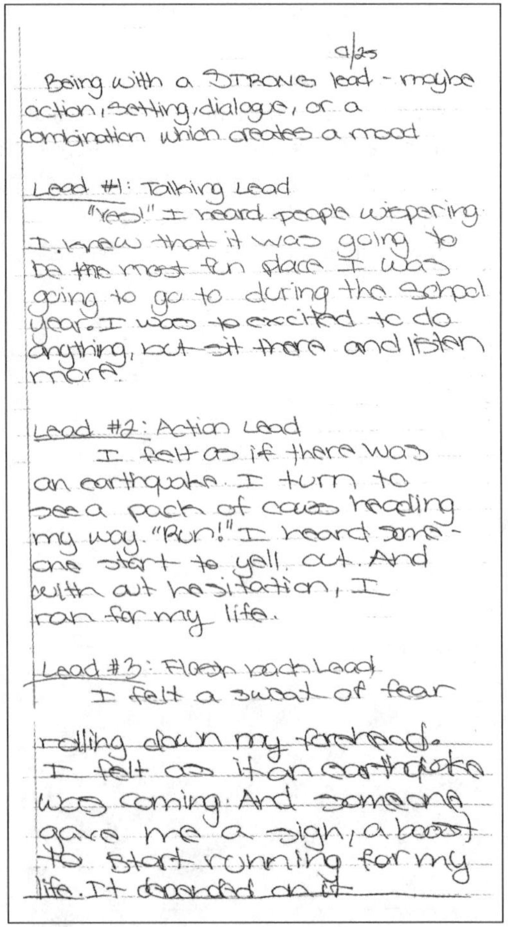

9/25
Being with a STRONG lead - maybe action, setting, dialogue, or a combination which creates a mood

Lead #1: Talking Lead
"Yes!" I heard people wispering I knew that it was going to be the most fun place I was going to go to during the school year. I was to excited to do anything, but sit there and listen more.

Lead #2: Action Lead
I felt as if there was an earthquake. I turn to see a pack of cows heading my way. "Run!" I heard some-one start to yell. out. And with out hesitation, I ran for my life.

Lead #3: Flash back Lead
I felt a sweat of fear rolling down my forehead. I felt as if an earthquake was coming. And someone gave me a sigh, a boost to Start running for my life. It depended on it

FIG. 7–1 Arlene has tried out three different leads in her notebook.

SESSION 7 HOMEWORK

REHEARSING YOUR STORIES

"At home tonight, you'll need to choose the lead that you think works best for setting you up to tell your story really, really well. Does that mean you'll need to write a couple more leads, to have more leads to choose from? Maybe you will. Or perhaps you'll want to go back and reread the start of 'Everything Will Be Okay' to see what other techniques you might try for starting a story."

Session 8

Flash-Drafting

Get the Whole Story on the Page

Dear Teachers,

Today is a big day, and you'll want to begin by rallying students' energy for the flash-drafting they'll do. Yesterday, you reminded them that rehearsing for how a piece of writing will go can empower them as writers, making the blank page less frightening. Now, they will put pen to paper and capture the best of those rehearsals.

Today you will ask students to take their seed idea from the previous session and flash-draft a first draft version of their stories. You might wonder about the purpose behind a day like today, where students draft in a flurry of writing. At the Teachers College Reading and Writing Project, it took us nearly a decade to recognize the magic that happens when writers fix their eyes on their topics, reimagine each and every detail of it, and then write to capture the intensity of the whole moment on the page, all in one session. These drafts, though rough, have proven to be far superior to those eked out across several days, paragraph by paragraph. Pieces that are written in a day tend to have a cohesiveness and a voice that just don't emerge when writers write one draft across many days.

MINILESSON

You might begin this session by explaining the process of flash-drafting to students. "Today, writers, you will venture outside your notebooks, working on clean sheets of paper to create the first draft of your story. These drafts won't be perfect—first drafts never are—but I'll give you some tips for doing them in such a way that you capture the truth of your small moment on the page."

For your teaching point, you might say something like, "Specifically, what I want to remind you of is that writers fill themselves up with the true thing that happened, recall how they've decided to start the story, and then, keeping their mind fixed intently on the mental movie of what happened, they let their pens fly down the page. When they do this, they finish a whole draft (or close to a whole draft) in one sitting."

Common Core State Standards: W.6.3, W.6.4, W.6.5, W.6.10, RL.6.2, RL.6.3, SL.6.1, SL.6.4, L.6.1, L.6.2, L.6.3

It is unlikely that you'll choose to model flash-drafting on this day. Instead, we recommend using your teaching time to give students a few pointers before sending them on their way. This is a day for fast and furious writing, and your goal will be to get the students off the rug as swiftly as possible.

Set students up for the day's work by explaining that there are a few things writers do before flash-drafting. Listing these things across your fingers, you might remind students that writers:

- Aim to get a first draft down, regardless of whether it is their best writing or not.
- Relive the story in their mind's eye before starting to write, remembering the best of their rehearsals from the day before.
- Listen and watch as the story unfolds in their mind, trying to remember what they can't quite recall.
- Work silently and intently, holding themselves to the highest of standards.

Before sending students from the meeting area, give them a moment to reread their entries in their writer's notebooks, recall their rehearsals, and give you a signal when they are ready to begin writing. As students signal, send them from the meeting area to begin writing.

CONFERRING AND SMALL-GROUP WORK

As you move around the room, be wary of interrupting your writers too much. After all, you have just charged them with a big task and want to do justice to the hard work and concentration they'll need to get the most out of today's writing workshop. Rather than conferring or pulling small groups, you might instead decide to do a few voiceovers to support velocity and stamina. "Remember the words of Donald Murray," you might say, "'You have to write fast to say what you did not know you needed to say.'" And later, "You should be on your second page by now. Keep writing. Fast and furious." You might remind your students, "Don't forget to write from inside of the story—hear the splashing of the waves, feel the sun on your shoulders."

Watch for students who seem stuck or as if they are moving too slowly. Crouch beside these writers and offer a bit of advice to get them started. Ask them to retell the memory, starting with the beginning, telling it with specifics. "Where were you, exactly? What did you notice, sitting there? What did you do next?" Other times a meaningful look or a whispered, "Keep going, I know you can do it," will be enough to reengage the writer.

SHARE

To celebrate today's achievements, choose four students at the end of their writing time to share their flash-drafts in small groups. You'll divide the class into four groups and assign each group to a different corner of the classroom. Then, in each corner group, a different student will read aloud his flash-draft while the other students in the group listen really intently to feel the way the story affects them and to take notice of some moves they might also try in their drafts.

Divide the class, and while those students are moving to their areas, collect the four students who will read aloud. Give your readers clear directions, something like, "Don't start reading until you have everyone's eyes on you. Read in your best storytelling voice: clearly and with lots of expression." And then send them off to join their groups.

To start them off, you might say, "Writers, your very important job is to *really, really* listen. Lose yourself in the story you are about to hear. Try to see and feel this powerful small moment just as the writer tells it."

In one corner of my classroom, Jose began reading (see Figure 8–1).

When the groups are finished, you might take a moment to acknowledge how hard your students worked to meet today's goal of writing a first draft and how excited you are to hear more of their stories tomorrow.

Good luck!
Lucy, Stacey, and Ali

Jose
Oct 5

Roller Coaster

I remember him approaching the door and I didn't want to go. In my head I heard the argument I had with my mom. "No I don't know him, no I don't want to go with him No he is just out of prison why should we trust him." But my mom was relentless. So here I am going to the door to meet the man I have never known.

We went to the car and I opened the door. All I could say to him was hey and all he can say back was hey. We never looked at each other just the road each in our own thoughts as we entered the fair. We parked and solely I closed the door in my head repeating no please don't make me go no please don't make me go. We walked around it felt like hours but only fifteen minutes past. Than we got to the roller coaster me with a stranger asking me, "do I want to go on". My reply "okay". We got on together as the roller coaster slowly started to go up the hill than down quickly then up to the biggest hill. That's where the story begins.

The ride slowly up, up, up, to the top than as we were about to get to the part where we go down the biggest part bam, crash it stopped just like that stopped at the top and all I could see was little figures. The announcement said, "We are sorry for the inconvenience but it will be a few moments. As we sat there I looked at him my father, hum blue eyes sunken and alert looking actually very much like my own, his hair was brown and wavy like my sister and the scar I heard about but never saw til now. He looked at me I looked at him and time stopped for me for a moment as he took my hand. He knew I was nervous maybe he heard my heart beating quicker and quicker as we stayed on top. We spoke for the first time ever how are you he asked. Fine I said you. He asked about school and baseball. We talked for awhile than he looked at me his eyes staring straight at me and said Im sorry! I messed up and am not the father you wanted. I looked and in my mind the wind blew faster and storm clouds began to appear all around us when I blinked and said its ok you are hear now.

At that point when we looked at each other we felt the chug the ride began again he let go of my hand and we sat together. We got out of the ride, he stopped bought that rip off picture that they take at the end of the ride and he began to walk towards the car separate again. I looked at him on the way home his eyes straight ahead more tired than I thought, his smile sad looking, and I knew that when the roller coaster separated us it was like it was a separation of the first time I felt a dad, a father and the last time I would ever see him again.

As he left it was like a piece of me left with him and has he waved goodbye I memorized him what he looked like how he spoke. My dad died that year in jail he got that disease. But me I got a present I got a dad!

FIG. 8–1 Jose's flash draft

Session 9

Using Writer's Notebooks for Mindful, Goal-Driven Work

IN THIS SESSION, you'll teach students that writers use their writer's notebooks as a place to try new things, to practice their skills, and to work hard at the writing goals they've set for themselves.

GETTING READY

- ✔ Students should bring their notebooks, a writing tool, and their copies of "Everything Will Be Okay" to the meeting area.
- ✔ An excerpt from "Everything Will Be Okay" for you to read aloud that highlights a craft move you will be emulating (see Teaching)
- ✔ A section of your story on chart paper, or ready to project, with which you will model revising (see Teaching)
- ✔ The anchor chart, "How to Writer Powerful Personal Narratives" (see Teaching and Link)

COMMON CORE STATE STANDARDS: W.6.3.a,b,c,d,e; W.6.5, W.6.9.a, W.6.10, RL.6.2, RL.6.4, RL.6.10, SL.6.1, L.6.1, L.6.2, L.6.3, L.6.4

I ONCE OVERHEARD A PIANO TEACHER tell her young student, "Don't think about how you need to get better at playing piano—think about how you need to get better at practicing." That bit of advice stuck with me, and I often point out to students that the elite athletes and masterful artists they admire aren't just naturally talented. Somewhere along their journey, they figured out how to practice effectively, how to practice in a way that would bring them closer to their goals.

Effective practice is focused and goal-driven, and it often hinges on following the same key steps. It begins with either honest self-assessment or critical feedback from a peer or teacher. Once a learner has identified a particular skill to develop, it's possible to set specific goals and make a plan for working resolutely and deliberately toward them. This kind of targeted and meaningful practice is more likely to yield noticeable results, and that, in turn, is highly motivating to learners!

In this session, just as students are on the brink of making large-scale, whole-new-draft revisions to their flash-drafts, you will support their growth as writers by teaching them how to practice really well. You will let students know that writers can work at tackling the goals they have identified by going back into their notebooks to practice. Writers can revisit many previous notebook drafts and practice honing a particular skill on certain portions of those stories. Imagine a student who wants to work on developing her characters more completely. She may decide to work across several different personal narratives that she generated in her notebook last week, perhaps drafting more visual details that bring the characters to life. Then, she might revisit her mentor text to search for specific help she could glean from the author and then try one of those techniques in another narrative.

Of course, some of your students will be eager to bring their newfound, freshly practiced skills to their flash-drafts or to a new draft they will just now generate. Because all of these alternatives are open to all the writers in the class, if you step back to scan the room, you'll find youngsters are engaged in a remarkably diverse array of activities. That is as it should be in a well-functioning writing community, so step back and appreciate your sixth-grade writing workshop!

MINILESSON

Using Writer's Notebooks for Mindful, Goal-Driven Work

CONNECTION

Rally your students to invest in themselves by recognizing that successful learners see hard tasks as challenges—and failures as opportunities to learn.

"Several years ago, J. K. Rowling gave a speech to the graduating class at Harvard University. Can you imagine how excited those graduates must have been to have the opportunity to hear the best-selling author of Harry Potter? Well, on that day, she surprised a lot of people with her message. She said, 'On this wonderful day when we are gathered together to celebrate your academic success, I have decided to talk to you about the benefits of failure.' The benefits of *failure*?" I raised my eyebrows at the students.

"It turned out that J. K. Rowling wanted to talk to the students about failure, because in her life as a writer, she has learned a lot about pushing on with her learning and her practice, even when it felt like a real struggle. J. K. Rowling must have looked out at all those college graduates and thought that the biggest gift she could give them was her honest story of learning to face hard tasks, not avoid them."

"Some people think of work—and especially of hard work as a negative thing, but we don't have to be those people. When I read J. K. Rowling's speech, it actually made me think that it is so much more inspiring to think about the hard work behind people's success than it is to imagine that their skills come easily to them. Some people think that the best writers or the fastest runners are people who were just born with incredible talent. But the truth is that in every field, the people who become pros are people who figure out how to work at it. Albert Einstein, the genius mathematician, liked to say, 'Genius is 1% talent and 99% percent hard work.'

"*You* have proven that you are not afraid of hard work when it comes to improving your writing. You have started to learn a lot of important lessons from your mentor author, Jim Howe, and it's not because you put a copy of 'Everything Will Be Okay' under your pillow. Nope, you are learning from Howe because you are finding parts of 'Everything Will Be Okay' that you admire, jotting in the margins about how those parts affect you, and then trying some of those techniques in your own writing. This is a solid *first* step. But if you really want your writing to get noticeably better, you need to deliberately practice writing in the ways that you admire."

◆ COACHING

People often think that experience alone is the most important factor in determining proficiency, but they are mistaken. To continue our growth curve, we must be deliberate learners who self-assess ourselves, work toward clear goals, and receive regular feedback.

Name the teaching point.

"Today I want to teach you how to use your writer's notebook as a place to deliberately practice the techniques and skills you want to see in your writing."

TEACHING

Explain to students that they can think of their notebooks, and all of the personal narrative drafts they hold, as an open invitation to practice their skills.

"Imagine a basketball player practicing layups in a gym, or a ceramic artist practicing his craft at a pottery wheel. Now, imagine yourself, practicing a particular writing skill. Instead of using gym equipment or pottery tools, you use your notebook, and your notebook becomes filled with your efforts to do that one thing better, better, better, over and over. So if you're not yet successful at making characters come to life through realistic dialogue, you work on that in lots of places in your notebook—not just in one draft but in several of your drafts. You'll work at this skill for a while, then pull back to look over your work and think, 'How is this working? Do I like what I just did?' The key thing is to keep trying, keep *practicing*, and each time you give it another go, you do it a little differently, a little better."

With focused, deliberate practice, students can build a sense of self-efficacy—the confidence they develop as they fill their notebooks with deliberate efforts to make their writing better and better, trying out strategies and applying what they glean from mentor texts. When students develop a high degree of self-efficacy, they see difficult tasks as challenges rather than things to be avoided, and they begin to turn failures into opportunities to learn and improve.

Demonstrate how you might use your own writer's notebook as a place to practice a lesson you have gleaned from a mentor text.

"Let me show you what I mean by showing you a bit of my writer's notebook, where I can practice doing something I spotted Jim Howe doing in 'Everything Will Be Okay.'" I pointed to the last bullet on the "How to Write Powerful Personal Narratives" chart and read it aloud: "'Writers zoom in on the small but powerful details that really capture big moments and feelings.' Do you remember Howe did that so powerfully in 'Everything Will Be Okay?'" I read aloud some sentences that showcased that craft move:

> *Smoky is inside a big old pretzel can with a hose attached, clawing at the can's sides as my brother pumps in the gas . . .*

"I have a personal narrative in my notebook that I'd like to practice this on. It's the story of one of the first times my friends and I had permission to go to the playground without an adult. My mother made us promise not to climb the trees at the playground, and of course that's exactly what we did. So I'm really going to work at trying to capture the tiniest details of the moment, the ones that made a lasting mark on me in that moment." I projected a page containing part of my narrative from my writer's notebook and looked at it with the students.

> "Don't look down, just keep climbing–you're almost to the top," Bobby urged. I swallowed and snuck one quick look.

I picked up my pen, clearly thinking hard about how to attempt this work. Then I added:

> Lydia was still standing at the bottom of the tree, holding my dark blue sandals with one hand and shielding her eyes, with the other, as she looked up at me.

I straightened up, rereading my work to myself. "How did I do? I've definitely added some small details—where Lydia was standing, what she was doing with her hands. But, now that I'm rereading it, I'm not totally convinced that these are the tiny details I was noticing in that moment, stuck high up in the tree. Let me try again."

It's important to show your students that writers don't get it right on the first try! The whole point of today's session is to reinforce the idea that professionals practice, practice, practice until they get it just right.

I stared at the entry for a moment and then added the lines:

> The tree swayed slightly, and I tightened my grasp on the trunk. A rough piece of bark dug sharply into my forearm, but I didn't dare move.

Then, I read aloud the next sentence and added more.

> "I think I need help getting down," I shouted, my voice high and tight. I thought about my mother's clear warning to stay out of the trees that bordered the playground. This must be why.
>
> "Hold on," Bobby called. He circled slowly around the tree and then walked towards Lydia, talking to her in a low voice. I couldn't hear him over the rustle of the tree's leaves. Suddenly, he grabbed Lydia's arm and pulled her away from the tree. "Run!" Bobby commanded, and they made a dash for the gate.

Debrief, explaining how, exactly, you used the strategy from the mentor narrative in your own story.

"Writers, did you see how I made myself try Jim Howe's technique of zooming in on the small details when the moment is really big? To do that, I really had to put myself back in that park and replay that scene in my mind. I could feel myself clinging to the tree trunk for dear life, I could feel the tree bark scratching under my arms, and I knew I had to include those precise details. I think they show how frightened and alone I felt. So now I am going to continue this same work in another place in my story."

One thing to notice here is that I don't just add sensory details for the sake of doing so. Just as you taught the students in Session 4, the sensory details need to be the true ones that the writer notices when reliving the story from the narrator's point of view. And so I model for students how I use the mentor text as a guide for practicing new techniques while being careful to do so purposefully.

ACTIVE ENGAGEMENT

Ask students to choose a technique the class has noticed the mentor author using that they want to use more in their own writing. Then, ask them to practice that craft move in several places in their notebooks.

"Writers, look between our chart on craft moves and your mentor text to pick out a technique Jim Howe uses that you want to try. Make sure you have marked places in the mentor text where Howe uses that technique. Keeping the annotated mentor before you, open up your notebook to one of your personal narratives and write at the top of the page today's date and the strategy you want to try. Then practice using that strategy in as many places as possible—but remember to try it *purposefully*, like I did. I didn't just throw any ol' sensory details into my draft, I only added ones that made sense to the moment and my point of view. Do that now."

I circulated as I watched the students work, and then I stopped next to Courtney, curious to see what she had chosen to practice. Courtney had bracketed the following portion of her story, about the day her mother let her get her cat.

> "Mommy, what's that?" I ask. We walk up and see it is a shelter and they are trying to give away saved animals to well homes.
>
> "So what are you guys doing?" my mom asks nicely.
>
> "We're trying to find these animals homes. There are more animals at our shelter," one of the girls says.
>
> "Please, can I get a cat?" I beg my mom.

"I want to show how badly I wanted a pet right then in my life and how I really didn't think my mom would go for it. I have a lot of dialogue, but I think I need to show more of what I was thinking and how my mom was acting. I can see how Howe does little bits of explaining between the characters talking. I can do that." I watched Courtney reread the portion of her story and then add in a couple of lines of reflection to show how a pet would keep her from feeling lonely over the summer. Leaning back to survey her work, she then added another line at the end of the passage.

> "Mommy, what's that?" I ask. We walk up and see it is a shelter and they are trying to give away saved animals to well homes.
>
> I've always wanted a dog, but I don't think I could always walk him/her everyday. I just wanted a pet who could keep me company over summer break since 2nd grade was coming to an end.
>
> "So what are you guys doing?" my mom asks nicely.
>
> "We're trying to find these animals homes. There are more animals at our shelter," one of the girls says.
>
> "Please, can I get a cat?" I beg my mom. She just looks at me and I knew I wasn't going to get one.

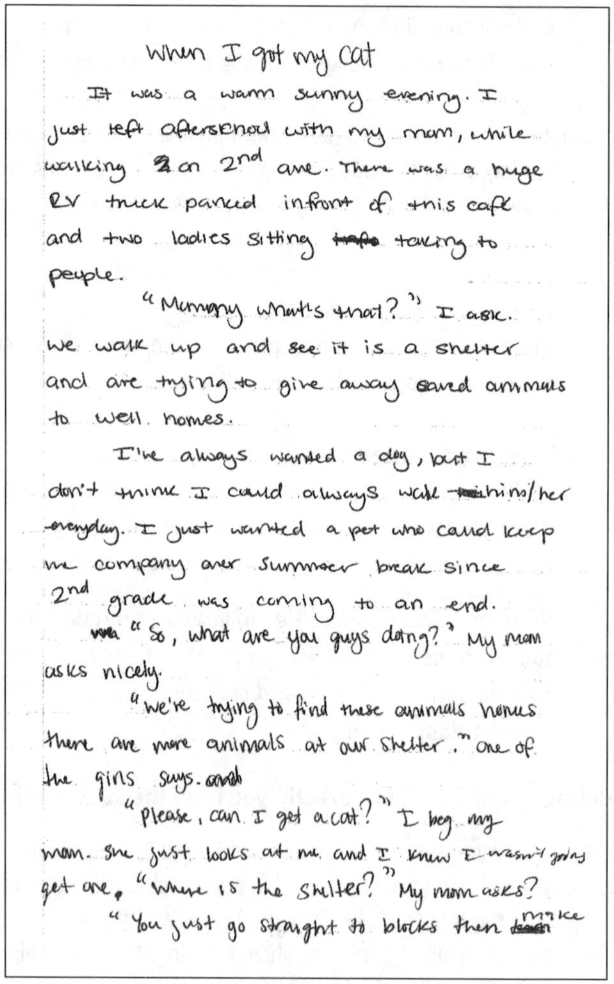
When I got my cat

It was a warm sunny evening. I just left afterschool with my mom, while walking on 2nd ave. There was a huge RV truck parked infront of this cafe and two ladies sitting talking to people.

"Mommy what's that?" I ask. We walk up and see it is a shelter and are trying to give away saved animals to well homes.

I've always wanted a dog, but I don't think I could always walk him/her everyday. I just wanted a pet who could keep me company over summer break since 2nd grade was coming to an end.

"So, what are you guys doing?" My mom asks nicely.

"We're trying to find these animals homes there are more animals at our shelter." one of the girls says.

"Please, can I get a cat?" I beg my mom. She just looks at me and I knew I wasn't going get one. "Where is the shelter?" My mom asks?

"You just go straight to blocks then make

FIG. 9–1 Courtney practices narrating, in between the characters' dialogue, to explain their choices and actions.

LINK

Synthesize today's minilesson, letting students know that from now on, you want them to use their writer's notebooks as a place to deliberately practice strategies, not just to collect new drafts.

"Writers, so far this year, and for many of you in the years prior, the writing process has unfolded sequentially: from gathering drafts in your notebook, to selecting a seed idea, to drafting out of the notebook and beginning to revise. My hope is that today's lesson offers a new vision for how you might use the writing process in general and your writer's notebook in particular. From now on, you can use your notebook for more than simply collecting one story after another. You can now use it as a place to practice certain strategies, to strengthen specific writing muscles.

"By now you know that if you want to learn from a mentor text, you can't simply read it. You need to study it. You need to scrutinize and analyze it, so that you can say, 'This writer is doing X, Y, and Z. I am going to try that now with my own writing.'

"Before you return to your seats, think about the work you will do today. As always, you have many choices, so as always, I will see people doing many different things as I circulate. Some of you will spend more time analyzing and annotating 'Everything Will Be Okay,' finding new things we could add to our chart on how to write powerful narratives. Some of you will use the work we've already done with our mentor to guide you today. You will pull from a part of your draft or from an entry and use your notebook to build a writing muscle—you will revise the excerpt you chose by practicing a technique from our chart that you want to get better at as a writer."

How to Write Powerful Personal Narratives

- Think of a person, place, or moment in your life (maybe a first or last time, or a time when you realized something) that matters, and write a story about it.
- Focus on one episode, write with detail (don't summarize a stretch of time).
- Help readers picture the episode–a small action and exact dialogue.
- Climb inside the moment and write within the narrator's point of view.
- Make characters say the words and use the tone that shows their personalities and hints at the bigger meaning of the moment.
- Explain why the characters act the way they do.
- Zoom in on the small but powerful details that really capture big moments and feelings.
- Use the Narrative Writing Checklist to ask, "As a writer, what are my strengths? What are my needs?" Then, plan your next steps as a writer.
- Craft a memorable lead.

CONFERRING AND SMALL-GROUP WORK

Working Steadfastly toward Goals

As you move around the room, from one conference or one small group to the next, remind students that the best way to keep their readers engaged is to write about compelling moments with compelling techniques—techniques that pull readers into a story and don't let them go. In the midst of such conversations, you might direct students' attention to relevant resources. Remind them to use the charts in the room, to recall strategies they have already learned, and to turn to partners for help, so they can practice crafting each bit of text with purpose and meaning. But also remind them that rarely does a piece of writing emerge well-crafted and meaningful the first time around—which is why writers try and try again.

Many of your conferences and small groups today will help students work toward the goals they set for themselves during the active engagement. As students read the mentor text and think and write, your work will also take many forms. Some students will benefit from more support with reading as a writer—from locating parts of the mentor text that stand out to them, to doing the challenging work of putting into words exactly what the mentor author is doing that the student wants to emulate. Others will need your help as they practice new strategies. You will ask students to show you what they marked in "Everything Will Be Okay" and where they are trying similar work in their own writing. Often, your help will come in the form of encouragement. Perhaps

(*continues*)

MID-WORKSHOP TEACHING **Writers Keep Their Tools Close at Hand**

"Writers, eyes on me. In today's lesson, we talked about using your notebook as a place to strengthen your writing muscles through repeated practice. And over the last many days, I have given you or we have created together certain tools that can help with that practice. All of you have a copy of the narrative checklist for sixth grade. All of you have a copy of 'Everything Will Be Okay,' which, by this point, should be marked up with plenty of underlining and annotations. And though you don't have your own copies, all of you also have access to the charts hanging in the room on different things strong writers do.

"However, as I work around the room today, I notice that too many of you aren't using those tools—and that many of you don't even have these tools on hand! Whether you're practicing a craft move on various drafts in your notebook or starting a new draft, you should have your eyes on more than just the excerpt on which you are working. When I sit at my desk and write, I surround myself with my writing tools. To my left, I might have a checklist of things I have to do and another list of things I might try. To my right, I might have a stack of mentors, and they don't just sit there! No, I refer to them often, flipping through the pages, underlining new parts, rereading my notes in the margins about things I love and want to try.

"Your work spaces should look similar. Your narrative checklists and mentors should be right next to you—and you should be using them, looking back and forth between these tools and your writing, even jotting notes to yourself in the margins about what you want to work on. Similarly, I should see some of you quietly getting out of your seats, writing in hand, to reference the charts we have in the room. They are hanging here for your benefit, to help you!

"Right now, get out your tools if you haven't already. And as you keep writing—today and from now on—*use* your tools."

you will compliment their efforts and say, "Now try it again. Look for another place to practice this strategy. Or, just as you did when you wrote several leads, try it again in this very same place. Is there another way this part could go?"

Other students will need more help emulating the mentor text. Often, this requires another, deeper look at the mentor text. For example, if students are saying, "Howe uses details" and then adding lots of details to their own writing, teach them to notice and name exactly what *kinds* of details—and then to revisit their own writing with the narrowed purpose of writing in that very specific way.

You might teach some students to turn to each other for mentorship. You could pull together a small group and say, "Jim Howe is not the only expert in this room. Each of you has strengths as a writer, and you can learn from one another's strengths." From here, you might proceed in a couple of ways. You could simply have them swap notebooks with a partner and study a peer's writing the same way they studied Howe's, finding places they want to emulate and doing that work in their notebooks. Or you might ask the group to reflect on what each of their strengths are and to find an example or two in their notebooks. Once they've done that, share everyone's strengths and then say something like, "If you want to work on developing the setting and tone in your stories like Abel often does, come sit next to him. If you want to work on conveying big feelings with tiny details, sit next to Bailey."

SHARE

Committing to a Goal—and Practicing, Again and Again

Gather students in the meeting area to remind them that writers try and try again.

"Writers, do you remember what I told you earlier—how J. K. Rowling gave that speech about the benefits of failure? The truth is, failure only benefits you when you get up and try again. It's not the falling down that helps you grow, it's the getting back up, and writers have to do that over and over again."

Remind the class to use the tools available to them—this time, to help them set a new goal.

"Right now, look across all the writing tools available to you—the charts hanging in the room, your mentor text, the narrative checklist. As you do that, think about a technique you want to try or get better at—and take a risk. Don't pick the thing that you already know how to do. Pick the thing you *wish* you knew how to do.

"Then, turn to the next blank page in your notebook. At the top of the page, write what it is you want to try and put a box around it. That is your goal for now. Work toward it, again and again, until you feel like you can say, 'I am a writer who knows how to do ______. I do it often and I do it well.'"

SESSION 9 HOMEWORK

WORKING TOWARD YOUR GOAL

"Tonight, whether you start a new draft or use excerpts in your notebook to practice smaller bits of writing, hold your goal in mind. Work those muscles. If they start to get tired, if you're feeling like it's just too hard, remember J. K. Rowling—and don't let yourself abandon the work you set out to try.

"Know that great writers are not born and great writing does not emerge with a magic 'poof.' Great writers and great writing come from hard work and from the courage to keep trying. Tonight, write with courage."

Session 10

Re-Angling and Rewriting to Convey What a Story Is *Really* About

FOR MANY WRITERS—and especially young writers—revision can be quite a daunting prospect. It is challenging enough to stare at a blank page and think, "What will I write today?" But to stare at an already-written page and think, "How can I do this *again*—but even *better*?" can be especially overwhelming. In the classroom, this can lead to increased chatter, frequent bathroom breaks, and the oversharpening of pencils—anything that leads to a reprieve from that draft staring back at them, begging for improvement.

This session will challenge students to loosen their hold on their first drafts and boldly take on the task of revision. Even more, it teaches students that to revise means to re-*envision*, which means much more than just inserting a word or a phrase or even trying out a new lead. Rather, re-envisioning—*true* revision—means seeing something in an entirely new way. It means creating something new. You must therefore instill this expectation in your students, that when writers revise, they in fact re-envision and then rewrite—not a word or a paragraph, but entire chunks of text, at the very least, if not the entire draft from beginning to end.

The beauty of this session is that it teaches students how to do that work with purpose and meaning and with concrete tools to help them navigate the process. Many of your students already know to ask themselves, "What is my story *really* about?" and have learned to hold tightly to the answer as they set out to revise the heart of their story. Once you remind students of how that work goes, you will extend it by teaching students to rehearse their storytelling in ways that allow them to hint at the larger meaning, early on in the story, and then to develop that meaning throughout the story.

You can teach sixth-graders to use the story mountain to rehearse how their new drafts will unfold. You will show them that on the outside of the arc of the story mountain, they will jot the sequence of external events, while holding close to that question, "What is my story *really* about?" On the inside of the arc of the story mountain, they will jot the internal story—what their characters (themselves and anyone else in their pieces) think and feel about each event. From there, students can consider, and even story-tell to a partner,

IN THIS SESSION, you'll teach students to kick off their substantial revision process by re-angling their storytelling to hint at the larger meaning, early on in the story, and then to develop that deeper meaning throughout the story.

GETTING READY

- ✔ Each student should bring his or her notebook to the meeting area for the minilesson.
- ✔ Your own story, ready to be planned in new ways (see Connection and Teaching)
- ✔ Story mountain for your story, sketched on chart paper (see Teaching)
- ✔ "How to Write Powerful Personal Narratives" chart (see Link)
- ✔ Blank Post-its to distribute to students (see Share)

COMMON CORE STATE STANDARDS: W.6.3, W.6.4, W.6.5, W.6.10, RL.6.2, RL.6.5, SL.6.1, SL.6.4, SL.6.6, L.6.1, L.6.2, L.6.3, L.6.4, L.6.5, L.6.6

the types of details they might include as they compose each dot on their timelines. Imagine, for example, that one student's story is *really* about facing her fears and realizing she is stronger than she realized. If the first event on her timeline is diving into a lake, and the feelings that go along with it are anxiety, fear, and apprehension, the writer won't consider just any ol' detail she could include to describe the lake or the dive or the character. Rather, she will think, "What details—what describing words and what inner thinking—might I include

"Re-envisioning—true *revision*—*means seeing something in an entirely new way."*

here to get across my intended meaning?" And rather than describing the serene blue and gentle ripples of the lake, she might describe the eerie stillness and dark depths.

The work of this session is many fold. It is about revising as re-envisioning and rewriting. It is about searching for a deeper meaning in one's story. And it is about using details in purposeful ways: not just plunking them in because we all know writers use details, but instead, making conscious choices about what to include and not to include to convey an intended message to readers. Finally, it is about doing all of these things simultaneously, spinning several plates at once without letting one or more drop to the ground.

MINILESSON

Re-Angling and Rewriting to Convey What a Story Is *Really* About

CONNECTION

Remind students that revising means rewriting—that it means *re-envisioning*, not merely crossing out a line here and inserting a phrase there.

"Most of you already know that revision is about a lot more than inserting a word here and a phrase over there. You know that revision means to *re-envision*—to see something in a whole new way. When writers can see a piece in a whole new way, they can write it in a whole new way.

"Of course, this is very hard work! Once you have a picture in your head of how something goes, it can be difficult to see it any other way. This is why writers often take a first draft and put it aside for a small stretch, like you did yesterday when you shifted your focus to practicing particular writing techniques in your notebook. When writers put a draft aside, they often keep thinking and even talking about it, exploring new possibilities for how that piece could unfold. And then, they start fresh. With blank paper and pen in hand, they write a new draft, incorporating all their new thinking and insight. *That* is true revision."

Acknowledge that many of them know how to write with the question, "What is my story *really* about?"

"I want to remind you of an important strategy for tackling revision, for tackling a second draft of your personal narrative with new insight. Many of you already know how to re-envision your story—especially the heart of your story—by thinking about what your story is *really* about. You know that when you rewrite with that question in mind and then place your new draft alongside the old, you see two very different pieces.

"Let's do that familiar work of asking ourselves, 'What's this story really about?' together right now."

Help students reflect on what their stories are really about by sharing your own example and giving them time to think about their drafts.

"I'd like to share one of my personal narratives with you. Do you remember the 'Moments I Realized Something' list from several days ago? The personal narrative I chose to publish is the story idea I jotted on that list—the story about the time my younger sister and I ignored my dad's directions and wound up destroying the garden. My flash-draft already tells what happened that day, and now I can think about the deeper meaning I want to convey and how to make

◆ COACHING

I am probably overstating students' experience with producing brand-new drafts as they revise. However, I do this because I want to set the expectation that students will write a very different version of their personal narratives today. Too often, I see students churning out two, three, four drafts that seem almost identical—which is not only a waste of time, but it is not true revision.

that happen throughout the draft. When I think about my story, I realize it could be about different things. Maybe I want it to be about my relationship with my sister and how, growing up, I often felt more like her mother than her sister. Or maybe I want it to be about my big realization, in that moment, that my dad would always help me sort problems out, even when I didn't listen to him. I was sure he was going to be furious with me, and instead he calmed me down, and together, we began to fix the mess. Hmm . . . now that I'm talking about it, I think I'm more interested in getting that second meaning across in my story.

"Right now, will you look back at your draft and decide what your story is *really* about? Maybe you're thinking about other people in your story and how your piece could be about the type of relationship you have with one of those people." I left a few moments of silence for students to do that thinking. "Or maybe," I continued, "you're thinking about how the events in your story changed you in some way—changed what you know or how you think or feel about something. Or maybe you're thinking about the big feelings in your story." Again, I left several seconds of silence, signaling to students to start that thinking.

"Writers, please put up your thumbs if you have at least one idea for what your story could really be about. If, like me, you've thought of multiple options, use your fingers to show me how many—and then be thinking about the one you will choose, the one that will guide you as you write your next draft." Seeing that the majority of students had at least one idea for their story's meaning, I continued to the next phase of my teaching. "Now that most of you are thinking about the significant meaning of your story, you're ready to think about how you might best convey that meaning to your readers."

I tuck this work into the connection because many of them learned to do this in past years. This way, I can use the teaching to extend their learning. This minilesson serves a dual purpose. First, I want to remind students to ask the question, "What is my story really *about?" I need to give them a little time to actually do that work, so they are ready to practice what comes next, during the teaching—using timelines and storytelling to figure out how they can hint at and then develop their story's deeper meaning.*

Name the teaching point.

"Today I want to teach you that when you let yourself be guided by the question, 'What is my story *really* about?' you find yourself wanting to tell your story in a completely new way. You can plan and rehearse your new draft in ways that will hint at the larger meaning, early on in the story, and develop that deeper meaning throughout the rest of the story."

TEACHING

Show students how realizing what your story is really about will lead to ideas for a brand-new draft where you can tell the story differently. Demonstrate using an external-internal story mountain as a tool for planning a new, more meaningful version of your story.

I quickly opened my notebook and drew a simple story mountain. Above the line of the mountain, I jotted "External Story (Physical Events)," and below the line, I wrote "Internal Story (What's my story really about?)."

"Let's see. If I want my reader to understand that my story is really about realizing that my dad would be there for me, despite my bad choices, then what do I need to show my reader? I think I first need to show my reader how impatient I was, at the beginning of the story, when my dad was trying to give me instructions. Then, at the end, I need to show how grateful I felt that my dad didn't give up on me." I jotted those feelings on the underside of my story mountain,

I am assuming some familiarity with story mountains and double timelines, but you might choose to say more about how they work. You might choose to explain that the arc of the story mountain represents how stories usually go: they introduce a main character who has hopes and wants. Usually that character's hopes lead to some sort of trouble. The problem gets bigger or more complicated, and then the story ends with a resolution. By making the story mountain a "double timeline," a writer can consider the relationship between the external and internal story arcs.

at each end. Above "impatient," on the outside of the story mountain, I wrote, "Dad showed Alison and me the new garden hose and went over the rules."

"Let me try rehearsing my story to see if I can hint at how impatient and frustrated I was with my dad in the beginning." I looked up, indicating that I was putting myself back into that moment and then began, "Dad motioned Alison and me closer, the new garden hose tucked under his arm. He began to say, 'Girls, you can do the watering for me, but there are a few important rules . . . ' Immediately, I looked at Alison and rolled my eyes and puffed out my cheeks, annoyed that he was starting one of his lectures. Alison giggled, but Dad's face was stern when I turned back around. 'Okay, okay, Dad,' I said quickly, 'I'm listening.' As my father began another one of his long explanations, I sighed and thought, 'Here we go again.'

"Do you see how I am trying to pop out my feelings of irritation, right from the beginning—it's in my details: my tone of voice, my inner thinking, my expressions. I can't just build the action of the story. I also have to build the characters' feelings. Together, those will show my reader what my story is really about.

It's not just your words that are pulling your students into the story—it's also the way you read aloud. You'll want to practice telling your story dramatically. You'll emphasize certain phrases, slow down or speed up at times, even pause to draw attention to how powerfully you are trying to compose your story.

"Let me try a bit more." I tapped what would be the second point on my story mountain to show that I was continuing and then said, "I aimed the hose at Alison's feet, and we laughed, as she hopped all over the garden to avoid the spray." I looked up and shook my head, "Wait a minute—I can't just hint at my story's deeper meaning at the beginning and then drop it. I want to show how much fun we were having, but I also need to show that I was deliberately ignoring my dad, that I felt like I shouldn't have to do everything exactly his way." I paused again, thinking, and then lit up, "Oh, I know!"

I resumed storytelling. "I aimed the hose at Alison's feet, and we laughed, as she hopped all over the garden. The spray pelted the side of the house and dug into the soft dirt of the flower beds. I felt a twinge of guilt, knowing Dad had just planted those. I shrugged the feeling off—*why was he always so picky about everything, anyway?* And then Alison screamed, 'Get me, get me! You can't get me!' and I couldn't resist. I chased her with the stream of water, both of us zigzagging through the flower bed. Suddenly, Alison changed tactics and ran at me, knocking the hose from my hands. First, we collided hard and then we ricocheted off of each other, both falling to the dirt, half-moaning, half-giggling. It wasn't until I fell down that I looked around. We had turned the garden into one giant, muddy mess."

I paused and looked at the students, "You know, those flowers were a big deal for my dad. He loved growing them from seeds, and he had silly names for them and talked to them in baby talk to make us laugh. He was good at taking care of things, at nurturing. I think I need to pop out those flowers, in this scene and later in the story, to make them an important symbol—a symbol of the kind of caregiver my dad was: faithful and patient. And then my sister and I literally trampled those flowers. We trampled his trust! Hmm . . . I'll need to keep that in mind as I rewrite today."

I am tucking in this quick demonstration of how writers might use symbolism to bring forth the deeper meaning of the story, but you'll notice that I am not pausing to debrief my writing move. Instead, I am offering this model to students who might be ready for it, knowing that I can follow up by pulling those students together for a small group to teach more explicitly about symbolism.

Debrief in ways that highlight the transferable skills that you hope the students will bring to their own revision process.

"Did you notice my process just now? When I started retelling my story, I pushed myself to angle my retelling so that it would bring out the deeper meaning that I want to convey. And, as I wrote to show how impatient and irritated I was with my dad at the beginning of my story, I didn't just add a bunch of details. Instead, I kept searching for the storytelling techniques that would allow me to bring out that specific meaning I have in mind."

ACTIVE ENGAGEMENT

Help students imagine how their new drafts might go. Encourage them to imagine multiple possibilities by asking the question, "What is my story *really* about?"

"Writers, before you go back to your seats, use this time to think about how your new drafts might go. Open up to the next blank page in your notebook so you can sketch a couple of different possible timelines for your stories. Try one, then another on the next page—you'll want lots of space to add the internal story. Holding close to what your story is really about, where might this new draft start? Earlier? Later? The same place as your old draft?" Between each tip, I left some silence for students to think and jot. "And how will the events unfold? In sequential order? Or out of order, with flashbacks or flash-forwards?" Again, I paused and then said, "*Which* parts will you choose to include this time? Will you stretch out different moments than before? Include new ones? Eliminate parts that no longer seem as relevant? Remember to keep in mind what your story might really be about, and consider which external events can help show that meaning."

I moved about the students as they worked, coaching them to try out different possibilities, all the while keeping their eyes on the meaning behind their story. "I see that several of you have already tried out one possibility for your revised timeline. Turn the page and try another!" And a minute later, "However far along you are, pause to focus for a moment on the internal story. Remind yourself about the deeper meaning of your story and then ask, 'What can I do or say or think in my story to show my reader what it is really about?"

Set students up to story-tell their revised pieces to a partner, making sure to weave together the internal and external story as they do.

"Okay, writers, if you have more than one timeline started, choose the one you will draft today, and think, 'What details will I include to get my meaning across to my readers?' Jot notes on your timeline as you get ideas." I left a bit of silence as students readied their timelines.

"Now, Partner 1, use your timeline to help tell your story to Partner 2 in a way that gets across your meaning. Partner 2, listen for that meaning. Listen so closely that you can tell your partner what you think his or her story is about and *why* you think that—what details hinted at that meaning for you."

Don't rush through this work. You have just asked students to do something challenging. When you pause for silence and give them a moment to think, you are communicating that this is difficult but worthwhile work.

As students told their stories, I circulated and whispered reminders. "Remember to use a storyteller's voice, just as I do when I read aloud. Tell your story in a way that pulls your readers in, makes them want to keep listening." And "You can use your voice to get your meaning across. You might emphasize important parts. You might slow down or speed up in certain places." And "Remember to be thoughtful about the details you include. What might your characters think here, to pop out your meaning?"

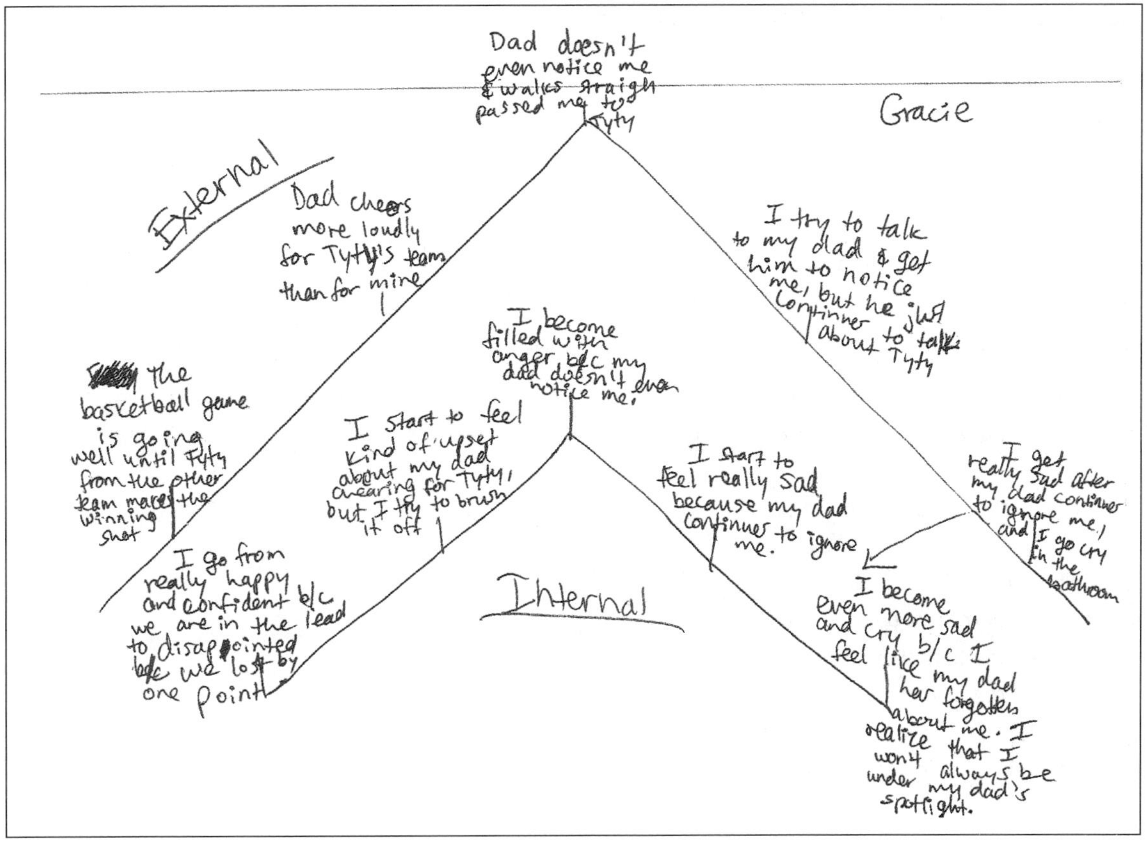

FIG. 10–1 Gracie uses an external-internal story arc to plan her revisions.

LINK

Restate your teaching point and send students off to write an entirely new—and more meaningful—version of their flash-drafts.

"Writers, please wrap up or pause your stories and give me your attention. Today you are going to put your first draft aside and write a new version, one that reads very differently than the first. Perhaps you'll begin in a new place. You might include whole new parts, just as you'll leave out some of what made it into your first draft. And certainly, you will include new details—descriptors, inner thinking, dialogue that will let your readers know what your story is really about.

"Usually at the end of a minilesson, I send you back to your seats with choices, knowing that each of you is in charge of your own writing. Today, however, I am going to ask everyone to keep working with a partner, so that all of you have the chance to rehearse your stories before you draft. So when you return to your seats, Partner 2 will story-tell to Partner

1, and this time, Partner 1 will listen so closely that he or she can pull out the meaning, as well as some of the details that get that meaning across.

"From there, all of you will get several blank pieces of paper and use your timelines and all your rehearsing to write a fresh and meaningful draft. Use our anchor chart, 'How to Write Powerful Personal Narratives,' as a reminder of how to write that draft well. I've added on today's learning. Off you go!"

How to Write Powerful Personal Narratives

- Think of a person, place, or moment in your life (maybe a first or last time, or a time when you realized something) that matters, and write a story about it.
- Focus on one episode, write with detail (don't summarize a stretch of time).
- Help readers picture the episode–a small action and exact dialogue.
- Climb inside the moment and write within the narrator's point of view.
- Make characters say the words and use the tone that shows their personalities and hints at the bigger meaning of the moment.
- Explain why the characters act the way they do.
- Zoom in on the small but powerful details that really capture big moments and feelings.
- Use the Narrative Writing Checklist to ask, "As a writer, what are my strengths? What are my needs?" Then, plan your next steps as a writer.
- Craft a memorable lead.
- **Ask, "What is my story really about?" and include descriptors, dialogue, and inner thinking that convey that meaning.**

CONFERRING AND SMALL-GROUP WORK

Rally Students for the Hard Work of True Revision

KNOWING THAT THE WORK you are asking of students today is especially challenging, you will want to rally their energy in ways that keep them going. Then too, you will want to give them the tools they need to successfully re-envision their stories. For some, what they will need most is for someone to listen in a way that gives their stories value. As you listen to writers tell their stories, you might respond with awe: "Wow, this feels like a really important story to tell." Let that sink in for them, and then decide how you could best support their work.

As you move around the room, especially during the first part of workshop when students are still storytelling to a partner, many of your conferences will help partners work more effectively. Rather than teaching the writer what to do, you might teach the listener how to scaffold a particular skill. Perhaps you'll teach him or her to listen closely enough to notice when the writer is moving too quickly, summarizing important parts, by saying, "I lost my picture of the story! Could you rewind and tell it again so I can see and hear what is happening?" You might teach others to help their partners angle a story, saying things like, "What do you want me to think and feel during this part of your story? Could you tell it again, and include character and setting details to get that across?"

Some students will struggle to begin anew, to make this second draft feel different. You might help them imagine a new place to start, so that from the first sentence, they are on a new track.

You might pull a small group of students that you think are ready to incorporate symbols in their writing, with just a little more support from you. You might ask them to identify central feelings in their stories and then brainstorm colors, objects, or setting details that might connect with those feelings and fit into their stories. For example, if a character goes from feeling anxious to relieved, perhaps the character first hides

(*continues*)

MID-WORKSHOP TEACHING **Keeping Partners Accountable—and Hence Effective**

"Writers, many of you are still rehearsing your stories with a partner, and I know the work you're doing now is going to make for much more powerful drafts! The more you practice telling your stories with rich, meaningful detail, the more likely it will be that you *write* them that way.

"I want to share something that Aidan and Emma are doing together, because I think it could help you be a stronger partner as well as a stronger writer. Rather than Aidan rushing through his story and then moving onto writing his draft, he's telling his story again and again—or parts of it, at least. And that's because Emma is *really listening*, in a way that allows her to notice when Aidan starts to summarize instead of show what is happening, or allows her to notice when Aidan includes parts or details that don't quite fit with the meaning of his story. For example, the first time I walked passed them, I heard Emma say, 'What's your story really about?' And then later she said, 'Could you tell that part again? I'm not really getting what you said the story was about—it seemed a little off-track.'

"Wow, writers, I wonder how many of you are doing that deep listening and thinking work. By now, you should all know what your partners' stories are supposed to be about. It is *your job* to hold your partner accountable to that meaning, just like Emma is doing. So if they slip off-track, ask them to rewind and tell that part again. The more you do this for your partner, the more you'll be able to do this for *yourself* when you write and revise your own story."

beneath a dark hoodie but later hangs it behind closed doors. Or perhaps shadows or dark clouds appear in the beginning scenes, to reflect the character's heavy mood.

> I could hear the squeaking of sneakers on the polished wood gym floor as I dribbled the ball.
>
> "Over here!" Jamie yelled, waving her arms around above her head. I made sure that there was nobody in the way, and I passed the ball to her. Jamie dodged her brother Jakie as he ran in front of her, and she caught the ball.
>
> Jamie dribbled the ball and passed it to Ayo. The basketball hit the gym floor, and went straight into her hands. From her hands it went straight through the hoop.
>
> "Yes!" I yelled. Tyty and Jakie's team had beat us the last time, but this time I was sure we had this. We were ahead by two, and there were only a few seconds on the clock. All of our team's hard work was finally going to pay off.
>
> The smile on my face instantly disappeared when Tyty got the ball. He was one of the best players on their team, even though he was only eight.
>
> Tyty dribbled the ball to the other side of the court. Ayo followed right behind him trying to get the ball. I looked at the clock. There were only seven seconds left.
>
> Tyty dribbled around Ayo's figure that towered above him, and shot the ball. It bounced off the backboard, and went through the hoop. A three point shot.
>
> The crowd of parents in the bleachers were all on their feet, clapping for Tyty. I remember feeling that huge wave of disappointment like it was just yesterday . . .

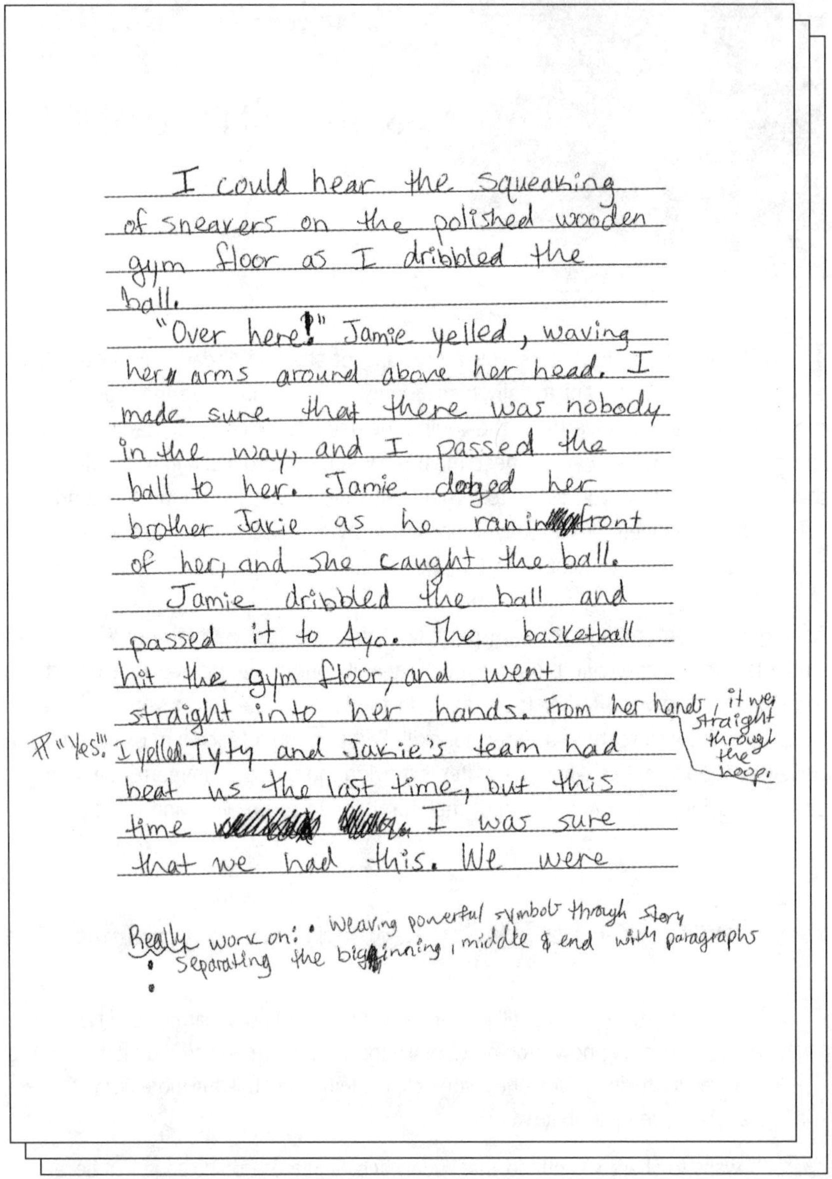
I could hear the squeaking of sneavers on the polished wooden gym floor as I dribbled the ball.
"Over here!" Jamie yelled, waving her arms around above her head. I made sure that there was nobody in the way, and I passed the ball to her. Jamie doged her brother Jacie as he ran in front of her, and she caught the ball.
Jamie dribbled the ball and passed it to Ayo. The basketball hit the gym floor, and went straight into her hands. From her hands, it went straight through the hoop.
¶ "Yes!" I yelled. Tyty and Jakie's team had beat us the last time, but this time I was sure that we had this. We were

Really work on: • Weaving powerful symbol through story
• Separating the beginning, middle & end with paragraphs
•

FIG. 10–2 Gracie's first draft

Work on Symbolism

Bracelet that dad gave me fell off—me realizing that my dad wouldn't always be paying attention to me, that I wouldn't always be in his spotlight.

As I punched the air in anger, the light brown beaded bracelet that my dad had given me slipped off of my wrist and fell onto the gym floor. I quickly gathered the small round beads and the broken string, but one of the beads rolled under the bleachers before I could reach it. I put the beads and string into the pocket of my gray shorts and walked over to Jamie.

You might find some students struggle to identify a deeper meaning—that a story about going to the fair remains a story about going to the fair. You might ask them why, of all the stories they could devote more time to, they chose this one. If they answer with a shrug of the shoulders, it might be that they have not chosen the best piece to publish. You might encourage them to return to their notebooks, this time with an eye out for stories that yield an answer to the question, "What might this *really* be about?" With a new draft idea in hand, set them up to make another timeline, orally rehearse a new story, and draft a new piece.

Others might respond differently when asked why they chose to write what they did. They might talk about how hard or how wonderful the experience was. Even if they focus more on feelings than a significant relationship or realization or theme, you can encourage them to retell and rewrite their stories in ways that truly show those feelings—and perhaps that do so in new ways, like through setting and character descriptors or symbols.

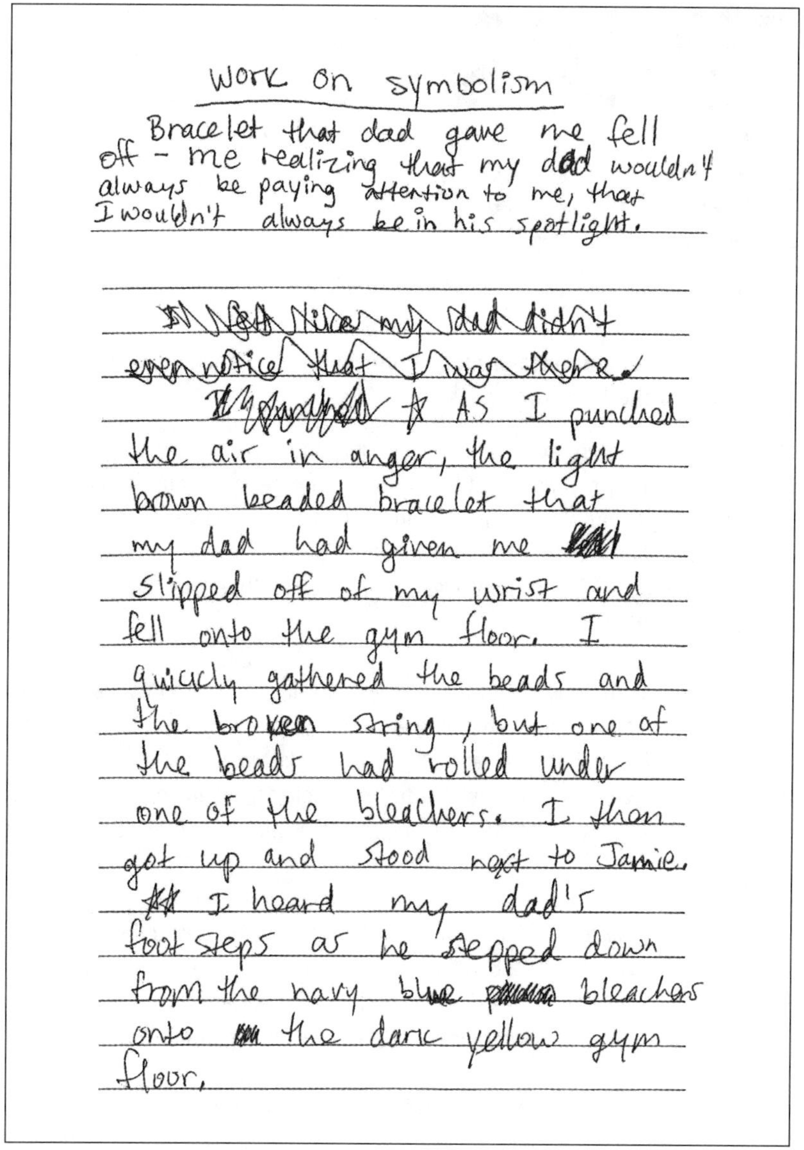
Work on symbolism

Bracelet that dad gave me fell off - me realizing that my dad wouldn't always be paying attention to me, that I wouldn't always be in his spotlight.

~~I Noticed my dad didn't even notice that I was there.~~

AS I punched the air in anger, the light brown beaded bracelet that my dad had given me slipped off of my wrist and fell onto the gym floor. I quicly gathered the beads and the broken string, but one of the beads had rolled under one of the bleachers. I then got up and stood next to Jamie. I heard my dad's foot steps as he stepped down from the navy blue bleachers onto the dark yellow gym floor.

FIG. 10–3 Gracie's notebook page, where she wrote about the broken bracelet as symbolism.

SHARE

Sharing Techniques with Other Writers

Combine partnerships into groups of four, and set up each small group to study one another's writing as they would a published mentor.

"Writers, would you and your partner please join another partnership and then find a place in the room to sit together? I will give you thirty seconds, then look at me for further direction." When all eyes were back on me, I said, "We have spent a good amount of time studying Jim Howe's piece, 'Everything Will Be Okay,' and from that, have gathered a lot of great techniques we can all try in our writing," I said, pointing to several items on our chart, "How to Write Powerful Personal Narratives." "Right now, you are going to do that same kind of work, but this time, you are going to study each other's writing.

"You can choose how you want to work in your small groups. You might swap stories, independently studying one, then another. Or you might work with a partner to study a piece together, then another piece. I'm coming around with blank Post-it notes so that when you see something you like, you can jot what the writer did and then name or describe the technique in a way that will allow *you* to try a similar move in your writing. By the end of our share today, everyone should have at least two Post-its. Everyone should be able to find at least two things another writer tried that you want to try."

As writers read, talked, and jotted, I circulated and coached, saying things like, "Instead of just saying 'the writer wrote with detail,' can you look a bit closer and say *how* he did that? What *kind* of details did he use? Where did he use them? How do they affect you as a reader? That will make it easier for you to do something similar." And, "If you're not sure how to describe what the writer did, talk with others in the group—study the part together."

After students had time to read and study at least one story, I said, "Writers, wrap up your work and give me your attention again. You should all have at least two techniques you want to try as writers."

REVISING YOUR STORIES

"Tonight for homework, keep revising your stories. Perhaps you'll find a part you want to rewrite, trying one or both of those techniques. Perhaps you'll find a place where you want to add something new, using those techniques. Whatever you do, whatever techniques you try, make sure you are using them to help convey what your story is really about."

Session 11

Elaborating on Important Scenes and Adding New Ones from the Past

IN THIS SESSION, you'll teach students to use everything they know about writing powerful scenes to further develop the most important parts of their stories and to incorporate new moments from the past that connect with their stories' meaning.

GETTING READY

- ✔ A copy of your own draft, including a part that has been rewritten with more elaboration (see Teaching and Active Engagement)
- ✔ "How to Write Powerful Personal Narratives" chart (see Teaching and Active Engagement)
- ✔ Students' drafts and writing tools (see Link)
- ✔ Students' copies of the Rubric for Narrative Writing and the section on paragraphs, enlarged for the class to see (see Mid-Workshop Teaching)
- ✔ "Everything Will Be Okay" or the mentor text you are using throughout the unit (see Conferring and Small-Group Work and Mid-Workshop Teaching)
- ✔ Work from a student to highlight (see Share)

Common Core State Standards: W.6.3, W.6.4, W.6.5, W.6.10, RL.6.2, RL.6.4, RL.6.5, RL.6.6, SL.6.1, SL.6.6, L.6.1, L.6.2, L.6.3

IN THE PREVIOUS SESSIONS, YOU REMINDED STUDENTS that writers ask the question, "What is my story *really* about?" and then taught them a few ways writers get that message across to readers. Your students now have a second draft of their story, and today they will consider more ways to convey meaning as they revise. Writing with elaboration is not new work for your students, but because it is not only a challenging but a foundational skill, we return to it again and again, for different purposes. Today the purpose for elaborating is to pop out a story's meaning, so you will remind students that once writers decide what a story is really about, they can stretch out whatever parts might show that meaning.

"Writing with elaboration . . . is a foundational skill . . . we return to again and again."

You will also teach students to use everything they know about writing strong personal narratives to draft new scenes, in which they remember important moments from the past that will further develop a story's meaning. You will teach students to dig for parallel moments, to think, "When was *another* time I felt like this, another time I experienced this relationship in this way?" Or in some cases, if their story is about a realization, they might dig for moments that highlight a change—moments that emphasize the shift between old and current thinking. Either way, you will teach students to embed these new moments into their current draft as if to say, "Look here, readers, I'm saying it again! *This* is what my story is really about."

MINILESSON

Elaborating on Important Scenes and Adding New Ones from the Past

CONNECTION

Point out for students that scenes are the building blocks for personal narrative. Explain that sometimes writers focus on crafting an individual scene, while at other times they focus on fitting individual parts together.

"Writers, none of you are new to writing powerful scenes. After all, we use the same muscles to write a powerful scene as we use to write a powerful personal narrative," I said, gesturing to our chart. "The reason we use the same techniques when drafting a single scene as we do when drafting an entire story is because scenes are the building blocks. We draft one, then another and another, and when we place them together just so, 'Poof!' we have a whole narrative. Often, our work as writers seems focused on crafting individual scenes—on choosing just the right words, on incorporating the best inner thinking and the most precise setting details. And of course this is critical. However, our work as writers is also about learning to first choose and then piece together individual parts in just the right way, so that our finished product presents the way we intended.

"This means that when writers revise for meaning, just as you all are doing, they often zoom in to revisit individual scenes. And they often zoom out to revisit how all the parts fit together."

Name the teaching point.

"Today I want to teach you that when writers zoom in to look at individual scenes, they often *elaborate* on the ones that are most important to the central meaning of the story. And when writers zoom out to see how all the parts fit together, they often pull in *new* scenes from the past and future to help get across what the story is really about."

TEACHING AND ACTIVE ENGAGEMENT

Show how you slowed down and stretched out an important scene in your own draft. Then demonstrate how you imagine new, possible scenes from the past.

"I'm going to use my own draft to show you what this work looks like. Remember that I decided my story about destroying the garden is really about my realization that my father will always be here for me, even when I make terrible mistakes," I said, projecting a section of my draft for the class. "When I read over my draft, one thing I did was look for

◆ COACHING

Because there are two parts to my teaching—slowing down a scene and incorporating new scenes from the past and future—I use an atypical structure for this minilesson. Rather than teaching everything up front, I break up the steps into more manageable chunks by moving back and forth between teaching a strategy and coaching students as they try it themselves (hence, the Teaching and Active Engagement are combined).

It's important to plan carefully for your modeling. To help students focus on the work at hand, choose small entries that allow you to clearly and efficiently demonstrate the use of a strategy. You may want to begin with an entry that is purposefully deficient (in this example, writing that does not elaborate on a key part of the story), so you can show your students how you are able to fix the problem.

parts that I'd already written that I could elaborate on to better convey my meaning. So in this particular story, I looked for parts where my father and I were interacting, like in this part, when he is handing off the hose to Alison and me. Do you see how I put brackets around that part of the scene? I realized that if my story is really about the kind of father my dad is, then I need to stretch out a part like this with the kind of details that will help my reader imagine more clearly how my dad was with me."

> Dad motioned Alison and me closer, the new garden hose tucked under his arm. He began to say, "Girls, you can do the watering for me, but there are a few important rules . . ." Immediately, I looked at Alison and rolled my eyes and puffed out my cheeks, annoyed that he was starting one of his lectures. Alison giggled, but Dad's face was stern when I turned back around.
>
> "Okay, okay, Dad," I said quickly, "I'm listening." As my father began another one of his long explanations, I sighed and thought, "Here we go again . . ." Then, I began to tune him out, letting my mind wander to what Alison and I would play with the new hose.

"Then, using our charts, 'Lessons from Mentor Narratives' and 'How to Write Powerful Personal Narratives' as guides, I rewrote those parts with more elaboration. For example, our chart says to climb right into the story and experience it as you write. That's the first thing I tried to do—I closed my eyes, took myself back in time to that moment in the yard. I tried to shift my focus from what I was doing and saying and thinking to *showing* my father's small actions and his exact words. Let me show you what I tried to do in my revision." I held up a different piece of paper, the one where I had redrafted that part of my story, and then projected it for the class.

> Dad's face was stern when I turned back around. But then, he took one of his deep breaths and relaxed his face. Instead of continuing his explanation, he put the hose down and bent his tall frame over me to come down to my height. Dad kept his eyes on mine and spoke softly, "You need to show me that I can feel comfortable leaving you in charge for a little while. If you can't even listen to my directions . . ." Dad trailed off, but his eyes searched mine. I leaned in, matching my expression to his serious one, wanting him to see that he could trust me. I could do it, I could be in charge.
>
> "Okay, okay, Dad," I said quickly, "I'm listening–it's okay, go ahead." But as my father began another one of his long explanations, I couldn't help but think, "Here we go again . . ." I kept my eyes on Dad and the hose, but I tuned him out and let my mind wander to what Alison and I would play with the new hose.

Debrief, highlighting that writers elaborate in ways that bring out their intended meanings.

"Writers, this is just one small place in my story that I elaborated, and I didn't pick just any place. I looked for a part that I knew connected to what my story is *really* about, and then I used what I know about writing powerful personal narratives to pop out my father's small, telling actions and bring his actual words into the story. I also tried to add another

Because I am essentially teaching two distinct techniques for getting across what a story is really about—to elaborate on existing scenes but also to pull in new scenes—I expect this minilesson to be a little longer than usual. For that reason, I teach through example and explanation rather than through demonstration. The former method allows me to prepare my examples ahead of time, and I know this is quicker than composing on the spot while thinking aloud to highlight the process, as is done through demonstration teaching.

layer to my internal story—through my inner thinking, I tried to show that even though I was annoyed with my dad's long explanation, I did want him to feel he could trust me."

Set students up to identify an important scene in their drafts and to story-tell a more elaborated version to their partners.

"Writers, I want you to practice this same work in your own drafts. Holding onto what your story is really about, reread your piece and put brackets around scenes that are particularly important—that really connect with your story's meaning. Do that now." After giving students a minute to do that, I continued, "Pick one of those scenes for now, put your draft aside, and close your eyes so you can climb back into that moment. Remember, don't ever let go of what your story is really about, because that will drive all the decisions you make about how to rewrite this part. Keeping your eyes closed, look around—where are you? What tiny details do you see in your scene that could pop out your meaning?" I paused, giving students time to "see" and "write" their surroundings. "Now scan your body—what actions are you taking? What are you thinking and feeling?" Again, I paused. "Are there any symbols you could incorporate into this part of your story for more meaning and elaboration?

"Now open your eyes. Today, Partner 2—without looking at your draft—you're going to story-tell just this scene to Partner 1 with as much elaboration and meaning as possible. Partner 1s, your job, of course, is to listen closely enough to hold your partners accountable to the meaning of the story *and* to stop and ask them to rewind if they start to summarize instead of elaborate."

As students worked, I circulated. Sometimes I whispered prompts for Partner 1 to repeat to Partner 2, such as "Slow down, tell that part again so I can really see and hear what is happening." Or I voiced over, saying things like "Remember to include what characters are thinking" and "Slow down your character's actions so I can see what is happening—and why this part is so important."

Reconvene the class's attention for part two of the teaching and active engagement and restate your teaching point.

"Writers, wrap up with your partner and turn your attention back to me. We know that elaborating on scenes that show our meaning is another way to write powerful personal narratives. I've added that to our anchor chart. Now I want to show you how writers can also pull in *new* scenes from the past. That's yet another way to get across your meaning and write powerful narratives, so I've also added that to our chart."

How to Write Powerful Personal Narratives

- Think of a person, place, or moment in your life (maybe a first or last time, or a time when you realized something) that matters, and write a story about it.
- Focus on one episode, write with detail (don't summarize a stretch of time).
- Help readers picture the episode–a small action and exact dialogue.
- Climb inside the moment and write within the narrator's point of view.
- Make characters say the words and use the tone that shows their personalities and hints at the bigger meaning of the moment.
- Explain why the characters act the way they do.
- Zoom in on the small but powerful details that really capture big moments and feelings.
- Use the Narrative Writing Checklist to ask, "As a writer, what are my strengths? What are my needs?" Then, plan your next steps as a writer.
- Craft a memorable lead.
- Ask, "What is my story <u>really</u> about?" and include descriptors, dialogue, and inner thinking that convey that meaning.
- **Elaborate on important scenes that show what the story is really about.**
- **Include new scenes, remembered from the past or imagined in the future, that help show what the story is really about.**

"Let me show you what that sounds like with my story. Since my story is about realizing my father wouldn't give up on me even when I exercised poor judgment, I thought about whether there was a place where I could jump back in time to bring out that understanding. First, I thought about jumping back to the day my dad spent so long working on the garden that he wound up with a blistering sunburn. That flashback would show how hardworking my dad was, but I realized that wouldn't help me show how my dad was always there for me. I remembered another time when my dad was right there for me when I needed him. I decided to insert that other moment as a flashback in which my dad comes back, just before he sees what Alison and I have done to his garden. Here's how that part of my story initially went." I read aloud.

> I aimed the hose at Alison's feet, and we laughed, as she hopped all over the garden. The spray pelted the side of the house and dug into the soft dirt of the flower beds. I felt a twinge of guilt, knowing Dad had just planted those. I immediately shrugged the feeling off–why was he always so picky about everything, anyway?
>
> Alison screamed, "Get me, get me! You can't get me!" Unable to resist, I chased her with the stream of water, both of us zigzagging through the flower bed. Suddenly, Alison changed tactics and ran at me, knocking the hose from my hands. First, we collided hard and then we ricocheted off of each other, both falling to the ground and half-moaning, half-giggling. Cold, muddy water seeped right through my clothes.
>
> I sat up quickly, startled to realize that the garden was more giant mud puddle than dirt. Then, my eyes fell to the scattered flower petals. They were everywhere–except where they were supposed to be, on the heads of the flowers.
>
> "Alison, stop . . . don't move," I hissed, "Look what we've done. Dad's going to kill us . . . no, Dad is going to kill me." I could hear my voice rising with panic. Alison and I scrambled up, and I frantically began to push uprooted, broken plants back into their spots.
>
> I was holding a handful of the purple petals, my dad's favorite, when he turned the corner. He was holding a box of plants, smiling broadly in my direction. From his bouncy walk, I could tell he was excited to show me his new plants.

And then I added this new scene from the past.

> As my dad closed the gap between us, I thought about how I was always the one running around that corner, running to the garden to find my dad. My mind drifted back to much earlier in the spring, when I had turned the same corner in a storm of hurt and tears, crying so hard that I could barely see my dad. He had dropped the heavy stone he was holding to run to me and wrap me in his arms, to comfort me after my run-in with neighborhood bullies. Only after I had totally regained my calm, did my dad plunk himself down on the grass and ease off his tennis shoe, revealing the toenail he'd smashed when he had dropped the stone. When I had gasped at the sight, Dad had stopped grimacing and had quickly put his arm back around me to joke, "You're worth it . . . and wait till those bullies see how tough your dad is."

"Writers, do you see how that flashback shows how my dad was always ready to drop everything and put me first—literally, drop everything! He couldn't even acknowledge his own pain until he was sure I was okay.

"Now, listen how I returned to the present time, when my dad is coming toward Alison and me."

I squeezed the crushed purple petals in my hand, afraid to watch his friendly greeting dissolve into anger and disappointment. "And why shouldn't it?" I chastised myself, "He trusted you to be in charge, and look at what you did." A few feet from me, Dad stopped suddenly. As he put the crate of new plants down heavily, his eyes traveled over the ruined flower bed and then stopped on me. I was expecting to see fury etched into his face, but instead it was a look of bewilderment and even worse, hurt.

"Dad . . ." my voice broke as I tried to apologize, "I'm sorry. I'll fix it, I promise." Dad swallowed and nodded. I could tell he was having trouble finding his words. He nodded again, still silent, and pulled me into his arms.

"Writers, do you see how I took this one tiny moment, when my dad rounds the corner, and added a flashback that pushes forward my deeper meaning that, no matter what, my dad was there for me?"

Ask students to consider new scenes, remembered from the past, that they might incorporate into their own stories to convey their deeper meaning.

"Before you go back to your seats, practice this next strategy with your own stories. What new scenes—remembered from the past—could you incorporate into your draft to further show what your piece is about?" As students thought, I voiced over with scaffolds, pausing in between each one to give students time to think. "When *else* have you experienced what you realized or felt in this story? If your story is about a relationship, what's another time you experienced that person in this way? If your story is about a change, is there another moment from your past that shows what things were like *prior* to the change?

"Put your thumbs up when you've thought of at least one new scene you could incorporate from the past that connects to what your story is really about."

LINK

Remind students of the teaching point but also that they have many choices as writers. Let them know they can choose from a repertoire of strategies as they revise their drafts today.

"Writers, today you've seen yet more ways that writers get across what their stories are really about. You've seen that you can elaborate on important parts that already exist in a draft, but also that you can incorporate whole new scenes from the past that connect with a story's meaning.

"As you continue to revise your pieces today, you will need to decide what work will best serve you as a writer and which techniques will do the most to lift the quality of your draft. Remember that you have many options, many of which are on our chart, 'How to Write Powerful Personal Narratives,'" I said, gesturing to the chart, "as well as on our Narrative Writing Checklist, which all of you have in your folders. Whatever you work on today, hold tight to what your story is really about so the answer can continue to guide you."

CONFERRING AND SMALL-GROUP WORK

Revising for Meaning in Myriad Ways

WHETHER SUPPORTING FIVE-YEAR-OLD, fifteen-year-old, or fifty-year-old writers, something I always find myself teaching is how to elaborate on key parts of a story—which highlights the fact that this is challenging work at any age. You can expect, then, to spend some of your time today supporting your students with this skill, perhaps pulling together a small group to study how another writer stretches out an important scene. Whether you use a strong student example or a published

(*continues*)

MID-WORKSHOP TEACHING **Using the Rubric for Narrative Writing to Self-Assess for Paragraphs**

"Writers, there is a lot of different work happening today, which is, of course, a great sign. It means that you are thinking hard about the choices you want and need to make as a writer and proceeding with independence.

"Interestingly, despite the variety of tasks today, I am noticing a pattern, which is that many of you are—or if you aren't, you should be—thinking about paragraphs as you write and revise and edit. For example, many of you who are pulling in new scenes from the past and future are using a new paragraph to show that the narrator is thinking back or jumping ahead—you use paragraphs to signal to your readers that there is a change in time. Some of you are using paragraphs to slow down or to emphasize important parts, to encourage your readers to pause and take in an important image or event or feeling.

"Right now, let's look at the part of our Rubric for Narrative Writing that focuses on paragraphs. You have your own copies, but I am also displaying that section up here. I just talked with you about using paragraphs to," I held up one finger, "signal changes in time and, two," I held up another finger, "to slow down or emphasize key parts. Looking at fifth and sixth grade on the Rubric for Narrative Writing, notice how the rubric lists some other reasons to use paragraphs." I continued to use my fingers to highlight distinct strategies. "To show when a new character is speaking. To show setting changes. To show new parts of the story. And to create suspense for readers.

"Let's look quickly at how Jim Howe uses paragraphs for different purposes—like to emphasize something important or create suspense for readers. On the first page, he has the sentence 'The kitten makes a pitiful noise' as its own paragraph. And on the next page, 'He is my father's dog, really' is also its own paragraph. Howe does that a lot—gives a sentence its own paragraph to emphasize important parts and help get across the story's meaning (which in part has to do with how sensitive he is, how much he wants to take care of animals like this helpless kitten, while his dad and brothers are more interested in hunting and 'tough guy' stuff).

"And let's look at the end of page 3, where Howe has four small paragraphs in a row. For me, the way he uses paragraphs here slows down this intense moment and builds tension. As I read this part, think about whether you agree."

> I pushed the venison away.
>
> My father said, "That's a waste of good meat."
>
> My brothers teased me. One of them called me a sissy.
>
> My mother said, "You don't have to eat it," and took the slab of gray meat off my plate.

"Take a minute right now to reread your draft through the lens of paragraphs. If you find places—and I'm sure you will—where you could use a paragraph for one of these reasons, make sure to insert this paragraph sign where you want to be sure to indent," and I jotted the symbol on the board.

mentor text like "Everything Will Be Okay," help writers notice and name the transferable strategies the author uses to set them up to try similar work in their own pieces.

As students work on elaborating on important scenes, you might also teach some of them about poetic license—namely, that while they need to stay close to the bigger truth of their stories, writers often take liberty to invent the smaller details that convey that truth. So when students say, "I don't remember what I was thinking," you can respond with, "Based on what was happening in that moment—and holding tight to what your story is really about—what *might* you have been thinking in that moment?"

Some of your writers will benefit from a conference or small group on the benefits of *deleting* scenes. Acknowledge how painful it can be to write and write and write—and then delete all that hard work. But also emphasize that once a writer identifies what a story is really about, they almost always have to cross out parts that detract from that meaning. You might prepare ahead of time a draft of your own story in which you included isolated details as well as bigger chunks of text that no longer belong. Demonstrate the process of reading with a critical eye, repeatedly asking yourself, "Does this part (this detail, sentence, scene, lead) connect with what my story is really about?" and crossing it out whenever the answer is, "No." Then direct students to practice similar work with their own drafts.

You might find other students wanting but struggling to find new scenes to include. Knowing that writers often return to the same topics again and again, you might teach them to look back in their notebooks for other stories—or parts of stories—they've already written that connect with what their current piece is about. Though you certainly do not want students copying over the same story and calling it a new draft, writers do often revise by plucking a line, a passage, a whole scene from other pieces they've written. If students don't find fodder in their notebooks, remind them that they already know how to generate story topics and that the only difference here is that they need to think about moments that connect with what *this* draft is about. So depending on what that is, they might consider other moments about a particular relationship, place, event, idea, strong feeling, and so forth. Whether pulling from old drafts or crafting new scenes, part of your work with these students might entail teaching them how to use transitions to seamlessly weave in these new parts.

SHARE

Highlighting Students' Revision Process and Their Growth as Writers

Share an example of a student's writing that shows moving to a new scene, in the imagined future.

"Writers, many of you are moving backward in time, but some of you are drawing on what you already know about personal narrative writing to move *forward* in time, as well. Some of you, like Shayna, are learning how to move forward in time by studying your mentor text. Shayna noticed that, in 'Everything Will Be Okay,' the narrator jumps to the future when he writes":

> *When I am older, I will go hunting with my father the way my brothers have done. I try not to think about this. I want to go, because I want my father to like me. But I don't want to kill animals.*

"And Shayna also noticed how this jump to the future, imagining himself going hunting, really connects to what the narrator has been trying to show in his story—that he has to become his own person. Then, Shayna looked at her story about trying to make her parents understand how badly she wanted to go to the Justin Bieber concert, and she added the following scene."

> "Mom, GUESS WHAT!" I yelled across the room to my mom.
>
> "What? What's the matter?" my mom said with a concerned look on her face.
>
> "Justin Bieber is coming to New Jersey on July 31st! Can you get me tickets?" I pointed to the screen that showed an advertisement to buy tickets.
>
> I imagined myself in the same room as Justin Bieber. Better yet, I imagined myself breathing the same air as him. I imagined him looking into my eyes and only mine, out of the thousands of screaming girls there. He might pick me as the OLLG ("One Less Lonely Girl").
>
> "Yeah, yeah . . . hold on, Shayna, I'm doing something really important right now." As my mom walked away, I was wondering if she had heard me, or was she just trying to shrug me off so she wouldn't have to hear my "nonsense"–according to her. I felt as if she never listened to me when it came to Justin Bieber, and it bothered me.
>
> As I watched the commercial finish, I noticed that is said, "HURRY, THEY'RE SELLING FAST!"

"Shayna's story is becoming more powerful, with this flash-forward, because it allows her to show how badly she wants this experience. Then, when she comes back to real time, and her mom dismisses Shayna and her 'nonsense,' the reader begins to understand that Shayna feels her parents don't understand what is important to her."

SESSION 11 HOMEWORK

VOLUME IS IMPORTANT

"Tonight, as you continue to work on your draft, you might add a scene from the past, or a scene from the future—or maybe you'll try both. Either way, you should keep in mind what your story is about and how the new scenes show that meaning to your reader.

"And remember that even when revising, volume is important. A goal for tonight, in addition to anything else you're working on, should be to produce two new pages of writing. Again, those pages might include an entirely new scene as well as a scene you've already written but want to re-envision and write again."

Session 12

Using All Available Resources to Aid with Final Touches

Dear Teachers,

Over the last few days, you have supported students as they moved from picking a piece to bring to publication, to drafting, and then to revising in significant and meaningful ways. Today you will teach them how to use all the tools available to them as writers to aid with final revisions and editing. Students will need easy access to the teaching charts you've created and used throughout the unit, as well as their own copies of the Narrative Writing Continuum. Students might also want to turn to the various mentor texts you've used, from your own writing samples to published pieces like "Everything Will Be Okay." In short, because you will remind students that writers draw on *all* the tools they have at their disposal when putting on the final touches, you will get ready for today's minilesson by making sure these tools are within students' quick reach.

MINILESSON

You might begin your minilesson by reminding students that writers have many tools, and that over the course of this unit, they have learned to keep those tools close at hand so they can use them often. You can tell students that many professionals use checklists to guide their work. Doctors and nurses use them as a reminder about proper procedures, as do attorneys, pilots, and even teachers. You can say that similarly, as writers near the finish line of a project, as your students are doing today, they often use checklists to remind them of all they need to do before they say, "Here you are, world!" and present a finished piece.

Of course, having a checklist is not enough. Writers must know how to *use* a checklist—which potentially becomes even more complicated when there are many of them to navigate at once. You will therefore want to demonstrate the process of making a plan for how you—and hence they—can use the many available tools to put the final touches on a piece of writing. You will certainly want to teach students that one cannot check for everything all at once. For example, it is never enough to read through a draft just one last

COMMON CORE STATE STANDARDS: W.6.3, W.6.5, RL.6.3, RL.6.10, SL.6.1, SL.6.6, L.6.1, L.6.2, L.6.3

time. To the contrary, one must read and read again, over and over, each time with a different lens. With an editing checklist in hand, the focus could be on periods and capitals the first time through, then paragraphs, then punctuated dialogue.

Your plan might entail using the Narrative Writing Checklist first, perhaps starting with organization, then shifting your focus to leads and endings during a second read, and lastly to transitions. From there, your plan might be to focus on conventions, again in several phases as suggested above, by using your "Questions to Ask Yourself as You Edit" chart as a guide. Perhaps the final step of your plan is to revisit the charts around the room to consider any last techniques you want to try.

Once you map out your plan, you can demonstrate how you implement the first step. Show students how you first study your tool—in this case, the "organization" section of the Narrative Writing Checklist—then return to your draft, looking for places where you still need to address any of those items. Tell students that at a later date, you will repeat the same process for each step of your plan.

During the active engagement, set students up to consider their own plans and then to work with a partner to self-assess. Everyone should identify a few goals and places for revision before they return to their seats and begin working toward those goals.

Narrative Writing Checklist

	Grade 6	NOT YET	STARTING TO	YES!
	Structure			
Overall	I wrote a story that has tension, resolution, realistic characters, and also conveys an idea, lesson, or theme.	☐	☐	☐
Lead	I wrote a beginning that not only set the plot/story in motion, but also hinted at the larger meaning the story would convey. It introduced the problem, set the stage for the lesson that would be learned, or showed how the character relates to the setting in a way that matters in the story.	☐	☐	☐
Transitions	I not only used transitional phrases and clauses to signal complicated changes in time, I also used them to alert my reader to changes in the setting, tone, mood, point of view, or the time in the story (such as *suddenly, unlike before, if only she had known*).	☐	☐	☐
Ending	I wrote an ending that connected to what the story is really about. I gave the reader a sense of closure by showing a new realization or insight, or a change in the character/narrator. I might have shown this through dialogue, action, inner thinking, or small actions the character takes.	☐	☐	☐
Organization	I used paragraphs purposefully, perhaps to show time and setting changes, new parts of the story, or to create suspense for readers. I created a logical, clear sequence of events.	☐	☐	☐
	Development			
Elaboration	I developed realistic characters, and developed the details, action, dialogue, and internal thinking that contribute to the deeper meaning of the story.	☐	☐	☐
Craft	I developed some relationship between characters to show *why* they act and speak as they do. I told the internal, as well as the external story.	☐	☐	☐
	I wove together precise descriptions, figurative language, and some symbolism to help readers picture the setting and actions, and to bring forth meaning.	☐	☐	☐
	I used language that fit my story's meaning and context (for example, different characters use different kinds of language).	☐	☐	☐
	Conventions			
Spelling	I used resources to be sure the words in my writing are spelled correctly.	☐	☐	☐
Punctuation and Sentence Structure	I used punctuation such as dashes, parentheses, colons, and semicolons to help me include extra detail and explanation in some of my sentences.	☐	☐	☐
	I used commas and quotation marks or italics or other ways to make clear when characters are speaking.	☐	☐	☐

CONFERRING AND SMALL-GROUP WORK

Before students revise and edit, you always want to collect their drafts to assess and to form small groups based on shared needs. The last day or two before publication can feel even more hurried than the rest of your days as you rush to support as many students as possible before letting them say, "I am done with this piece." Small groups will be critical, then, to maximize your face time with as many writers as possible. Based on your read-through of their drafts, you might pull one group of students to teach them how to re-envision their endings as a way to convey their meaning, perhaps by wrapping up their stories with a realization or change in character. With another group, you might focus more on conventions, teaching students that writers use paragraphs for different reasons; for example, sometimes it is to signal a change in time or place so readers do not get confused, but other times, it is to build suspense. You might pull yet another group of students who need help making a plan and using the tools at their disposal as a guide for revision and editing. Together, you might look closely at another part of the Narrative Writing Checklist, identifying what each writer does well and what they might work on when they return to their seats.

SHARE

Tomorrow you enter into the final bend of this unit of study, during which students will begin new personal narratives. You may wonder why students don't publish these pieces first. Remember, you want students to get more adept at moving through the writing process, and taking a day to copy or type their pieces and make them beautiful for the world will slow that process. Students *will* publish one of their stories from this unit, and what they learn during Bend III will lead to stronger pieces the second time around—so better to wait, so they have their second pieces from which to choose something to publish.

Still, you will want to celebrate all their hard work and accomplishments before you shuttle students to the next phase of this unit. Create an opportunity for students to share their writing with an audience. Perhaps you will group students with two or three other writers and ask them to read their stories aloud to one another. Or perhaps you'll ask each writer to choose a favorite part to read to the entire class. You might also offer a small gift, something that says, "Congratulations!"—a special pen or pencil, or celebratory poem or passage to tuck into their notebook for inspiration.

Another way to celebrate their hard work is to highlight their growth. You might ask students to sit alongside their partner and notice what looks different about the drafts they wrote in the first days of sixth grade and the one they are sharing today. Each student could write her name on a Post-it note and record one or two things she has learned as a writer, already, in just the first couple of weeks of school. Or perhaps each writer hangs his finished draft on the bulletin board with three or four highlighted passages or phrases, alongside which he jots a couple things he has been working on that are exemplified in these parts.

More than anything, you want to rally students' energy for the final phase of this unit. Help them feel proud—and ready to dig into the work ahead.

HOMEWORK

In anticipation of launching a second cycle of personal narrative writing tomorrow, you might ask students to return to their notebooks and do some rereading of earlier drafts. You might say to them, "I bet, if you go back and reread those early notebook drafts, you will notice how much you have already grown as a writer, and you will find yourself energized to write. So that's your job tonight, to feel your accomplishment and to use everything you have learned to generate a new and powerful personal narrative—at least two new pages of writing. Remember your generating strategies, the ones you arrived with and the ones you may have just learned. Or, perhaps, as you're rereading your notebook, you'll stumble across a powerful story idea that you never had a chance to write! With your idea in hand, hold onto everything you've learned about writing powerful personal narratives, and let that knowledge guide you through your very first draft."

Best of luck,
Lucy, Stacey, and Ali

Writing a Second Personal Narrative with New Independence

BEND III

Session 13

Taking Charge of the Writing Process

Deciding Where to Begin and How to Revise from the Get-Go

IN THIS SESSION, you'll rally students to take charge of their writing process and their plan as they embark on a second personal narrative. You'll remind them to draw on everything they know how to do, keep an eye on their goals, and make use of their many writing tools.

GETTING READY

- ✓ Students should bring their notebooks to the meeting area for the minilesson, along with their copies of "Everything Will Be Okay" or the mentor text they are using throughout the unit, their copies of the Grade 6 Narrative Writing Checklist, and their completed personal narratives from Bend II.
- ✓ Chart from Session 11 titled "How to Write Powerful Personal Narratives" (see Share)

Common Core State Standards: W.6.3, W.6.4, W.6.5, W.6.10, RL.6.1, RL.6.2, RL.6.3, RL.6.6, SL.6.1, SL.6.6, L.6.1, L.6.2, L.6.3

TODAY MARKS THE START OF BEND III. You won't be surprised to learn that your goal in this session is twofold: you'll need to rally your sixth-grade writers to embark on a whole new personal narrative, but you'll also need to convey expectations that they are ready to take charge of their writing process and lift the level of their work from their first generating right through their last revisions.

When sixth-graders, who are rapidly embracing independence in all areas of their lives, feel they have earned ownership of the writing process, they step into this role with enormous seriousness. Of course, even as students make decisions about how to move themselves through the process, your teaching will support their transference of the previous bends' strategies and skills. Thus, in this third bend of the unit, you will teach students how to use what they have just learned—especially their careful study of mentor texts and their use of the writer's notebook as a place to deliberately practice writing techniques—from the very beginning of their process.

Today, when students return to their notebooks, they are not repeating the same involved generating process of Bend I. Instead, they return to their notebooks with the understanding that their notebooks already hold many untapped possibilities. Given the number of personal narratives that many students generated earlier in the unit, it is reasonable to expect that after today's session and homework, most students will be ready to choose a seed idea. And it won't be just any old seed idea that they just pluck from their notebook. You'll remind students of how steadfastly they worked toward their writing goals by practicing specific writing techniques on drafts in their notebooks and urge them to continue to bring the same awareness and work ethic to their early writing process. Today, as they mine their early entries, they can already ask, "Is this story idea as powerful as it can be?" "Is my deeper meaning coming out in this draft?" "Is there a writing move that I know I admire that I can study and bring to my first draft, right now?" From there, they can proceed to make substantial revisions early on, when their story ideas are still flexible and it isn't as difficult to make big changes to a piece.

MINILESSON

Taking Charge of the Writing Process

Deciding Where to Begin and How to Revise from the Get-Go

CONNECTION

Establish a shared knowledge base about the writing process by asking students to share what they know about how the writing process will go in this upcoming bend.

"Writers, over the course of this week, you'll have the chance to use all that you have learned from the personal narrative work you've done so far to write a brand new, especially powerful, personal narrative. You'll take charge of your writing process, writing and rewriting at least two pages a day, until your piece is fully revised and edited and ready to publish at the end of the week. If that sounds too fast to you, you should know that the personal narratives you wrote last week show otherwise!

"For homework last night, you grabbed a generating strategy or a story idea you already had in mind, and you wrote fast and furiously, producing another compelling, true story. So tell me, knowing all you know about the writing process, what will you do in today's writing workshop? And then what will happen next?"

Several students called out that they would write one or two more personal narrative drafts and then pick their seed idea. I nodded and complimented them. "Absolutely. Do you see how you've developed a strong sense of how the writing process goes? You can see yourself generating, choosing, imagining your story, and then writing and rewriting until it's unbelievably beautiful."

Name the teaching point.

"Today I want to teach you that when writers are in charge of their own writing process, they think back over everything they know how to do, they eye their personalized writing goals, and they gather all their tools. Then they make a work plan, and they start working really hard at it."

◆ COACHING

When you ask a question of the whole class, let one or two students answer, and then keep going. It's also entirely fine to add to their answers, if they don't grasp what you are asking. Today's connection is not about assessing your students' developing understanding of the writing process; it's about acknowledging where they are as a class and where they are about to go.

TEACHING

Rally your students to believe they can make their own process decisions by listening to their own writing and letting their writing lead the way.

"Writers, I can tell from that look in your eyes that many of you are already making big decisions about your next steps. Some of you are certain you want to start by collecting one or two more powerful personal narrative drafts, and you're already flipping through your mental files of generating strategies." Brianna pointed to the "How to Write Powerful Personal Narratives" chart, and I nodded. "That's right, or you are consulting the chart, one of the many writing tools you have on hand, for reminders about how to get ideas.

"And some of you are already flipping between several drafts in your notebook, starting to suspect that you might already have your seed idea. It is entirely possible that you do, and that will be up to you to decide!

"Shayna just pulled out her marked-up copy of 'Everything Will Be Okay.' She must be thinking that, as she begins her second personal narrative, she must purposefully draw on all she has learned from Jim Howe about writer's craft. From the beginning, she is determined to write in ways that will make the reader want to stick with her story. So she is absolutely right in her thinking that she should go back to all those places she marked in her mentor text and remember the lessons she learned." Shayna nodded and sat up a little straighter. I continued, "Then, as she generates today, she'll apply all of those lessons to her new writing, just as she has practiced doing across her notebook. When you practiced techniques across your notebook, you tried a move, drew a line under your work, tried it again in another part of your writing, drew a line under your work, and tried it again elsewhere. Going forward in your writing process, you'll continue to write fast and furiously, but you'll also use those revising muscles that are so nicely toned from all of your notebook practice. You'll be able to bring out all of your writerly tricks as you go. That will mean writing for a stretch, quickly rereading to think, 'What have I done here? What would make this writing more powerful?', doing whatever immediate revision work you think is needed, and then continuing on.

Narrative Writing Checklist

	Grade 6	NOT YET	STARTING TO	YES!
	Structure			
Overall	I wrote a story that has tension, resolution, realistic characters, and also conveys an idea, lesson, or theme.	☐	☐	☐
Lead	I wrote a beginning that not only set the plot/story in motion, but also hinted at the larger meaning the story would convey. It introduced the problem, set the stage for the lesson that would be learned, or showed how the character relates to the setting in a way that matters in the story.	☐	☐	☐
Transitions	I not only used transitional phrases and clauses to signal complicated changes in time, I also used them to alert my reader to changes in the setting, tone, mood, point of view, or the time in the story (such as *suddenly, unlike before, if only she had known*).	☐	☐	☐
Ending	I wrote an ending that connected to what the story is really about. I gave the reader a sense of closure by showing a new realization or insight, or a change in the character/narrator. I might have shown this through dialogue, action, inner thinking, or small actions the character takes.	☐	☐	☐
Organization	I used paragraphs purposefully, perhaps to show time and setting changes, new parts of the story, or to create suspense for readers. I created a logical, clear sequence of events.	☐	☐	☐
	Development			
Elaboration	I developed realistic characters, and developed the details, action, dialogue, and internal thinking that contribute to the deeper meaning of the story.	☐	☐	☐
Craft	I developed some relationship between characters to show *why* they act and speak as they do. I told the internal, as well as the external story.	☐	☐	☐
	I wove together precise descriptions, figurative language, and some symbolism to help readers picture the setting and actions, and to bring forth meaning.	☐	☐	☐
	I used language that fit my story's meaning and context (for example, different characters use different kinds of language).	☐	☐	☐
	Conventions			
Spelling	I used resources to be sure the words in my writing are spelled correctly.	☐	☐	☐
Punctuation and Sentence Structure	I used punctuation such as dashes, parentheses, colons, and semicolons to help me include extra detail and explanation in some of my sentences.	☐	☐	☐
	I used commas and quotation marks or italics or other ways to make clear when characters are speaking.	☐	☐	☐

"My plan might start in a different place. I might be planning to look back at my Narrative Writing Checklist, at the goals that I've already crossed off and the goals that I've circled. To me, this feels like the right time to pause again and take stock of the work I have started to do and the work that still needs to happen. If that's part of my writing plan, then I might assess the personal narrative I just finished revising to come up with some new goals. So part of my writing plan can be thinking about how I will push myself to work toward those new writing goals, even as I am generating a new draft or choosing a seed today."

Shayna may have just pulled out her mentor text, or I might be imagining that she pulled it out. Either way, I am certainly assuming a lot about her thinking and her intentions for her writing! But students have come to expect that I will take liberties when I voice over their work, for the sake of bringing particular strategies to the class's attention. Sixth-graders are also capable of reading your voiceover as an acknowledgment of the hard work you believe they are capable of doing.

Debrief, emphasizing that no matter what decisions they make about where to start their work, they must continue to draw on all they have already learned about writing powerfully.

"The very important thing about today is that every one of you is taking charge of your writing process. That means that you'll reflect on where you are right now, in your generating process, and how you'll use the craft techniques you have studied and practiced from the get-go, from right now!"

ACTIVE ENGAGEMENT

Set the students up to begin planning their own writing process.

"Right now, while you are all still together, will you take a minute to flip through the pages of your writer's notebooks? Figure out if you already have a compelling story idea on one of those pages or if flipping through those pages reminds you of another powerful story idea you've been meaning to write." I looked down at my writer's notebook, doing the work along with the students.

After a moment, I began to voice over their reading and thinking. "This is a good time to ask yourself the kinds of questions you know lead to stronger storytelling: 'Is this story idea as powerful as it can be? What is this story *really* about?' When you take charge of your writing, you take charge of bringing out all of your tricks right away. You don't wait until you have a draft that needs a lot of revising."

Ask students to work with a partner to share their ideas for their own writing plans.

"Go ahead and tell your partner what work you will do today and what strategies you'll use. Also, share the writing goals that are foremost on your mind. What do you know that you, as a writer, need?" I circulated and listened in as the partners shared their plans.

As you walk around and listen closely to students sharing their writing goals, try to take mental notes (or jot quick notes) about what they are saying about their goals. Though many students will be right on target, some may need a little coaching as to the goals themselves or how they plan to use strategies. Are their goals about areas of writing they really need to improve on or something less important but perhaps easy to fix? Or do students identify good writing goals but don't know exactly how to achieve them? Listening in will help you pinpoint students and issues for conferring and small-group work.

LINK

Send the students off to begin their second personal narrative.

"Writers, you are taking charge of your writing today, but really, you are taking charge of your writing for the rest of your life!

"Keep in mind that when you come to class tomorrow, you'll have chosen one personal narrative as the seed idea for your second personal narrative. You only have today and tonight's writing time, so really draw on all of your resources and be in charge of doing your strongest writing yet."

CONFERRING AND SMALL-GROUP WORK

Encouraging Independence

IN YOUR CONFERRING TODAY, continue to emphasize and teach independence. Instead of suggesting solutions to problems you can see, invite students to identify and attempt to solve their own writing problems. It can be difficult for teachers to resist the urge to teach content, but today you can strive to teach writers something even more valuable: resiliency in the face of challenges.

Your goal in today's workshop is to turn issues and problems back to the writer. If a student is reading through her earlier personal narratives, and then says she doesn't have any powerful ideas for her next seed idea, make moves to support her problem-solving process. Empathy can be a good place to start, because it allows you to restate the student's problem and recognize the legitimacy of the writing issue. You might say, "This happens to me, too—that feeling that I just don't have anything to say." Then, instead of generating a list of things the writer could do next, try turning it back to the writer. You could say, "I know when I am really stuck, I try to reach for a strategy that just might help me. Why don't you try that right now? Go through all of those strategies you are carrying with you, and reach for one, just to see if that helps." Then, rather than lingering to coach the student through that work, say, "I'll check back with you in five minutes to see how things are moving along for you." When you establish that you expect a writer to rise to the occasion, she typically does.

You can also help writers find their ways out of their current predicaments by asking them to reflect on what they know about the writing process. If a writer claims to be stuck, try guiding that student toward finding his own next steps by asking, "Where are you in the process? What do writers typically do next?" Of course, it can be challenging to strike a balance between supporting a writer's independence and supporting a writer's engagement in the writing process. Writing with independence should not amount to students rushing through a new personal narrative. Instead, the goal is for students to become resourceful and strategic problem solvers. With a growing awareness of how the writing process works, writers will begin to internalize the role that teachers have played for them, especially assessing and planning their work.

MID-WORKSHOP TEACHING **Coaching Writers to Plan**

"Writers, I am impressed by the way you are really taking charge of your writing lives today. But I'd like to remind you that taking charge of your writing is not necessarily the same thing as *charging into your writing*. Can you honestly say that you did take a moment to decide what your work would be today, before you got started?

"I had a chance to observe Brandyn doing something that professional writers do. He picked up his pen as soon as he arrived at his desk, but he didn't just begin writing. Instead, he spent a couple of moments thinking. He must have been asking himself important, reflective questions like, 'Where am I in my work, as a writer?' and 'What next steps make sense for me?'

"And then Brandyn did something really strategic—something that you might like to try, as well. In the upper corner of his notebook page, he jotted a little planning box. In other words, he made a little To-Do list to guide his work today. Remember, when writers create planning boxes, or lists, they try to plan how they'll go about writing. So that list is likely to name specific strategies that you'll want to remember to try as you go about your writing today."

SHARE

Carrying Forward All You Know

When you convene the students, ask them to bring last week's finished piece of writing. Then ask them to examine the qualities in their finished pieces.

"Writers, I was so impressed today to see how each of you made important decisions about the steps you need to take. Many of you left the meeting area with a new and powerful story idea—and quite possibly your seed idea—in hand, and you used your writing time strategically. Some of you wrote a new personal narrative, producing a long and strong notebook draft. And others of you used your notebook to rehearse ways you might tell the story you are choosing as your next seed idea.

"I watched most of you surround yourselves with your writing tools: your checklists, your mentor texts, your finished piece from last week. Honestly, it filled me with glee to see those tools come out. *But*—I am worried that too many of you are forgetting to actually incorporate the techniques you studied, practiced, and used in your writing last week! What good are these tools, if you don't hold yourself to using everything you have already learned about writing powerful personal narratives?

"Right now, look at the finished personal narrative that you wrote last week. I'm going to read off the chart that lists the qualities of powerful personal narrative writing. As I read, give me a thumbs up for a quality that you know you can find evidence of in your final piece." I read the bullets aloud, pausing at the end of each for students to signal.

Most students were able to recognize how much they had done in their finished pieces. "Now, take a very honest look at the writing you did today. How does today's writing measure up to what you've established you can do?

"Please talk to your partner and share what you noticed. Which qualities of powerful narrative writing do you need to push yourself to remember? Set a goal for tonight's writing."

How to Write Powerful Personal Narratives

- Think of a person, place, or moment in your life (maybe a first or last time, or a time when you realized something) that matters, and write a story about it.
- Focus on one episode, write with detail (don't summarize a stretch of time).
- Help readers picture the episode—a small action and exact dialogue.
- Climb inside the moment and write within the narrator's point of view.
- Make characters say the words and use the tone that shows their personalities and hints at the bigger meaning of the moment.
- Explain why the characters act the way they do.
- Zoom in on the small but powerful details that really capture big moments and feelings.
- Use the Narrative Writing Checklist to ask, "As a writer, what are my strengths? What are my needs?" Then, plan your next steps as a writer.
- Craft a memorable lead.
- Ask, "What is my story really about?" and include descriptors, dialogue, and inner thinking that convey that meaning.
- Elaborate on important scenes that show what the story is really about.
- Include new scenes, remembered from the past or imagined in the future, that help show what the story is really about.

SESSION 13 HOMEWORK

SETTING YOURSELF UP TO DO YOUR MOST POWERFUL WRITING

"Tonight you have one last chance to generate one more personal narrative draft in your notebook. You will definitely want to use all of your important tools: "Everything Will Be Okay," your Narrative Writing Checklist, and your personal narrative from last week. After you write those powerful two pages, you will commit to a seed idea to take through the writing process. Remember to read over all your entries when you set out to choose your seed idea—even the ones you collected right at the start of the unit."

Session 14

Slowing Down and Stretching Out the Story's Problem

ONE REASON WE PARTICULARLY LOVE "Everything Will Be Okay" is that Jim Howe's craft is so visible to the reader. Each time we read this story with sixth-graders, they are deeply affected as readers and then see something in it that dazzles them as writers. They are then inspired and well positioned to try out Howe's beautiful writing moves.

Donald Murray once wrote, "Writing is a craft before it is an art; writing may appear magic, but it is our responsibility to take our students backstage to watch the pigeons being tucked up the magician's sleeve." Earlier in the unit, writers had the opportunity to study and experiment with the particular bits of Jim Howe's story that most struck them. Often those bits are the characters' dialogue—especially the way the author can write dialogue to reveal the characters' personalities and hint at the bigger meaning of the moment. Sixth-graders react strongly to Paul's tone, to his condescension and cruelty. When Paul tells Jim to "be a man" and help him end the kitten's life, students ache for Jim. They find themselves jumping to his defense, wishing they could protect him from his brother's insensitivity. While students may still be reaching, as writers, to emulate Howe's techniques, they recognize the power of such craft moves and can continue to work toward writing this way in their own drafts.

There is another aspect of Jim Howe's craft, in this same scene, that could significantly raise the quality of your writers' drafts. You'll notice how closely he controls the tension in the scene at Dr. Milk's office, carefully maintaining a sense of uncertainty and building emotion. These qualities make the scene especially gripping for readers who are pulled along, anxious for Jim about what they suspect and dread might happen. Jim Howe is an extraordinary storyteller. By studying his text closely, students can begin to learn how to structure their own story to stretch out the problem and give the character and the reader, alike, more time to absorb the events.

In this session, you'll lead your writers in a study of Howe's advanced storytelling structure and help them to consider how they can story-tell, just as powerfully, as they begin planning and then drafting. From the start, just as they are putting their story on

IN THIS SESSION, you'll teach students that when writers draft, they think carefully about how to slow down the problem in their story and build tension.

GETTING READY

- ✔ Students should bring their copies of "Everything Will Be Okay" and their notebooks, with their seed ideas identified with paper clips to the meeting area for the minilesson (see Connection and Teaching).
- ✔ Narrative Writing Checklist, Grade 6, and sixth-grade writing samples (see Conferring and Small-Group Work)
- ✔ Piece of rope and index cards (or Post-its) (see Share)

COMMON CORE STATE STANDARDS: W.6.3, W.6.4, W.6.5, W.6.10, RL.6.1, RL.6.3, RL.6.5, SL.6.1, SL.6.2, SL.6.4, L.6.1, L.6.2, L.6.3

paper, students can dedicate themselves to slowing down the problem, telling it bit by bit, and creating multiple moments of building pressure. Your students are ready to learn that when they craft the tiny moments of their narratives with this kind of merciless attention to detail, it marks the difference between reporting an event and writing an incredibly compelling story.

"Writing is a craft before it is an art; writing may appear magic, but it is our responsibility to take our students backstage to watch the pigeons being tucked up the magician's sleeve."

—Donald Murray

MINILESSON

Slowing Down and Stretching Out the Story's Problem

CONNECTION

Remind writers of how this week will go.

"Writers, I am glad to see you are ready for today—that you have a paper clip marking your seed idea in your notebook. As you know, over the course of this week, you'll need to take yourself through the writing process. That means you'll probably draft more than one draft, you'll use all your available tools to revise, and you'll edit. Finally, by the end of this week's workshops, your fully revised and edited draft will be ready for publication. That way we can begin to look forward to celebrating your accomplishments from this unit."

Call to mind the way time seems to stretch out in slow motion, in a bit-by-bit manner, when they find themselves in real trouble.

"So, today I know you'll be drafting, and I also know that you have a lot of strategies at your fingertips for writing a whole new draft really, really well. Right now, will you turn to your partner and list three things you will absolutely want to remember to do as you write your first draft?" I gestured for them to do that immediately.

After a few moments, I continued. "Now, I'd like to teach you about one more thing you can push yourself to do as you write your draft today. Have you ever noticed that in your favorite Hollywood blockbuster movies, the most intense and perhaps even action-packed scenes actually take their time unfolding? There are even top ten lists dedicated to the best 'action-packed *slow-motion* scenes.'" With that, students began to call out some favorite movie titles and demonstrate their own silly slow-motion effects. I refocused the students and continued, "Of course, it's not always mayhem that needs time to unfold—sometimes it's a really sad or scary moment in a movie, too." I looked around at the students' nods and even grimaces as they recalled chilling scenes from horror movies.

"I can see you are thinking of those parts of particular movies that you just can't forget. Right now I'm thinking about *The Hunger Games*, the part in the movie when Katniss first enters into the arena and it's like time freezes. Things are so incredibly tense in that moment. I wanted it to be *over*, I was so anxious! And yet, time moves excruciatingly slowly as Katniss goes up, up, up in the elevator to the arena, then looks around to see where she is, and looks at everyone else who is there, and then the countdown as they wait, wait, wait for the signal to begin. It was almost *unbearable* for me to watch!

◆ COACHING

In classrooms—as well as in life—people benefit from knowing exactly what is expected of them.

You, too, might choose to introduce this concept by detailing one specific movie moment, like when Katniss enters the arena in The Hunger Games, *that you think is current and accessible to your students. You might even show a short video clip of one such unforgettable movie scene.*

Some of your students may also be thinking about their own intense, real-life experiences that felt like slow motion, with each moment seeming to take forever. It might be a moment of exhilaration, like when you're "in the zone" playing basketball or dancing or painting a picture, when everything feels effortless and amazing, but weirdly, strangely in slow motion. Or it might be a moment of fear, like when you're witnessing a car crash or a tornado descending—or when you're taking a dramatic tumble off your bike.

"Writers, I think you can take inspiration from some of your favorite movie directors today as you begin planning and drafting. You'll want to keep in mind what they know about building a problem and building tension in ways that keep their viewers on the edge of their seats."

Name the teaching point.

"Writers, today I want to teach you that when writers set out to draft, they make an effort to story-tell in the most compelling way, even if it's not exactly how the events happened in real life. To do this, it's helpful to study how your mentor writers slow down the problem in their writing and build the tension in a slow-motion, bit-by-bit way."

TEACHING

Demonstrate that when writers want to craft an especially compelling story, they can begin by studying a mentor text and asking, "How has this author structured the story? What has this writer done to story-tell powerfully?"

"It is probably a bit of a challenge for you to stop thinking that you have to stick to telling the story *exactly* as it happened, but that's what writers do. They ask themselves, 'What do I want my reader to feel and understand about this moment? How can I tell my story in a way that will make that happen?' I want you to be that kind of writer. Go ahead and take your poetic license!

"Let's give this a try together with 'Everything Will Be Okay.' We're going to look closely at the part where Jim Howe tells the story of when he and Paul bring the kitten to Dr. Milk's office, after hours." When a couple of students sigh, I know they are picturing this terrible scene. "Jim Howe doesn't just let Paul turn on the lethal gas, right? No, Howe really stretches out this tense moment in a way that makes all of us tense, right? Let's look at what he writes and list across our fingers each tiny step of events."

> *Dr. Milk is not there when my brother pulls the car into the parking lot. It is after hours. My brother has a key. I am impressed by this.*
>
> *"Come on," Paul says in his take-charge voice, "get that box now. Bring it on in here."*
>
> *He flicks on the light in the waiting room. "You're coming in back with me," he commands. "I'll need your help."*
>
> *"What are you going to do?" I ask. I am holding the box tight against my chest. I feel Smoky moving around inside.*
>
> *"What do you think?" he says. "You heard your mother. That kitten is sick, bad sick."*
>
> *"She's your mother, too."*
>
> *"Well, she happens to be right," Paul tells me. "With an animal that far gone, you don't have a choice. It's got to be put to sleep."*

The teaching section of this session will look closely at "Everything Will Be Okay" again, so you want to move directly from your connection into teaching, leaving time to unpack the structure of the text there.

For your teaching, you will want to have a copy of "Everything Will Be Okay" on hand.

I think the tears I jam back into my body are going to kill me. I think if I don't let them out they will kill me. But I won't let them out. I won't let Paul see.

"You do have a choice," is all I say. I hug the box for dear life and move to the door. Paul moves faster.

"Come on now," he says, gently taking hold of my arm, "be a man."

"I'm not a man," I tell him. "I don't want to be."

"You've got to do what's right. That kitten is half dead as it is."

"Then it's half alive, too."

He shakes his head. "You always have to one-up me, don't you?" he says.

I don't know what that means, but I do know that no matter what I say he is going to do what he wants to do.

A few minutes later, we are in the back room. The box is empty. Smoky is inside a big old pretzel can with a hose attached, clawing at the can's sides as my brother pumps in the gas. He is telling me it is good for me to watch this, it will toughen me up, help me be more of a man. Then he starts to lecture me about different methods of putting animals out of their misery, but all I can hear is the scratching. And then the silence.

"Okay, so the first thing that happens is that Paul makes Jim get out of the car with the box and follow him into Dr. Milk's office," I said, as I underlined that part, then held up my first finger, signaling to students that they should do the same on their copies. "What happens next?"

Jelena began, "Paul turns on the light and tells his brother he has to come in back and help him." I underlined that part to show we weren't missing a step, and we all held up a second finger.

Ben raised his hand and continued, "But, Jim doesn't move. He wants to know what Paul is going to do, so he asks Paul. And Paul doesn't say it, at first, he just says, 'What do you think?' in a mean way."

As I underlined that part, we saw that we were missing something. "Wait," Kei said, "Before Paul answers, Jim is holding Smoky's box really tightly, and he says he can feel the kitten moving around."

I pointed at Shayna and she added, "The narrator describes how he won't let his tears out, even if it kills him, because he doesn't want Paul to see him cry." The class continued on with their detailed retelling, each student adding more details of the narrator's terrible ordeal.

"Writers, when you study the sequence of events like you just did, it really brings out how the author made Jim's ordeal at Dr. Milk's office more and more intense, with each passing second. Paul didn't just grab the box from Jim and administer the deadly gas. Instead, Howe create a series of tiny, pressure-filled moments where bit by bit, things only get more devastating for Jim."

As students retell the various parts of the scene at Dr. Milk's, be sure they name each and every detail that occurs. Direct them to return to the text to capture the nuanced way Howe stretches out this one moment. If possible, help them notice the tiny, minute ways that Howe builds tension—Jim's physical pain as he keeps his tears inside, the way Paul gently takes hold of his brother's arm. These are the details that grab us and keep us in the clutches of the scene, even as it feels unbearable.

Model for students how, like Jim Howe, you can slow down trouble and build tension in your own story.

"I think that, with some deliberate planning, you can do this too. It's a matter of slowing things down, making sure you don't get to the worst part of the problem too quickly.

"I'll try this right now, with my own story. I'm actually going to work on my story about destroying the garden. This is an opportunity for me to deliberately practice a technique. I can work at it on this story, and then I can practice some more as I draft my new seed idea. Remember how my story goes, how I planned on drafting across these scenes." I held up a finger for each part as I spoke. "First, my dad put me in charge before he left. Second, the part where Alison and I destroyed the garden. Third, there's the part where I frantically try to fix the mess, and my dad comes back. Fourth, finally, at the end, would be the part where my dad surprises me by helping me calm down and, together, we set about fixing the garden."

Notice how I quickly transfer the work we saw Jim Howe doing to my own story, modeling with my own story before asking the students to transfer the strategy to their own writing.

I said these parts once more over my fingers. "Listening to Dad, destroying the garden, panicking and trying to fix it, Dad helping me."

Slow down your demonstration. Think aloud for your students, really emphasizing how you'll plan out the parts of your story to slow down the trouble and build tension.

I looked up at the ceiling as if thinking and then began to muse aloud. "So, if I were to story-tell like Jim Howe, structuring my story so that it builds lots of tension, I'd have to stretch out the problem and tell it in bits. With each bit, I'd have to make my emotions more intense, too," I paused, visibly thinking. "I'm thinking it starts when my dad has just left the yard. I could watch him turn the corner, my fingers just itching to twist the faucet as high as it would go. Maybe Alison would make wide eyes at me, surprised at how deliberately I was disobeying Dad. I could squeeze the nozzle tentatively—the crazy water pressure probably making the whole hose jump off the ground. And I could glance at Alison, plotting to spray her, but Alison could always tell what I was thinking, so maybe she would quickly run to the garden, maybe even yelling that the garden was 'base.' Irritated, I would probably glance back at the end of the yard, just to make sure my dad wasn't coming back, and then back to Alison, taunting me and daring me to get her. Then, I would blast the hose on her and the garden. Once she knocks me down, that's when the mood of the piece really changes, when things get worse, and my emotions get more intense, too."

I looked up at the students again. "Writers, I have to tell you, I think I would have just told my story the way it happened—and it felt as if it happened so fast—had we not talked about this. But studying and thinking about what Howe did with 'Everything Will Be Okay' really helped me plan out how to build tension into my retelling. I'll keep working on this, planning to slow down the trouble in different parts of my story, so it doesn't pass by too quickly."

Share particular insights gained from trying this work.

"Writers, after trying this myself I'm realizing something important. I'll have to escalate the tension in more than one part of my story. I have to build from the part where my dad leaves to the part where I wreak havoc with the hose. But I also have to build tension again when I try to repair the damage I've caused, before my dad returns. I also have to think about how my emotions get more serious—and how I'll show that—as the trouble in each scene intensifies. I have a lot of thinking and planning to do as I draft."

ACTIVE ENGAGEMENT

Invite students to rehearse with their partners as they think through the parts of their stories and plan out how the problem will escalate across these parts.

"Writers, it's your turn to plan how you'll structure the problem in your drafts as well. Think about the parts of your story, like I did, either on your fingers or in your mind." I waited a moment until students nodded at me.

"Now, think about just the problem in your story. How could you slow down and stretch out the problem so that the tension really builds for you readers? Imagine how your problem can get worse and worse. Use your partner to rehearse a bit of that storytelling right now."

Ruby turned to her partner, Fionna, and began to rehearse. Holding one finger up, she said, "First, I grabbed the lunch tray and entered the cafeteria." Then, raising her second finger, she continued. "I was surprised that the tables were already so filled up, but I spotted Lisa, that girl who sat next to me in math class." She continued on, raising a finger to tick off each new part of her story. "As I walked to the table, I smiled directly at Lisa, but she didn't acknowledge me. Instead, she quickly turned back to her friends."

I briefly interjected, saying, "It sounds like you've just arrived at a point of tension in your story. Make sure you slow that moment down. As you keep rehearsing, use your fingers to stretch out just that one moment." I then moved on to listen in on other partnerships as Ruby continued to story-tell. I continued to scaffold, prompting students to "ask your partner to slow down—ask them to tell that part again across five fingers instead of one!" And "Remember all the strategies you know for elaborating! Rehearse that part again with more inner thinking and precise actions to slow things down and build tension."

As you listen to your students tick off events and story-tell, make sure they're thinking of ways to stretch out the tension inherent in a problem or conflict, and not just ticking off points in the story plot. You may want to suggest to some students that they try to visualize the stretched-out event in slow motion, like in a movie, with tiny actions or a few words or even silence imbued with huge amounts of meaning. Once that significant event is over, the story will snap back to real time or even speed up.

LINK

Remind writers of how their writing might go today, and send them off to work.

"Writers, with your piece due in just four days, I know you are very eager to get right to work. Some of you will want to spend some more time developing your stories. I think many of you will make some quick plans and then throw yourself into the work of drafting. Before you dive into your individual processes, you should all take a moment to remind yourself of the writing goals you're aspiring to."

CONFERRING AND SMALL-GROUP WORK

Using Leveled Student Writing to Help Students with Next Steps

TO GET READY FOR CONFERRING AND SMALL GROUPS TODAY, you'll want to grab the sixth-grade leveled student samples for narrative writing, along with the checklist. As you read a student's story and listen to him describe what he's doing, you can think, "Where does this student's work fall on the learning progression of narrative writing?"

I saw Darian rereading his on-demand narrative and jotting notes in the margins of his draft (see Figure 14–1).

"Merry Christmas," I said out loud.

"Merry Christmas," they all replied.

I loved when my family was together on a special event like Christmas. We were all having fun, eating, talking, and playing. It was around 12 o'clock in the morning. We were all opening each gift one by one, celebrating each gift.

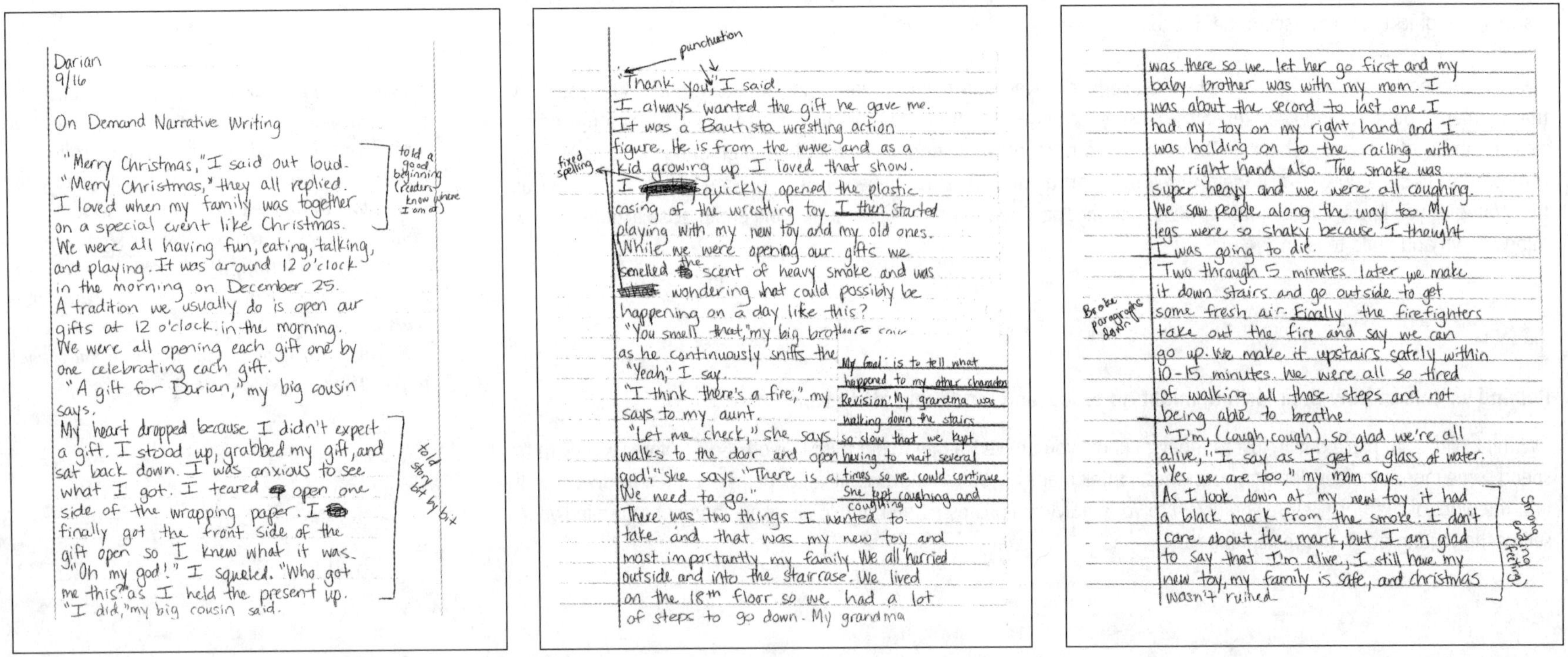

Darian
9/16
On Demand Narrative Writing
"Merry Christmas," I said out loud.
"Merry Christmas," they all replied.
I loved when my family was together on a special event like Christmas.
We were all having fun, eating, talking, and playing. It was around 12 o'clock in the morning on December 25.
A tradition we usually do is open our gifts at 12 o'clock in the morning.
We were all opening each gift one by one celebrating each gift.
"A gift for Darian," my big cousin says.
My heart dropped because I didn't expect a gift. I stood up, grabbed my gift, and sat back down. I was anxious to see what I got. I teared open one side of the wrapping paper. I finally got the front side of the gift open so I knew what it was.
"Oh my god!" I squeled. "Who got me this?" as I held the present up.
"I did," my big cousin said.

(margin notes: told a good beginning (readers know where I am at); told story bit by bit)

"Thank you," I said.
I always wanted the gift he gave me. It was a Bautista wrestling action figure. He is from the wwe and as a kid growing up I loved that show.
I quickly opened the plastic casing of the wrestling toy. I then started playing with my new toy and my old ones. While we were opening our gifts we smelled the scent of heavy smoke and was wondering what could possibly be happening on a day like this?
"You smell that," my big brother [illegible] as he continuously sniffs the [illegible].
"Yeah," I say.
"I think there's a fire," my [illegible] says to my aunt.
"Let me check," she says. walks to the door and open god," she says. "There is a We need to go."
There was two things I wanted to take and that was my new toy and most importantly my family. We all hurried outside and into the staircase. We lived on the 18th floor so we had a lot of steps to go down. My grandma

(margin notes: punctuation; fixed spelling; My Goal: is to tell what happened to my other characters. Revision: My grandma was walking down the stairs so slow that we kept having to wait several times so we could continue. She kept coughing and coughing.)

was there so we let her go first and my baby brother was with my mom. I was about the second to last one. I had my toy on my right hand and I was holding on to the railing with my right hand also. The smoke was super heavy and we were all coughing. We saw people along the way too. My legs were so shaky because I thought I was going to die.
Two through 5 minutes later we make it down stairs and go outside to get some fresh air. Finally the firefighters take out the fire and say we can go up. We make it upstairs safely within 10-15 minutes. We were all so tired of walking all those steps and not being able to breathe.
"I'm, (cough, cough), so glad we're all alive," I say as I get a glass of water.
"Yes we are too," my mom says.
As I look down at my new toy it had a black mark from the smoke. I don't care about the mark, but I am glad to say that I'm alive, I still have my new toy, my family is safe, and christmas wasn't ruined.

(margin notes: Broke paragraphs down; Strong ending (feeling))

FIG. 14–1 Darian annotates his writing.

"A gift for Darian," my big cousin said.

My heart dropped because I didn't expect a gift. I stood up, grabbed my gift, and sat back down. I was anxious to see what I got. I tore open one side of the wrapping paper. I finally got the front side of the gift open so I knew what it was. "Oh my god!" I squealed. "Who got me this?" as I held the present up.

"I did," my big cousin said.

"Thank you," I said.

I always wanted the gift he gave me. It was a Bautista wrestling action figure. As a kid growing up, I loved that show. I quickly opened the plastic casing of the wrestling toy. I then started playing with my new toy and my old ones. While we were opening our gifts, we smelled the scent of heavy smoke and were wondering what could possibly be happening on a day like this?

"You smell that?" my big brother said as he continuously sniffs the air.

"Yeah," I said.

"I think there's a fire," my big brother said to my aunt.

"Let me check," she said while she walked to the door and opened it. "Oh my god," she said, "There is a lot of smoke. We need to go."

There were two things I wanted to take and that was my new toy and most importantly, my family. We all hurried outside and into the staircase. We lived on the 18th floor, so we had a lot of steps to do down. My grandma was there so we let her go first and my baby brother was with my mom. I was about the second to last one. I had my toy in my right hand and I was holding on to the railing with my right hand also. The smoke was super heavy and we were all coughing. We saw people along the way too. My legs were so shaky because I thought I was going to die.

Two through five minutes later, we made it down the stairs and went outside to get some fresh air. Finally the firefighters took out the fire and said we could go up. We were all so tired of walking all those steps and not being able to breathe.

"I'm (cough, cough) so glad we're all alive," I said as I got a glass of water.

MID-WORKSHOP TEACHING **The Emotions of Secondary Characters Can Grow in Intensity, Too**

"Writers, as you were busy drafting, I saw Lydia was looking intently again at 'Everything Will Be Okay.' When I asked her what had caught her attention, she said she was interested in rereading the bits where the tension in the story escalated, trying to see how the author was able to pull this off.

"Lydia was specifically examining parts of 'Everything Will Be Okay' where Jim's brother Paul is talking to him in Dr. Milk's office. Lydia noticed that while Jim is becoming increasingly upset, Paul is *also* getting more emotional. At first Paul attempts gentleness, but tension mounts as he slips into annoyance and then even starts to lecture Jim in a condescending way. I know we all felt tense reading this part because of Jim getting more and more upset. But don't you also feel increasingly on edge as Paul's emotional state intensifies? Howe builds tension by stretching out what's happening internally and externally for the main character as well as the secondary character in this scene.

"Lydia realized she can do something similar in her story. In her draft, she is planning not only for how her conflict or problem will get worse, and how her own emotions will get more intense, but also how the other characters' emotions will gain intensity. If you are attempting to escalate tension, you might try the technique Lydia discovered. You might think about the emotional arcs of not only your major but also your secondary characters."

"Yes, we are too," my mom said.

As I looked down at my new toy it had a black mark from the smoke. I don't care about the mark. I am glad to say that I am alive, I still have my new toy, my family is safe, and Christmas wasn't ruined.

I asked Darian why he'd written notes such as "I love being with my family at Christmas," "I wasn't expecting a gift," and "My cousin is really generous." He explained that he liked the entry and had decided to rewrite it, so he was making notes on the important parts of his story so he could add details. For example, in the part of the story about his cousin handing him the gift, he planned to show more emotions about how his cousin felt about giving him such a wonderful present.

For a moment, I sat confused. On the one hand, I was excited that Darian had taken the idea of annotating the draft seriously, and it was great he was planning his next draft. And I was even more pleased that he had chosen key parts of his story and was planning to elaborate on his characters in the next draft, purposefully referring to his narrative checklist. But on the other hand, I wasn't sure that he understood how to choose key parts of his story to stretch out in order to build tension.

Since I had the sixth-grade checklist and the two benchmark writing examples, I was able to scan them quickly and find what I thought Darian needed help with. His story was about learning what really matters to him—his family. He had a strong central dramatic moment that could be used as the basis of a vivid, moving story, but he needed to be able to escalate tension in parts of his story to make for more effective storytelling and writing.

I pointed out to Darian that he didn't just need to find the key parts of his story and add details about characters. He needed to think about the important points of the disaster on Christmas and plan how to slow down or stretch out the action to help intensify the tension in that crucial scene. I left Darian with some benchmark texts, pointing out where the writers had stretched the moments of crucial parts of their stories and asked him to try out those moves in his own story.

Narrative Writing Checklist

	Grade 6	NOT YET	STARTING TO	YES!
	Structure			
Overall	I wrote a story that has tension, resolution, realistic characters, and also conveys an idea, lesson, or theme.	☐	☐	☐
Lead	I wrote a beginning that not only set the plot/story in motion, but also hinted at the larger meaning the story would convey. It introduced the problem, set the stage for the lesson that would be learned, or showed how the character relates to the setting in a way that matters in the story.	☐	☐	☐
Transitions	I not only used transitional phrases and clauses to signal complicated changes in time, I also used them to alert my reader to changes in the setting, tone, mood, point of view, or the time in the story (such as *suddenly, unlike before, if only she had known*).	☐	☐	☐
Ending	I wrote an ending that connected to what the story is really about. I gave the reader a sense of closure by showing a new realization or insight, or a change in the character/narrator. I might have shown this through dialogue, action, inner thinking, or small actions the character takes.	☐	☐	☐
Organization	I used paragraphs purposefully, perhaps to show time and setting changes, new parts of the story, or to create suspense for readers. I created a logical, clear sequence of events.	☐	☐	☐
	Development			
Elaboration	I developed realistic characters, and developed the details, action, dialogue, and internal thinking that contribute to the deeper meaning of the story.	☐	☐	☐
Craft	I developed some relationship between characters to show *why* they act and speak as they do. I told the internal, as well as the external story.	☐	☐	☐
	I wove together precise descriptions, figurative language, and some symbolism to help readers picture the setting and actions, and to bring forth meaning.	☐	☐	☐
	I used language that fit my story's meaning and context (for example, different characters use different kinds of language).	☐	☐	☐
	Conventions			
Spelling	I used resources to be sure the words in my writing are spelled correctly.	☐	☐	☐
Punctuation and Sentence Structure	I used punctuation such as dashes, parentheses, colons, and semicolons to help me include extra detail and explanation in some of my sentences.	☐	☐	☐
	I used commas and quotation marks or italics or other ways to make clear when characters are speaking.	☐	☐	☐

SHARE

Make Sure that Each Character Has a Strong Arc

Show writers a way to check that each character has an arc that leads to a satisfying conclusion.

"Writers, I want to share a marvelous tip from Sarah Weeks, the author of *Pie* and *So B. It* and many other books that you all love. She taught me that every character needs to have an arc in the story, and this is her special way of working on that. Before beginning to write a story, she takes a long piece of rope and lays it out on the floor like this in the shape of a mountain." As I spoke, I enacted what I was explaining to kids, first laying a piece of rope in the meeting area. "Then she takes index cards or Post-its and writes the major events of the story, making sure the story is structured with plenty of rising tension and a stretched-out climax. Each of these Post-its has a different scene from my story on it," I said as I placed my own notes along the rope. "But then on other index cards or Post-its Sarah jots down the different emotions the characters will experience through the course of the story, and she uses the rope arc to check that those emotions naturally build and escalate and then resolve—that as scenes move up the arc, so do emotions intensify, and as scenes move down the arc, emotions mellow. So look here at my story, for example. Down here at the bottom of the rope or arc, when my dad is directing my sister and me, I'm tuning him out, feeling slightly annoyed but mostly just kind of bored with him. But then, aha! I move up the rope and arc when my sister and I flood the garden, and suddenly I'm panicking! My emotions are definitely rising as tension rises and as we rise up the rope.

"Sarah Weeks does this—adds a note with feelings—for every character in her story. I won't go through every one of my Post-its, but do you see how the rope helps give me a visual to check myself to make sure tensions really are rising and falling in appropriate places? Can you also see how the rope helps me pinpoint which moments are the most tense—the ones I might want to stretch out?

"Sarah says that an arc is one of the most important aspects of a story and that without a strong, full arc, the story just won't work. Making sure each character has an arc is a way for readers to go on a journey with the people in your story, to experience their emotions and feel satisfied at the conclusion—just like we feel satisfied at the end of 'Everything Will Be Okay' when Jim makes that amazing transition from feeling alone and scared to suddenly knowing that his life is about to change, that he'll be strong and decide what kind of person he is and will be. That moment completes the arc of his character. We've been rooting for Jim, and we feel gratified that the story ends in this completely satisfying, believable way."

Set writers up to check that each of the characters follows a strong arc.

"I know that by now, most of you have already planned your stories and are deep into drafting, so it may feel odd to pause and revisit your plan. But actually, it's important to periodically pull back from a draft and make sure it's heading in the best direction. Even when we plan first, we can lead ourselves astray in the midst of writing. So right now, sketch an emotional arc for your main character and if you can, for a secondary character, as well. Make sure that your plan will lead that character on a journey with a satisfying conclusion for the reader."

SESSION 14 HOMEWORK

CHECKING THAT EACH CHARACTER TAKES AN IMPORTANT JOURNEY

"During today's share, you began to check that your narrator goes on a journey and comes to some kind of resolution at the end. So many of you came to the conclusion that you still need to develop your characters.

"Tonight, take time to think about what you noticed today and to revise in ways that round out your character's arc. What do you need to make your story work? Do you need to slow down a moment of tension? Or craft a more meaningful ending? Do what you need to make sure each of your characters takes a journey in your story. Finish sketching out your arcs—or if you have some rope and index cards, try using Sarah's method for checking story and character arcs.

"If you finish this work quickly, go through the same process for a secondary character. You should also begin revising your piece in other ways. Step back, reread your piece, and be a critical reader. Ask, "What is this piece of writing missing? What part feels weak to me?" And then use your backpack of revision strategies to make it better."

Session 15

Ending Stories in Meaningful Ways

SOME AUTHORS KNOW THEIR ENDINGS before they finish drafting their first page, whereas other authors expect the ending to emerge as they move through their writing process. There is no right or wrong approach to crafting a story's ending, but writers and readers alike agree that a good story needs and deserves a good ending.

Good endings provoke strong emotional responses, sometimes causing readers to cheer, sometimes causing readers to sob. Good endings are ones that stay in readers' minds long after they have turned the last page of the story. Good endings are the ones that inspire readers to think and feel and live a little differently. For all of these reasons, writers labor over the endings of their stories, never willing to risk a disappointing ending.

"There is no right or wrong approach to crafting a story's ending, but a good story needs and deserves a good ending."

Authors end their stories in many different ways. With this in mind, long before (and after) you teach this lesson, you should use your read-alouds to consider the techniques that authors use to end their stories powerfully. For today, you will need to decide how to nudge students to take on the challenge of writing a good ending. Teach them that endings can be a place to fashion a new insight, develop a new thought, resolve an issue, or learn a lesson. Because the truth is that when we consider ways to end our stories, we are also inventing ways to resolve our problems. This is life work at its richest!

IN THIS SESSION, you'll teach students that writers don't just end stories; they create resolutions that connect to the big meaning of their story.

GETTING READY

- ✔ The ending from *The House on Mango Street* by Sandra Cisneros, to project for the class or copied onto chart paper
- ✔ Your ongoing writing with one ending ready to be revised in front of students (see Teaching)
- ✔ Each student's draft, with them in the meeting area for the lesson and the share (see Active Engagement and Share)
- ✔ "How to Write Powerful Personal Narratives" chart (see Link)

Common Core State Standards: W.6.3.a,b,c,d,e; W.6.5, RL.6.2, RL.6.5, SL.6.1, L.6.1, L.6.2, L.6.3

MINILESSON

Ending Stories in Meaningful Ways

CONNECTION

Explain that writers use endings to resolve problems, but endings also tie back to the big meaning of the story and leave readers with a final message.

"Writers, you are well into your second personal narrative. As I looked over your busy shoulders yesterday and conferred with some of you, I could see how hard you were working to bring forth the deeper meaning of your stories. You've been asking yourself, 'What is my story *really* about?' from the first moment you cupped your hands around your story idea, and that awareness is shaping the way you tell your story and develop your characters.

"As I've been thinking about this, I've realized that we must talk about how authors resolve their stories. Endings are about tying up and completing your story, but strong endings also have the power to make your reader understand your story's big meaning in deeper, more complicated ways. Your endings are the last words you leave with your reader. They must resonate and bring your whole message to light.

"Some of you have turned to excerpts from *The House on Mango Street* by Sandra Cisneros in your search for your own mentor texts. When I reread her vignette, I knew I had to share her powerful ending with all of you. It's full of all sorts of lessons about what it means to struggle and the importance of not just having a house, but having a home. But, looking closely at the end of the vignette, I see another big truth." I revealed the end of the story and read the last five paragraphs of the vignette aloud.

"This is such a powerful ending, isn't it? When I read that final passage, I really understand that Sandra Cisneros means for her readers to know that the real struggle in Esperanza's life is about how she will learn to define herself in a world that is so eager to do it for her. When I feel that powerful message, at the end of the story, it makes me reconsider Esperanza and the story in a whole new way."

◆ COACHING

You could choose any powerful example for this lesson. You might look to your previous class read-alouds or to a well-known picture book. Any ending that leaves readers with something new to think about will work!

Name the teaching point.

"Today I want to teach you that you can write an ending that leaves your reader with profound understandings. Writers think back to what they tried hardest to express through their stories and ask, 'What do I want my readers to truly understand about my journey, as a character, in this story?' Then they write an ending that reveals this to the reader."

TEACHING

Let students know that writers rehearse and draft different endings by asking themselves important questions about their story's real meaning.

"Take a moment to think back to the time you spent rehearsing and drafting and revising different leads for your first personal narrative. I think you'll agree that your hard work paid off when you saw how changing your lead could actually change the direction of your story and set you up to tell your whole story more powerfully. What I really want to tell you today is that writers put just as much effort into drafting and revising alternate endings for their stories.

"It probably won't surprise you to hear that when authors think about how they'll end their stories, they don't think right away about *how* they'll end their stories. Instead, they return to that all-important question, the one that has guided them from their first words, and ask, 'What is my story *really* about?' Writers pause to reflect on what they want their readers to really understand about their struggle and journey in the story.

"For example, let me pull out my first personal narrative, the one on which I've been practicing specific writing techniques and skills."

Notice how this same text threads through the unit yet again. By now you know that we don't use a published text as a writing mentor until we've read and discussed it first as readers, so that students can focus on how something is written versus what it is about. Similarly, by returning to my same topic, my same story, throughout a unit, students can more easily focus on the writing strategies I aim to teach without getting distracted by content.

I projected a page of my draft. "First, I have to remind myself what this story is *really* about. Well, in this story, I was really trying to show how important it was to realize that that my father would always be there for me, even when I made terrible mistakes. In the story, I'm overcome with panic and fear over how my dad is going to react to my thoughtlessness, especially after he trusted me to be in charge. As my dad was returning to the garden, just before he would discover the destruction I had caused, I flash back to the time my dad dropped the garden paver on his toe in his hurry to comfort me. I think this flashback shows how available my dad was when I needed him. Then, my story returns to the present moment, beside the destroyed garden, and my dad reacts with sadness, instead of anger.

"But I'm noticing my story sort of drops off after that." I reread the next part of my story aloud, showing them how sudden the ending is. "I feel terrible, and my dad hugs me and that's it. It's awfully abrupt and perhaps a little too tidy, considering how big the moment was."

"Alison, stop . . . don't move," I hissed, "Look what we've done. Dad's going to kill us . . . no, Dad is going to kill me." I could hear my voice rising with panic. Alison and I scrambled up, and I frantically began to push uprooted, broken plants back into their spots.

I was holding a handful of the purple petals, my dad's favorite, when he turned the corner. He was holding a box of plants, smiling broadly in my direction. From his bouncy walk, I could tell he was excited to show me his new plants.

As my dad closed the gap between us, I thought about how I was always the one, running around that corner, running to the garden to find my dad. My mind drifted back to much earlier in the spring, when I had turned the same corner in a storm of hurt and tears, crying so hard that I could barely see my dad. He had dropped the heavy stone he was holding to run to me and wrap me in his arms, to comfort me after my run-in with neighborhood bullies. Only when I had totally regained my calm, had my dad down plunked himself down on the grass and eased off his tennis shoe, revealing the toenail he'd smashed when he had dropped the stone. When I had gasped at the sight, Dad had stopped grimacing and had quickly put his arm back around me to joke, "You're worth it . . . and wait till those bullies see how tough your dad is."

I squeezed the crushed purple petals in my hand, afraid to watch his friendly greeting dissolve into anger and disappointment. "And why shouldn't it?" I chastised myself, "He trusted you to be in charge, and look at what you did." A few feet from me, Dad stopped suddenly. As he put the crate of new plants down heavily, his eyes traveled over the ruined flower bed and then stopped on me. I was expecting to see fury etched into his face, but instead it was a look of bewilderment and even worse, hurt.

"Dad . . ." my voice broke as I tried to apologize, "I'm sorry. I'll fix it, I promise." Dad swallowed and nodded. I could tell he was having trouble finding his words. He nodded again, still silent, and pulled me into his arms.

"Do you see how sudden and sort of disappointing that is? I build up to this big moment where my dad finally returns and sees what I've done, and then it ends. I have to think, what is it that I really want to show here?" I looked at my story and then shifted my eyes up and away, visibly thinking. "You know, I think this ending shows that I feel bad about my actions, and it shows that my dad doesn't blow up at me. *But* I don't think it shows just how profound a moment it was for me to realize that my dad wasn't just there for me when I was well behaved. I realized my dad would love me through my mistakes, as well.

"So I can see that I definitely need to make some changes if I want to convey that understanding to my readers and leave them with something big at the end. Let me think, how can I show my message? Let me remind myself of techniques I could use to write powerful personal narratives, since I know those same techniques will help me here," I thought aloud, focusing my attention on our anchor chart. After scrolling my fingers and eyes down the items on our chart, I continued to think aloud, "I have action and dialogue and small details in my ending now, but I think I can use those techniques better, to pop out my meaning." I looked upward, to show I was deep in thought. "Let's see, how might I start? I'm sure I started to apologize, and I felt so badly, my voice was probably small. Maybe it even cracked, I felt so bad. Let me try some of that." I picked up my pen and began writing, crossing out the lines "I could tell he was having trouble finding his words. He nodded again, still silent, and pulled me into his arms."

> "Dad . . ." my voice broke as I tried to apologize, "I'm sorry. I'll fix it, I promise."

I looked up and said, "Okay, so that shows my actions and words. Now let me think about my dad. He probably didn't hug me *right away*. After all, he had to be pretty devastated about his garden! He was probably working hard to collect himself, nodding, swallowing all the things he could yell at me!" I turned back to the page and kept writing.

> Dad swallowed and nodded. Then he looked away from the wrecked garden and fixed his eyes on my teary face. Placing his strong hands on my heaving shoulders, he said gently but firmly, "You made a huge mess, you really did–these flowers are ruined."

"Wow, I can feel the shame in my gut even now, as I write all these years later. But then my dad hugged me. He loved me despite this awful mistake! Okay, let me get that down."

> A wave of shame rolled through me, and I looked down. Dad was quiet for a moment before he pulled me into his arms and murmured into the top of my head, "But, you'll help me. We will fix it, we'll make it nice again."

"Do you see how I did that? How I thought back to what was most important about this moment and then I put myself back in that moment, using all the techniques we've learned for writing powerful narratives to make sure that my ending really shows that meaning to my reader? I showed how even when my dad is disappointed in me, he doesn't push me away. He is still there for me."

Whenever possible, we want to show students how we turn to the tools at our disposal to help us as writers, just as I turn to the anchor chart here to help me craft an ending.

Notice how, when I teach through demonstration, I don't simply write in front of students. I also think *in front of students. I slow down enough to highlight for students the* process *of composing, thinking aloud each step of the way to reveal the many, many steps a writer takes to actually get text on a page!*

ACTIVE ENGAGEMENT

Ask students to revise their endings the same way.

"I want you to try now. Take out your drafts and start by reminding yourself what your story is really, really about. As a character in your narrative, what were you wanting or struggling with? When you're ready, turn and talk to your partner about how you might revise your ending to bring forth what your story is truly about."

I listened in to Maizy and Jose as the students talked.

Maizy began to explain her concern. "I think my story kind of drops off. I'm pretty sure nobody would be able to say what I wanted, from the end of my story."

"Yeah," Jose said, "I think I did the same thing." Then, he asked Maizy, "Well, what's your story really about? What do you have to show at the end?"

Maizy tilted her head, thinking, and then answered, "I guess that when I thought about it the other day, I wanted to show that everything stays the same on my block. There are the ladies on the folding chairs and the guy with the shaved ice cart. And I like that. I like seeing all of them, knowing that they'll always be there."

Jose coached Maizy, helping her to brainstorm an ending that might show that. "So maybe you can end with something that shows you know you'll see everyone the next day and the next. Like, when you walk by them, you could give your usual wave and say 'Same time tomorrow,' or something like that?"

"Hey, I kind of like that idea," Maizy said. "I'll work on it."

I gave them a thumbs up and moved on.

Even the most seasoned professional writers struggle with the art of writing endings, so don't worry if your students don't fully grasp the complexity of today's teaching. Do expect, however, that your students are thinking about their story endings, rather than letting a series of actions dictate some finite place where their story must end.

LINK

Recall the teaching points, then remind writers of the repertoire of choices they can draw upon.

"Writers, you have quite a bit of work to do, but first, you need to make some decisions about how that work should go today. What you just saw me do, and what you began to try with your partner, is a powerful revision strategy. Whenever you're revising your stories you can work on the endings. Remember, first remind yourself what you most want to show in your story. Then, use your strongest storytelling to show that meaning to your reader. I am going to add this strategy to our chart. I'll tuck it in next to leads, since leads and endings go together."

How to Write Powerful Personal Narratives

- Think of a person, place, or moment in your life (maybe a first or last time, or a time when you realized something) that matters, and write a story about it.
- Focus on one episode, write with detail (don't summarize a stretch of time).
- Help readers picture the episode—a small action and exact dialogue.
- Climb inside the moment and write within the narrator's point of view.
- Make characters say the words and use the tone that shows their personalities and hints at the bigger meaning of the moment.
- Explain why the characters act the way they do.
- Zoom in on the small but powerful details that really capture big moments and feelings.
- Use the Narrative Writing Checklist to ask, "As a writer, what are my strengths? What are my needs?" Then, plan your next steps as a writer.
- Craft a memorable lead.
- Ask, "What is my story really about?" and include descriptors, dialogue, and inner thinking that convey that meaning.
- Elaborate on important scenes that show what the story is really about.
- Include new scenes, remembered from the past or imagined in the future, that help show what the story is really about.
- **Craft an ending that delivers a powerful message.**

"But remember, you already know so much about revision. As usual, you shouldn't work on only what you learned in today's minilesson. So take a moment to tell your partner two or three things you might do to revise today." I gave them a moment to do this before sending them off to work.

CONFERRING AND SMALL-GROUP WORK

Supporting Effective Use of Revision Strategies

MANY OF YOUR STUDENTS will focus on revising their endings to try to add depth and bring out the meaning of their story conclusions. For some students, it will help to think about endings as a way to tie up loose ends. Writers ask themselves, "Have all the major questions in the story been answered or resolved?" Readers don't usually like to be left hanging or wondering (though, of course, that is the conscious intent of some writers, but that's not what today's lesson is about). In a story about a character that struggles with a problem of some kind, the writer could ask himself, "How is the struggle resolved? Does this character overcome the challenge or not? Why does this matter?" Or in a story about someone who wants something (love, to achieve a goal, to reach a destination), the writer might ask, "In the end, does the character get what she wants? Why does this matter?" Such questions will help some students pinpoint and convey a story's deeper meaning.

When working with stronger writers, you might teach them how to craft an ending that mirrors the beginning. You might pull aside a small, advanced strategy group today and model how to open a story with an image or a phrase that you then revisit at the end. Of course, this literary device does not work for all stories, and students should only attempt this if it makes sense for their story; it shouldn't be imposed artificially onto a story structure. The key to using this device effectively is choosing something meaningful to mirror. That is, you wouldn't mirror an unnecessary detail, but rather, one that holds significance. In my story about my dad, for example, I might add the words very similar to "You'll help me" to my beginning (as my dad says to me at the end), perhaps with my dad saying, "Girls, if you really want to help me, you can do the watering for me, but there are a few important rules . . ." Then the story goes on to tell all the ways that the main character and her sister were *not* helpful.

MID-WORKSHOP TEACHING **Creating More Powerful Story Endings**

"Writers, do you remember Jose's story from earlier in our unit? He wrote a story about how he met his dad for the first time, and his dad took him on a roller coaster ride. Now he's not sure how to end the story. In his first draft, the story ends with him saying good-bye to his dad after their day at the fair, which turned out to be the last time he ever saw him. Jose thinks the ending feels kind of weak, considering how meaningful it was—that it was the last time he ever saw his dad, and his dad died later that year in jail.

"Let's suppose that Jose will end his story thinking about the day he spent with his dad and their special time on the roller coaster. So far, he's written, 'As he left me at my house, it felt like a piece of me left with him. As he waved goodbye, I memorized what he looked like and how he spoke. Later that year, my dad died in prison from a terrible disease. I still remembered how it felt like that day we spent together. I got a dad that day!'

"But Jose realizes his ending doesn't really say how he felt about having just that one day with his dad and how it felt to lose him soon afterward. He wants the ending to express his feelings about how important it was to have that experience, that connection with his dad, even that one time. He knows he has to focus on making the ending as strong as his story. How can we help Jose write a stronger ending?"

Students soon chimed in with suggestions. "Maybe at the end, he should remember a detail from the roller coaster ride, like how his dad's hand felt in his own hand," said Ruby. Shayna added, "Or maybe he could talk about what it feels like to have a dad, how it feels when someone is really talking to you and interested in what you're doing, and when your own dad even apologizes to you." When Jose had a few more suggestions, I sent the students back to work on their own writing and to get ideas for endings just as they'd done for Jose.

In the meantime, you'll want to ensure that your students are using other revision strategies today, so you may also confer with students to see what revision work they're doing. Perhaps you could remind them that a good ending can highlight a story's meaning, but so can other parts in the story. Writers can ask themselves, "What is this story really about?" repeatedly as they revise and then check to be sure they've focused on that throughout the story. They could tweak a story's beginning to be sure it invites the reader in—and packs an emotional wallop.

Students could find other revision strategies helpful, as well. They could run their story, or part of it, by their partner to see if it reads the way they intended. They could use the class's personal narrative checklist or their own personal goal sheet to uncover what may still be lacking in their story. There are plenty of ways to revise, and at this stage students should be diligently trying out one strategy, then another, then another, taking charge of their choices as writers and aiming for their pieces to be as strong and as meaningful as they can make them. Encourage students to believe in their own power as writers—they've developed the skills and knowledge by now to intelligently assess and revise their work.

SHARE

Sharing Many Powerful Endings

Give students the opportunity to create a class poem of sorts by sharing a few lines from their endings.

"Writers, when you know you've written something powerful, something beautiful, it's hard to keep it under wraps. Is anyone feeling that way today?" Many students' hands shot into the air as they volunteered for a chance to read their endings aloud. I gestured for students to put their hands down, and I explained. "Today you are each going to share a few lines from your ending, reading them aloud in your best storytelling voice."

After giving the students a moment to prepare, I directed them to form a quick circle around the room. "We'll start right over here with Garrett. He'll read his lines, and then Ai and so on, all the way around the circle. We won't clap or say anything in between. We'll let your writing do the talking, forming a class poem of sorts." Garrett began, and each child read his or her line in turn.

> "Now I knew. Things would never be the same."
>
> "I turned around, looked at my friend's back as he walked away. 'Good-bye,' I whispered to myself. 'Good-bye.'"
>
> "I wrapped my arms around my mother and squeezed. I wasn't five years old anymore, but I would always be her little girl—and I realized I wanted it that way."
>
> As I watched the sun dip behind the horizon, I nodded to myself and walked inside.
>
> "'This is why I came,' I thought to myself. 'To see this moment. To feel this moment.' I squeezed my father's hand and smiled."

"Wow, writers, can you feel how powerful those lines from your endings are? I am proud! You should be, too."

SETTING A CLEAR WRITING TASK

"Today some of you wrote an ending that seems to connect well to the bigger meaning of your personal narrative. Others of you are still reaching for an ending that promises to resonate with your reader. Remember, even published authors struggle with their endings, often drafting many, many versions before deciding which one works. Tonight, even if you feel you've already found the 'right' ending, continue to draft a few different ways your ending might go.

"You might also spend some time thinking about your lead. Does it set readers up to understand what is going to be most important in your story? Does it grab your readers' attention and begin right at the start of the action?"

Session 16

Editing Sentences for Rhythm and Meaning

Dear Teachers,

Today you'll help your writers move to final revisions and editing, in anticipation of the quickly approaching celebration. Just as you did at the end of Bend II, you'll want to remind students to draw on all of the important tools that can help them as they engage in big-picture editing. Those tools certainly include their Narrative Writing Checklists and their list of "Questions to Ask Yourself as You Edit," but students should also have ready access to all of the teaching charts from the unit and to their mentor texts as well.

With this session, you'll build on the work you began in Session 12 by teaching students to read their drafts over and over and to listen—really listen—to the rhythm of their writing. Do their word choices, their punctuation decisions, and their sentence structures work to communicate their intended meaning? Does the rhythm of their writing convey the mood and feelings of their piece? Of course, students will still edit to correct the errors that are sure to be lurking in their spelling and mechanics, but they must begin to grasp that when writers edit, they consider how they want their writing to sound and feel to their reader.

MINILESSON

You might begin with a minilesson that emphasizes how important it is for writers to read their writing out loud, to really hear the sounds and rhythms of their words and sentences—and, of course, to still catch errors. You could talk about how published writers know that the sound of their words, the way they flow together, plays a very important role in communicating their meaning and tone.

You will probably want to demonstrate how to read a piece of writing aloud in a way that helps students listen for the rhythm that particular words and sentences create. You could choose to use your own writing for this, or you might model with a student's piece, if you know that student would be comfortable thinking aloud about his writing in front

Common Core State Standards: W.6.3, W.6.5, RL.6.3, RL.6.4, SL.6.1, L.6.1, L.6.2, L.6.3

of classmates. Either way, we recommend that you model reading an excerpt of writing out loud, pausing to consider the meaning and feelings you are really trying to convey and then rereading to see if that's what the writing communicates. It will be powerful for your students to see how right then and there, you can edit parts of your draft to change the sound of your writing so that it creates clearer images and feelings for the reader.

You can teach students how to read aloud with an ear toward sentence length. Show your writers how shorter and longer sentences affect the mood of a scene. You might also teach students to pay attention to the ways their sentences tend to begin and to notice if they usually start with a similar construction. Again, help your writers to hear that when they vary the way they begin their sentences, they change the sound of their writing and convey a different feeling and meaning. You may also want to point out that instead of varying sentence patterns, writers sometimes purposefully repeat sentence beginnings or patterns to communicate or emphasize certain emotions or ideas. The important thing to get across to your writers is that there is not one correct pattern or formula for how writing should sound. Writers read their piece out loud, thinking about what they are trying to communicate, and they listen to the rhythm of their sentences to see if that is coming across. Only then can they make decisions about how to vary their sentence beginnings and lengths.

Ask students to work with partners to examine their own work and to practice listening for the way the rhythm of their sentences do and do not create the mood they intended. After identifying a couple of parts of their writing that could use more variety (or a more repetitive rhythm), they'll be ready to return to their seats and begin working.

CONFERRING AND SMALL-GROUP WORK

As you move around the room today, you might notice students preferring to read their stories to partners, instead of reading aloud to themselves. Reinforce that this is a good idea, because sometimes it is difficult for writers to hear the sound of their own words, especially if they have already read them many times.

You will want to have several possibilities in mind for today's conferring. You might, for instance, teach students to vary the rhythm of sentences by using commas to combine sentences and set off each action. Or, you might pull together a group of writers who could stretch themselves by using something other than a series of actions to story-tell. You could remind these students that narrative writers often vary the rhythm of their sentences by varying the kinds of details they use: some small actions, some details about the time or place, some thoughts they are experiencing. All together, they will bring forth the meaning of the story. You might also teach your students that in addition to varying word choice and sentence lengths and the kinds of story details, writers make important punctuation choices. To do this, you might show students a short excerpt from a mentor text, like Cynthia Rylant's *Night in the Country*:

And, if you lie very still, you may hear an apple fall from the tree
in the backyard.
Listen:
Pump!

You could help your writers to see how Rylant uses a colon to set up the reader for the sound of the apple falling and then an exclamation point after *Pump* to make that single sound almost startling in the quiet of the night. This kind of example of will inspire students to play with punctuation to bring out the tone of their writing.

SHARE

You'll want to find a way to remind students that another important aspect of editing for meaning is editing for clarity. As students revise and edit, they need to keep an eye out for any language or details that might come between the readers and a clear image of the narrative's story world.

You might ask students to seek out fresh eyes by working with a new partner for another phase of editing. Have them sit together, with one person's writing between the two of them, and urge them to read aloud again, pausing often to ask each other whether each sentence creates the clearest vision of what is happening and moves along the ideas and feelings of the piece.

Best wishes,
Lucy, Stacey, and Ali

Session 17

Publishing and Celebrating as a Community of Writers

THE FIRST CELEBRATION OF THE YEAR is especially significant for both you and your students. You are certainly celebrating the students' tremendous progress as writers. Your writers have not just *finished* a personal narrative; they have learned to set and monitor their own writing goals and to take on all aspects of their writing process with independence. From generating to choosing to drafting and revising ideas, your students have proven that they believe their lives are worth writing about and that they are capable of telling their powerful stories with honesty and precision. That is worth celebrating!

Today is also about celebrating the writing community that you and your students have grown and nurtured with each passing day of workshop. Just a few weeks ago, your students stepped into the new context of your classroom—and perhaps the new context of middle school, as well. Take a moment to appreciate what you have created together: a place where it is acceptable, and even inviting, for adolescents to identify themselves as people who like to write. Take a moment to consider how momentous it might be for your students, at this particular stage of their lives, to look at what they have accomplished and to realize that they have used writing to make sense of their rapidly changing lives and to reach out to others with their stories.

All of this is to say that author celebrations, just like all other aspects of writing, are serious business. Your students' personal narratives are, well, personal. It's not only because they chose compelling topics from their own lives—though that is part of it, of course—it's also because their pieces are the result of their dedication and hard work to grow and outgrow themselves as writers. Teach your students to honor their peers' commitment by listening deeply to each other's words today. Help your students to regard each and every writer in the classroom as *authors* and to celebrate their efforts to make every word of their story resonate and matter.

IN THIS SESSION, students will share their final personal narratives with their writing colleagues and their families.

GETTING READY

- ✔ Select four students to read their writing or an excerpt from their writing to the whole group.
- ✔ Preassign each student to one of four groups.
- ✔ Prepare the rest of the students to read their writing or an excerpt from their writing to their small group.
- ✔ Set up the room to allow for all present to hear the first four students and then divide into four groups.
- ✔ Invite guests—parents, another class, teachers—as appropriate.
- ✔ Prepare refreshments.
- ✔ Provide each person with about ten small note cards. Each person will need one note card for every author they hear today (first in the whole group and then in the small group).

COMMON CORE STATE STANDARDS: W.6.3, RL.6.6, RL.6.10, SL.6.1, SL.6.6, L.6.1, L.6.2, L.6.3

MINILESSON

Publishing and Celebrating as a Community of Writers

CELEBRATION

Welcome everyone to the celebration, and with a brief introduction, set the tone for today's ceremony.

"Writers and guests, you are in for such a literary treat today. You are about to be magically transported, through the power of writer's craft and amazing storytelling, into so many different worlds. In a few moments, you'll feel Jose's roller coaster ride screech to a halt. Then, just like that, you'll walk alongside Courtney as she pleads with her mother outside the animal shelter. And then a few moments later, this classroom will disappear again and you'll find yourself plowing through the tall grasses in Arlene's story, wondering if she'll ever find her way.

"You will also have the satisfaction of hearing these authors read their very own words aloud. When authors read to us, they invite us into their minds and another layer of their story. No two people will ever read the same piece with the exact same intonation, but authors are especially in tune when they read their own work. Listen to the way today's authors read—notice their emphasis, consider the places where they pause, try to detect the smallest of sighs or the start of a chuckle. Those small details can be thrilling to attentive audiences, and they can even enhance our understanding of what the story is *really* about."

Explain the plan for today's author celebration. In this case, explain that after a few students read to the group, everyone will disperse to a corner to share writing in small groups.

"Today we'll listen to four stories together as a community. And then you'll move to one of the four story corners. Writers, remember, you already know your corner, and guests, you can follow along. In those corners, you'll read your pieces aloud with the pride and attention that your work deserves."

Tell writers that after each reading, instead of giving applause, listeners will respond by writing a short note to the author.

"Guests and writers, there are many ways to say thank you, to acknowledge somebody's achievement. Ai is coming around to give each of you a packet of note cards. At this authors' celebration, after a writer reads, please keep the room absolutely silent (so, no clapping). Then, to acknowledge the gift that writer has just given you, you'll write a short note to him or her. You might compliment a particular quality of his or her narrative or describe the effect his or her story had on you.

◆ COACHING

After putting oneself on the line, as writers always do, it is a rather extraordinary thing for someone to write back and say, "Your words mattered."

"To start us off, will the four whole-class readers come and sit in the chairs here at the front of the room?" After each of the four students read his or her final personal narrative, I prompted the audience to write their notes of gratitude and hold on to their notes.

Remind the readers to honor each other's writing with a short thank you note.

"Let's disperse into our corners. As you move, will you please drop your notes into the mailbox I have up here? I'll give them out to the authors later today.

"Writers, you lead the way. Guests, please follow. Begin right away with one student reading, and remember to honor each reading by pausing to write a short response to the author. When every author in your group has read, you'll want to drop those notes into the mailbox as well."

Here is Shayna's final personal narrative (see Figure 17–1).

"Needing to Be Heard"
by Shayna

"Mom, GUESS WHAT!" I yelled across the room to my mom.

"What? What's the matter?" my mom said with a concerned look on her face.

"Justin Bieber is coming to New Jersey on July 31st! Can you get me tickets?" I pointed to the screen that showed an advertisement to buy tickets.

I imagined myself in the same room as Justin Bieber. Better yet, I imagined myself breathing the same air as him. I imagined him looking into my eyes and only mine, out of the thousands of screaming girls there. He might pick me as the OLLG ("One Less Lonely Girl").

"Yeah, yeah . . . hold on, Shayna, I'm doing something really important right now." As my mom walked away, I was wondering if she had heard

<u>Needing to Be Heard</u> by Shayna

"Mom, GUESS WHAT!" I yelled across the room to my mom.

"What? What's the matter?" my mom said with a concerned look on her face.

"Justin Bieber is coming to New Jersey on July 31st! Can you get me tickets?" I pointed to the screen that showed an advertisement to buy tickets.

I imagined myself in the same room as Justin Bieber. Better yet, I imagined myself breathing the same air as him. I imagined him looking into my eyes and only mine, out of the thousands of screaming girls there. He might pick me as the OLLG ("One Less Lonely Girl").

"Yeah, yeah… hold on, Shayna, I'm doing something really important right now." As my mom walked away, I was wondering if she had heard me, or was she just trying to shrug me off so she wouldn't have to hear my "nonsense"--according to her. I felt as if she never listened to me when it came to Justin Bieber, and it bothered me.

As I watched the commercial finish, I noticed that is said, "HURRY, THEY'RE SELLING FAST!" I started to come to conclusion that I'm probably not gonna get them since my mom never listens.

About two days after I mentioned the concert to my mom, I tried to talk to my dad.

"Dad," I sat down across from him. "You know Justin Bieber's coming to town and I asked mom if I could get tickets but--"

"Shayna," my dad interrupted me with a concerned look on his face. " I'm sorry to say this, Shay, but concert tickets are very expensive and it's kind of out of our budget. I know how excited you are about this concert, but we just can't do it right now. Maybe another time."

I popped up, out of my seat and starting walking away quickly. I didn't want to hear what he had to say. *Didn't he know how much this concert meant to me*? Over my shoulder, I said sarcastically,

FIG. 17–1 Shayna's final draft

me, or was she just trying to shrug me off so she wouldn't have to hear my "nonsense"–according to her. I felt as if she never listened to me when it came to Justin Bieber, and it bothered me.

As I watched the commercial finish, I noticed that is said, "HURRY, THEY'RE SELLING FAST!" I started to come to conclusion that I'm probably not gonna get them since my mom never listens.

About two days after I mentioned the concert to my mom, I tried to talk to my dad.

"Dad," I sat down across from him. "You know Justin Bieber's coming to town and I asked mom if I could get tickets but–"

"Shayna," my dad interrupted me with a concerned look on his face. " I'm sorry to say this, Shay, but concert tickets are very expensive and it's kind of out of our budget. I know how excited you are about this concert, but we just can't do it right now. Maybe another time."

I popped up, out of my seat and starting walking away quickly. I didn't want to hear what he had to say. Didn't he know how much this concert meant to me? Over my shoulder, I said sarcastically, "Thanks, Dad. I really appreciate you crushing my dream." At that moment, I knew my words were probably hurting my father deep down inside, but I didn't care because he was hurting me.

I still tried to persuade my dad into getting me the tickets but the message was not getting through my dad. I went back to my living room in disappointment because I knew I wasn't getting the tickets. As I sat on my couch, scrolling through my Twitter feed, I saw about five different girls, in bold captions, explain that they have the best parents in the world because they had just bought them tickets to the July 31st Justin Bieber concert. It was the the concert I had been begging my parents about, the same concert that I knew I should be attending! In that moment, I was furious at my parents. Didn't they care about me? Didn't they care about what's important to me and what would put the biggest smile on my face?

The days dragged by. Every day I begged my parents until one day they snapped.

"Shayna, that's enough!" they both yelled at me, their faces turning bright red.

"Okay, okay. I get it, I'm sorry for asking!" I snapped back at them. I walked away and slammed my door shut as I lay on my bed. I thought to myself, "When it comes to Justin Bieber, the only time they listen to me is when I'm getting annoying and they can't take it anymore."

By July 30th, the day before the concert, I had accepted the fact that I was not going to see Justin Bieber. It was a beautiful sunny day, with just a bit of a breeze, but I was not myself. And, I was not in the best of moods, especially because I was stuck babysitting my younger cousins, Xavier and Avien. When my mom called me downstairs, I thought maybe my bad mood had started to show a little too much, because the tone of voice she had didn't make me feel very comfortable at all. As I walked downstairs I thought about all the things my mom might be mad about. I got downstairs and walked towards my mother. She looked me in the eye and said, "There's an envelope on top of the coffee table. Go get the envelope and come back downstairs now!"

I walked away, my heart is racing. I thought maybe the envelope was related to school. It could be a letter about bad grades or even talking about me going to summer school! I took the last step of my stairs and there it was, laying on the table. I picked it up, extended my thumb out to open it . . . one more tear to open it . . . and then it was open. I shut my eyes but still peeked a little, with just my left eye, as I pulled the letter out.

The first words I saw was "**BELIEVE TOUR**." I freaked out because I knew that was the name of the Justin Bieber tour. I screamed out loud and ran downstairs. When I got to my mom, I hugged her so tightly she turned red! In that moment, I realized that my mom actually does listen to me and pay attention, even when it seems like she's not. It made me feel so happy and overwhelmed that I might have even shed a tear or two. And, of course, I had an amazing time at the concert. Well, I did sprain my foot with all my wild jumping up and down, and I did lose my voice for four days. But it was all worth it.

"The Catfish"

by Cale

The catfish in my bucket were silent and still. Their black eyes looked empty, their whiskers twitched very slightly, and their fins were stuck to their sides. I was carrying the bucket up a hill to my grandparents' cabin, where I knew my grandpa and dad were waiting.

My grandpa is from West Virginia. He knew all about the wilderness, and he was always teaching me about it. He knew the forest we were in like the back of his hand, as he practically lived there. I figure that when he was a kid, he could live off the land for weeks. My dad on the other hand had lived in Virginia when he was a kid. He had spent his summers on the wild Scabby Island with his brother. They had to take a row boat to and from the island, and only their cabin and the wilderness were on it. I didn't have any of this experience. I had lived in Virginia and New York my whole life. My trips to West Virginia had always been short, and besides that I had just been in the city.

"Cale!" my dad yelled down. "Are you coming?"

"Yeah dad," I yelled back, too tired to say anything else. I took a few more steps with the bucket, hearing the water slosh rhythmically against the sides. A bead of sweat dribbled down my neck, as my shoulders and arms throbbed.

Several minutes before I had been in front of a pond, squeezing a worm onto the hook of my new fishing rod. I had whipped my arm forward, letting the line go. The hook and bobber hit the water, breaking the tranquil green surface. It only took a few minutes before I felt a sharp tug at my wrist. I excitedly reeled in. Soon enough I had seen a blurred dark shape under the surface, and pulled it up. My first fish. I had run up to the cabin, and brought my dad back to proudly show it off to him. While he was down by the pond, I had caught two more catfish.

"Those are really big," he had told me, patting my back. "Do you want to eat them for dinner tonight?"

"Yeah!" I had enthusiastically exclaimed. I was proud of my catch, and it was my right to have a prize. I thought about how cool it would be to tell my friends that I had caught and ate a catfish. All I would have to do is let my grandpa and my dad prepare it and stick it in the oven.

<u>The Catfish</u> by Cale

The catfish in my bucket were silent and still. Their black eyes looked empty, their whiskers twitched very slightly, and their fins were stuck to their sides. I was carrying the bucket up a hill to my grandparents cabin, where I knew my grandpa and dad were waiting.

My grandpa is from West Virginia. He knew all about the wilderness, and he was always teaching me about it. He knew the forest we were in like the back of his hand, as he practically lived there. I figure that when he was a kid, he could live off the land for weeks. My dad on the other hand had lived in Virginia when he was a kid. He had spent his summers on the wild Scabby Island with his brother. They had to take a row boat to and from the island, and only their cabin and the wilderness were on it. I didn't have any of this experience. I had lived in Virginia and New York my whole life. My trips to West Virginia had always been short, and besides that I had just been in the city.

"Cale!" My dad yelled down. "Are you coming?"

"Yeah dad," I yelled back, too tired to say anything else. I took a few more steps with the bucket, hearing the water slosh rhythmically against the sides. A bead of sweat dribbled down my neck, as my shoulders and arms throbbed.

Several minutes before I had been in front of a pond, squeezing a worm onto the hook of my new fishing rod. I had whipped my arm forward, letting the line go. The hook and bobber hit the water, breaking the tranquil green surface. It only took a few minutes before I felt a sharp tug at my wrist. I excitedly reeled in. Soon enough I had seen a blurred dark shape under the surface, and pulled it up. My first fish. I had run up to the cabin, and brought my dad back to proudly show it off to him. While he was down by the pond, I had caught two more catfish.

"Those are really big," he had told me, patting my back. "Do you want to eat them for dinner tonight?"

"Yeah!" I had enthusiastically exclaimed. I was proud of my catch, and it was my right to have a prize. I thought about how cool it would be to tell my friends that I had caught and ate a catfish. All I would have to do is let my grandpa and my dad prepare it and stick it in the oven.

When I was climbing back up the hill and saw my grandpa's knife for the first time though, I began to realize what I had signed up for.

"C'mon Cale," my dad said. "We're going to need your help cleaning these. It's pretty hard to do." He took out a catfish from the bucket and slapped it down on the wooden table he had gotten out of the cabin.

What does that mean again? I asked myself, racking my brain. It seemed like a familiar term, but I just couldn't put my finger on it.

"I think I'll just go inside while you guys cook it or whatever," I said.

"No Cale, you have to help us clean it," my dad repeated. I suddenly remembered where I had heard that before. In my copy of The Dangerous Book for Boys there was a chapter devoted to hunting and fishing. It had said that you have to clean a rabbit before eating. I realized that they were trying to get me to help them decapitate the fish and pull the guts out of it. I was shocked. I was only nine, and to me that seemed like I should have a free pass from any type of fish cleaning.

FIG. 17–2 Cale's final draft

When I was climbing back up the hill and saw my grandpa's knife for the first time though, I began to realize what I had signed up for.

"C'mon Cale," my dad said. "We're going to need your help cleaning these. It's pretty hard to do." He took out a catfish from the bucket and slapped it down on the wooden table he had gotten out of the cabin.

What does that mean again? I asked myself, racking my brain. It seemed like a familiar term, but I just couldn't put my finger on it.

"I think I'll just go inside while you guys cook it or whatever," I said.

"No Cale, you have to help us clean it," my dad repeated. I suddenly remembered where I had heard that before. In my copy of The Dangerous Book for Boys there was a chapter devoted to hunting and fishing. It had said that you have to clean a rabbit before eating. I realized that they were trying to get me to help them decapitate the fish and pull the guts out of it. I was shocked. I was only nine, and to me that seemed like I should have a free pass from any type of fish cleaning.

"Wait a second," I said slowly, getting ready to straighten things out. "Couldn't you guys just cut it up by yourselves? I think I would just mess you up."

"We need someone to help us hold the fish for us," my grandpa said. "And I don't think your mother is going to be too thrilled with that idea." I realized I wasn't going to get out of helping them, and a sense of dread came over me. I considered telling them that I had changed my mind, and going back down to the pond to let the fish go, but I decided against it. I didn't want to look foolish in front of my dad and grandpa. I put my hand on the fishes slippery tail and held on tightly waiting for the struggle. My grandpa lifted the knife up, prepared to bring it down in a deadly strike.

My grandpa chopped at the fishes neck several times before I heard the dull thunk of wood beneath the knife. The fishes bloody head rolled to the side, and to my my horror the jaw started moving up and down, as if it were talking without any sound coming out. It let out a loud croak that sounded a bit like a frog. I remembered the stories about chickens that stayed alive hours after they had their heads cut off. I tried to block that thought from my mind, but I was not very successful.

"Cale, calm down," my dad said, seeing the look on my face. "It's not alive anymore those are just nerves."

"Are you sure?" I questioned, still keeping my distance from the moving head.

"Of course, of course," my grandpa said. "I used to clean rabbits and fish all the time when I was much younger than you." I nodded nonchalantly, trying to hide how surprised I was of this. I had been thinking that I was too young to be doing this, but now I was changing my mind.

My dad put the knife to the top of the fishes body. He pressed hard, and made an incision downward.

"Will you help me peel the skin away John?" My dad asked my grandpa. He did, and I saw the intestines and stomach slide out of the opening. I felt myself beginning to become sick so I took a step back.

"Cale, could you be a really big help and take these guts over to the bucket over there?" My grandpa asked.

I took a deep breath and tried to not think about what I was doing. I walked a few yards over to the bucket (a different one than the one I had carried the fish in) and let the guts slide off my hands into it. I walked as slowly as I could back to the table, until it looked like my dad and grandpa were done.

"One down, two to go!" My dad shouted triumphantly.

One down, two to go.

We had managed to produce two fillets of meat from the fish, which I secretly thought was a very small amount from the work we had put in. They were both white and speckled with blood. They reminded me of the cuts of yellowtail and haddock you see in sushi restaurants, only I had just realized what they did to those fish.

"Cale, why don't you take these inside to your mother and ask her to clean them off," my grandpa said.

"Sure," I whispered, not wanting to open my mouth too wide. I laid the fillets out on each hand with care. I was not going to ruin all of the hard work we had put in by dropping them on the dusty ground.

My dad and my grandpa exchanged a knowing look. My dad said gently, "You might as well just stay inside. I think me and John have this under control." He must have noticed that I was a looking sick. I was grateful in my head, though, thanking him silently. But then I began to wonder if I might be disappointing him, too. It was no big deal for my dad and grandpa to clean a fish, so why couldn't I be a little tougher, too?

I walked inside and handed the fish to my mom.

"Dad wants you to wash these," I told her.

She looked at me, and she seemed concerned. "You look a little sick. Maybe you should go in to the bathroom."

I did, closing the door behind me and looking in the mirror. I was a bit of a mess, drenched in sweat and fish blood. As I looked at myself, I thought about what I had just done. I wanted to feel proud of helping my dad and grandpa, but I just felt kind of sad.

Is it easy for other people the first time they kill something? I thought. It wasn't for me, and in that moment, I didn't want to be that type of person. I wanted to be able to step up. I wanted to be able to impress my dad and grandpa. I wanted to live up to their expectations.

Maybe I was more grown up than I had been before that morning fishing with my dad and grandpa, but being grown up is harder than anybody realizes.

"The Unexpected Brother"

by Gracie

I could hear the squeaking of sneakers on the polished wood gym floor as I dribbled the ball.

"Over here!" Jamie shouted, waving her arms above her head. I made sure there was nobody in the way, and passed the ball to her. Jamie dodged her brother Jakie as he ran in front of her, and she caught the ball.

Jamie dribbled, then passed the ball to Ayo. The basketball hit the gym floor, and went straight into her hands. From her hands it went straight through the hoop.

"Yes!" I yelled. I looked over at the stands and saw my dad cheering. That smile on his face made me feel supported, it motivated me to win the game. Tyty and Jakie's team had beat us the last time, but this time I was sure we had this. We were ahead by two and there was less than a minute remaining on the clock. All of our team's hard work was finally going to pay off.

The smile on my face instantly disappeared when Tyty got the ball. He was one of the best players on their team, even though he was only eight.

He dribbled the ball to the other side of the court. Ayo followed right behind him trying to get the ball. I looked at the clock. There were only seven seconds left.

Tyty dribbled around Ayo who towered above him, and shot the ball. It bounced off the backboard and went through the hoop—a three point shot. As I punched the air in anger, the light brown beaded bracelet that my dad had given me slipped off of my wrist and fell onto the gym floor. I quickly gathered the small round beads and the broken string, but one of the beads rolled under the bleachers before I could reach it. I put the beads and string into the pocket of my gray shorts and walked over to Jamie.

The crowd of parents in the bleachers were all on their feet, clapping for Tyty. I remember feeling that huge wave of disappointment like it was just yesterday.

I gave Jamie a high five even though I was still frowning.

The Unexpected Brother by Gracie

I could hear the squeaking of sneakers on the polished wood gym floor as I dribbled the ball.

"Over here!" Jamie shouted, waving her arms above her head. I made sure there was nobody in the way, and passed the ball to her. Jamie dodged her brother Jakie as he ran in front of her, and she caught the ball.

Jamie dribbled, then passed the ball to Ayo. The basketball hit the gym floor, and went straight into her hands. From her hands it went straight through the hoop.

"Yes!" I yelled. I looked over at the stands and saw my dad cheering. That smile on his face made me feel supported, it motivated me to win the game. Tyty and Jakie's team had beat us the last time, but this time I was sure we had this. We were ahead by two and there was less than a minute remaining on the clock. All of our team's hard work was finally going to pay off.

The smile on my face instantly disappeared when Tyty got the ball. He was one of the best players on their team, even though he was only eight.

He dribbled the ball to the other side of the court. Ayo followed right behind him trying to get the ball. I looked at the clock. There were only seven seconds left.

Tyty dribbled around Ayo who towered above him, and shot the ball. It bounced off the backboard and went through the hoop -- a three point shot. As I punched the air in anger, the light brown beaded bracelet that my dad had given me slipped off of my wrist and fell onto the gym floor. I quickly gathered the small round beads and the broken string, but one of the beads rolled under the bleachers before I could reach it. I put the beads and string into the pocket of my gray shorts and walked over to Jamie.

The crowd of parents in the bleachers were all on their feet, clapping for Tyty. I remember feeling that huge wave of disappointment like it was just yesterday.

I gave Jamie a high five even though I was still frowning.

"We tried our best," I said. I was terribly sad because we had practiced so much. all to lose by one point.

When I looked over at the parents, they were still on their feet cheering.

I then found my dad's face. He was cheering loudest of all. There was a huge smile on his face as he chanted Tyty's name along with the rest of the parents.

"Tyty, Tyty," echoed through the gym. Every time I heard his name, my heart sank a little lower.

I could hear my dad's voice above the other adults! Why hadn't he cheered like that for my team? That was what filled my mind. I knew that Ayo and Tyty's dad had left when they were young, and my dad had tried to be there for them, so I tried to calm down.

I tried and tried but I just couldn't calm myself down. I felt like my day didn't even notice that I was there.

I heard my dad's footsteps as he stepped down from the bleachers and onto the dark yellow gym floor. I saw him start to walk in my direction, so that began to make me feel better.

I remember thinking everything was going to be okay, my dad was going to make me feel better. I was used to my parents being very supportive and of me, and making me feel better when I was sad. It then turned out that the complete opposite of what I thought, would happen.

My dad didn't even look at me as he walked straight past me and right up to Tyty. I felt as if my heart had dropped from my chest.

"Great job buddy!" my dad exclaimed seeming to forget that I was even there.

I was standing right next to them, and yet it was as if I was invisible.

My dad gave Tyty a high five and continued to praise him as I stood there alone. I walked directly in front of my dad to see if he would notice me, but he did not even look up.

I didn't understand why my dad couldn't even acknowledge me. I was his daughter after all. Tyty wasn't even related to us! I wish my mom would have come to our game instead of him. He was going to far and I could feel the anger burning inside of me. I wasn't used to my dad acting like this.

FIG. 17–3 Gracie's final draft

"We tried our best," I said. I was terribly sad because we had practiced so much, all to lose by one point.

When I looked over at the parents, they were still on their feet cheering.

I then found my dad's face. He was cheering loudest of all. There was a huge smile on his face as he chanted Tyty's name along with the rest of the parents.

"Tyty, Tyty," echoed through the gym. Every time I heard his name, my heart sank a little lower.

I could hear my dad's voice above the other adults! Why hadn't he cheered like that for my team? That was what filled my mind. I knew that Ayo and Tyty's dad had left when they were young, and my dad had tried to be there for them, so I tried to calm down.

I tried and tried but I just couldn't calm myself down. I felt like my dad didn't even notice that I was there.

I heard my dad's footsteps as he stepped down from the bleachers and onto the dark yellow gym floor. I saw him start to walk in my direction, so that began to make me feel better.

I remember thinking everything was going to be okay, my dad was going to make me feel better. I was used to my parents being very supportive and of me, and making me feel better when I was sad. It then turned out that the complete opposite of what I thought, would happen.

My dad didn't even look at me as he walked straight past me and right up to Tyty. I felt as if my heart had dropped from my chest.

"Great job buddy!" my dad exclaimed seeming to forget that I was even there.

I was standing right next to them, and yet it was as if I was invisible.

My dad gave Tyty a high five and continued to praise him as I stood there alone. I walked directly in front of my dad to see if he would notice me, but he did not even look up.

I didn't understand why my dad couldn't even acknowledge me. I was his daughter after all. Tyty wasn't even related to us! I wish my mom would have come to our game instead of him. He was going too far and I could feel the anger burning inside of me. I wasn't used to my dad acting like this.

My dad had still not stopped chattering about Tyty. It was just one shot, but my dad seemed to be explaining the plot of an action movie.

I took a deep breath and started to walk over to him. I tried to push the lump in my throat down as I made my way up to him.

"Dad, I'm really sad that we didn't win," I said, desperately seeking his support

The huge smile stayed on his face. His light brown eyes were full of light.

"Did you see that shot Tyty made?" he said. "It was amazing."

It was as if he hadn't even heard what I just said. I could feel the anger bubbling up inside of me. I just wanted to scream at the top of my lungs.

Now, being older and thinking about this, I know I shouldn't have been so jealous, but I wasn't used to my parents paying more attention to other children than to me. My dad really did hurt me that day, and I still think about it now. I am more mature now than when I was ten, but if this happened again I still think that I would feel pretty horrible.

I then walked over and stood by the wall, trying hard not to cry. I slammed my fist on the beige wall. I had thought my dad cared about me. I know that he does now, but at that time it sure seemed like he didn't.

I was trying so hard to hold my tears down. I swallowed. Thoughts of sadness and hatred ran through my mind. This just wasn't right. Fathers were supposed to care about their own children more than other people's children.

I looked up to see Jamie's dad patting her on the back, and that was the breaking point. I felt tears start to stream down my face. I was crying in the corner and my dad didn't even notice.

Ayo then noticed that I was crying.

"Are you okay?" she asked, leaning down to talk to me as her short brown hair fell over her eyes.

"Yeah," I said, trying to stop my tears. But I wasn't okay. I wasn't okay at all. I was sure that my dad had completely forgotten that I existed.

At that point I just couldn't hold it in anymore and I could feel sobs rising in my throat. I looked over my shoulder to see my dad standing with Tyty, and more anger joined my sobs.

I kicked the basketball on the floor as hard as I could and charged down the stairs toward the bathroom. I turned to my right and ran into the the girls' room.

I held a brown paper towel to my face as I sobbed into it.

To this day I still think about every moment of that game. It made me stronger and helped me grow up a little bit. It made me more mature than I was before, and it helped me realize that even though I am an only child, my parents won't always be thinking about me.

"Hard Work Beats Talent"

by Austin

Bam! "Oh my god," the little kid said to me. He said, "I wish I could be as good as you," and I remembered back to when I was his age, just six years old, and I was nothing. I couldn't touch the backboard back then, either. I remember a guy on the court said to me, "You will never make it. You will keep doing this over and over, but you will not make it to the NBA. You will never be able to dunk."

At that time, I thought to myself, "What if he is right? What if everything he says is true?" I wanted to be something, not someone who tries so hard but still doesn't go anywhere. I wanted people to support me, to say to themselves, "Wow, I believed in him, I knew he could do it."

As soon as I got home, I asked my dad, "Can we work out some day? I know you know a lot about working out, and I want you to be the person to push me, Dad."

The next day my dad came up to me and said, "You wanna be what you want to be?" When I nodded, my dad said, "Well, get up then. You're not going to get any better by sitting there." My dad made me work out every single day during the summer. He made me do three sets of pushups, sit ups, chin ups, toe ups, and squats. Most days, I thought I was too sore to keep going but every time I slacked off, my dad said, "No pain, no gain. Keep going, son, prove them wrong. If you give up now, you will be the loser. Remember, they're testing you, and they want you to give up!"

I kept going, I didn't want my dad to look at me and see a quitter. Over and over, in my head, I said, "I will achieve my goal. I will not give up. Everyone who doubts me will watch me prove them wrong!" Every day and every night I practiced the same exercises, trying to get in excellent shape so I could do what I had always wanted to do on the court.

My dad took me into the open gym and said, "Touch the backboard. Now." I jumped as high as I could and I just nipped the backboard by luck. My dad nodded and told me, "This is a good start, but now we gotta do more workouts, and don't give up, Austin. We are going to need more heart."

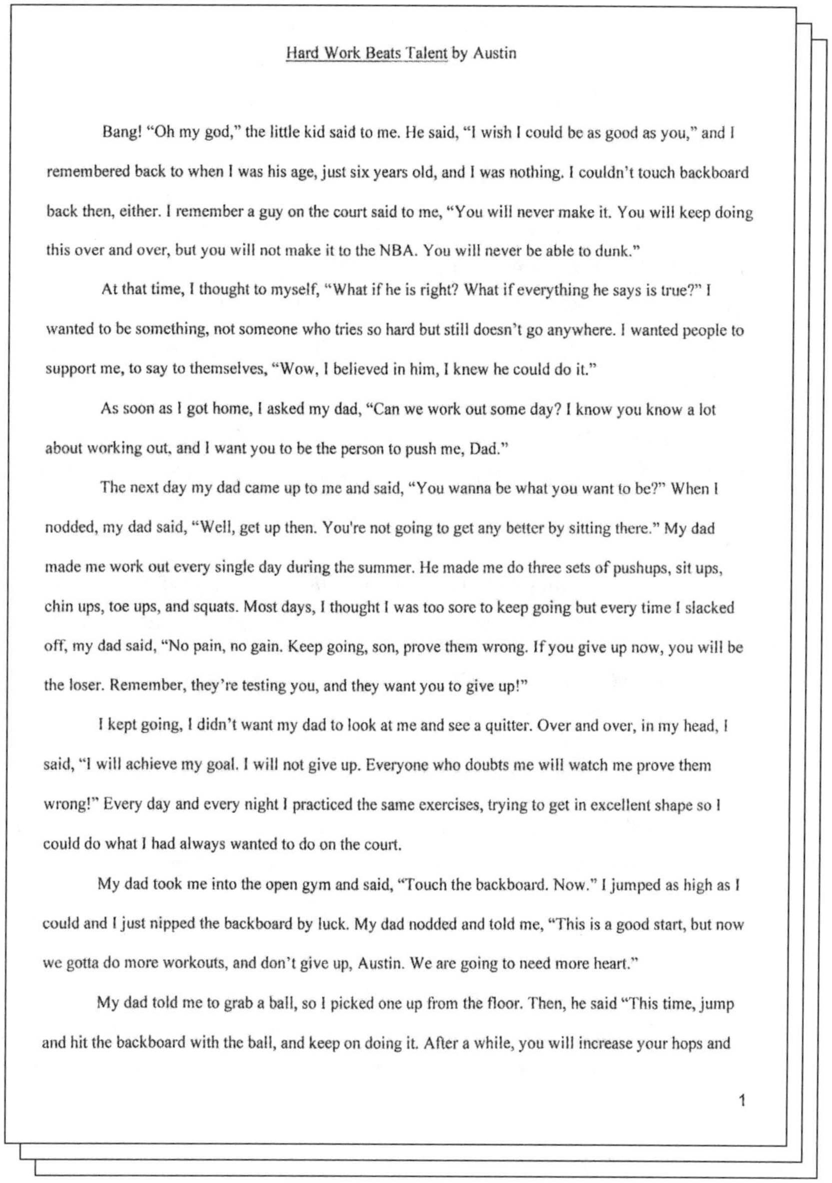

Hard Work Beats Talent by Austin

Bang! "Oh my god," the little kid said to me. He said, "I wish I could be as good as you," and I remembered back to when I was his age, just six years old, and I was nothing. I couldn't touch backboard back then, either. I remember a guy on the court said to me, "You will never make it. You will keep doing this over and over, but you will not make it to the NBA. You will never be able to dunk."

At that time, I thought to myself, "What if he is right? What if everything he says is true?" I wanted to be something, not someone who tries so hard but still doesn't go anywhere. I wanted people to support me, to say to themselves, "Wow, I believed in him, I knew he could do it."

As soon as I got home, I asked my dad, "Can we work out some day? I know you know a lot about working out, and I want you to be the person to push me, Dad."

The next day my dad came up to me and said, "You wanna be what you want to be?" When I nodded, my dad said, "Well, get up then. You're not going to get any better by sitting there." My dad made me work out every single day during the summer. He made me do three sets of pushups, sit ups, chin ups, toe ups, and squats. Most days, I thought I was too sore to keep going but every time I slacked off, my dad said, "No pain, no gain. Keep going, son, prove them wrong. If you give up now, you will be the loser. Remember, they're testing you, and they want you to give up!"

I kept going, I didn't want my dad to look at me and see a quitter. Over and over, in my head, I said, "I will achieve my goal. I will not give up. Everyone who doubts me will watch me prove them wrong!" Every day and every night I practiced the same exercises, trying to get in excellent shape so I could do what I had always wanted to do on the court.

My dad took me into the open gym and said, "Touch the backboard. Now." I jumped as high as I could and I just nipped the backboard by luck. My dad nodded and told me, "This is a good start, but now we gotta do more workouts, and don't give up, Austin. We are going to need more heart."

My dad told me to grab a ball, so I picked one up from the floor. Then, he said "This time, jump and hit the backboard with the ball, and keep on doing it. After a while, you will increase your hops and

1

FIG. 17–4 Austin's final draft

My dad told me to grab a ball, so I picked one up from the floor. Then, he said "This time, jump and hit the backboard with the ball, and keep on doing it. After a while, you will increase your hops and be a step closer to do what you've always wanted to do." I started, and in no time, the back of my calves were burning, but as I kept at it. It hurt more and more–more than I could have imagined. When I looked over at my dad, he immediately yelled, "Don't give up, keep going! Go!"

I couldn't say anything, but in my head, I thought, "But I'm getting lower and lower here–how am I ever going to increase my ability to hop?" I started to wonder if I would ever get to the point that I could dunk a basketball. When my dad said, "If you take a hit, you get up and keep fighting. So, keep fighting for what you want!" I knew he was right, I knew I couldn't give up. I had to keep fighting!

Then, the first time my dad took me to the gym and I saw how muscular the guys were, I was very scared. The first thing my dad said was, "Don't give up, keep trying."

I looked around again and said, "I won't, Dad. Never."

After two long months of hard work, my dad said it again. "Try to touch the rim." I surprised myself by getting really close and said, "This is going to be easier than I thought."

My dad answered, "We've worked harder than this–try like you want it!" Then, I jumped as high as I could and that time, I touched the rim.

I started to smile but then I said quickly, "I don't know if I can hang on it."

My dad said, "Try, I think you can." So I tried–I pushed and stretched–and I did it! My dad smiled his biggest smile and told me, "Hard work pays off."

This wasn't just any dunk. It was something I had always wanted to do. For my entire life, I had wanted to be like Kobe Bryant, touching the rim at such a young age, and suddenly, here I was. I was going to be that person that everyone wanted to watch on the court. Now I am looking forward, hoping I'll be known and be one of the greatest, too. I'm ready to show this world what I've got. I'm ready to be a better player, a better person, than that guy I watched back when I was six years old.

I understand that no matter what you want to do, you have to be willing to work hard for it. Nothing is ever going to be handed to you. Hard work really can beat talent.